ENGLAND'S LAST WILDERNESS

A JOURNEY THROUGH
THE NORTH PENNINES

PHOTOGRAPHS BY

John Beatty

ENGLAND'S LAST WILDERNESS

A JOURNEY THROUGH THE NORTH PENNINES

David Bellamy and
Brendan Quayle

YORKSHIRE
TELEVISION

B⭕XTREE

For Walter, Old Willie and all the Wild Men

First published in hardback by
Michael Joseph 1989
Paperback edition published in 1992 by Boxtree Ltd
36 Tavistock Street, London WC2E 7PB

Text copyright © David Bellamy Associates Limited, 1989, 1992
Photographs copyright © John Beatty

Historical Consultant: Don Wilcock

Pages 2 and 3: Hartside Moor
Pages 6 and 7: Looking south-east towards Cross Fell from the Alston–Penrith road

The extract from 'Strike' from *Selected Poems: new edition*, Routledge 1988,
© by Jon Silkin, is reproduced by permission of Jon Silkin.

Jacket design by Dave Goodman, Millions Design

Typeset in 11/12½pt Cheltenham Light by Goodfellow & Egan Ltd, Cambridge

Printed and bound in Italy by New Interlitho s.p.a.

A CIP catalogue record for this book is available from the British Library

ISBN 1 85283 184 7

CONTENTS

Introduction   8

1. TEESDALE: VALLEY OF THE ICE FLOWERS   22
   A Walk among the Ice Flowers

2. WEARDALE: LAND OF THE LEAD MEN   46
   A Lead and Silver Walk

3. DERWENTDALE: VALLEY OF THE BLACK MOOR   72
   The Walks of the Monks

4. ALLENDALE: VALLEY OF THE SHINING WATER   94
   A Walk Around and Above Allenheads

5. THE WEST ALLEN: VALLEY OF THE FIVE BRIDGES   116
   A Ravine and River Walk

6. THE OLD STONE DALE: VALLEY OF THE SOUTH TYNE   138
   A Walk of Railways and Romans

7. THE VALE OF EDEN   160
   A Walk on the Edge of Eden

Index   189

Acknowledgements   192

Authors' Note

It is recommended that the Outdoor Leisure 1: 25 000 map number 31 is used in conjunction with the text maps which illustrate the walks in Chapters 1, 2, 3, 4 and 7.

INTRODUCTION

Excuse us while we catch our breath . . . and take a look around. That's better – and what a view it is. For we have climbed to the peak of Cross Fell, some 2930 feet above sea level – it sounds more breathtaking in feet than in metres. Cross Fell is the highest point in the North Pennines, England's last great wilderness area, and now an officially designated Area of Outstanding Natural Beauty.

From here, except on the very cloudiest of days, you can look down into the upper catchments of three great historic rivers, the Tyne, the Tees and the Eden, all grinding busily away at the rocks beneath this, the high spot on the backbone of England. Their erosive power is a creative one, revealing mineral wealth in the rocks below, and watering the homes and workplaces of settlements great and small, country and city, from coast to northern coast.

Beyond the immediate shadow of Cross Fell run four more rivers. Three of these, the East and West waters of the Allen, and the River Derwent, though great rivers in themselves, are mere tributaries of the greatest of them all – the Tyne. The fourth – the Wear – is a legend in itself, a river which, in its course towards the docks and former grimy shipyards of Wearside, does its famous U-turn around the World Heritage Site of Durham Cathedral, a genuflection to the great grey towers, half church of God, half epitaph for Walter Scott.

The highways of these seven great rivers, as they forge their relentless passages down out of the moors around Cross Fell, ever on to their salty union with the sea, are the North Pennine dales. The production of action by glacier and river, these seven valleys cut deep into layers of limestone and millstone grit, provide shelter for sheep and a working living for farmers, foresters and gamekeepers. A sharp colour contrast with the moors and fells on the high horizon, the dales are lush green and grassy places, which have sustained human life for many centuries, and animal and plant life for many, many centuries more.

The seven dales are fed by the seven rivers, part and parcel of their ecology and economy. For in those rivers' train is left a rich diversity of habitats, homes for plants and animals, for creatures great and small; and a rich panorama of wilderness landscapes. Together with the hills and moors above, the green wilderness corridors provide a retreat for some, rich pickings for the historian and the natural scientist, and sport and recreation for many, not just for the seasoned walker or backpacker,

The view from High Cup Nick ▶

but for the casual motorist looking for beauty, peace and solitude.

We reached the top of Cross Fell by path and foot but even high Cross Fell itself is reasonably easy of access. For although it is the highest point on the Pennine Way and the epicentre of both England's last great wilderness area and largest National Nature Reserve, or NNR, both Cross Fell and its North Pennine hinterlands are easily reached by the average, car-travelling family. There is a good system of cross-Pennine roads which skirt and serve the area, yet do not puncture the wild wonder of the place. You can even drive all the way up to 2500 feet on Cross Fell itself, on the highest motor road in the country. From the A66, you take a side road to the village of Knock. From here an even smaller road takes you behind Knock Fell and up the steep fellside to a parking place used by skiers in winter and providing a marvellous view on sunny days all the year round. From there it is but a short distance by leg, foot and toe up to the high-domed radar station on Great Dun Fell.

Stretch those legs and before long you're on the Pennine Way itself, following in the tracks of an army of would-be Wainwrights who have measured the fell with bootprints of just about every size under the sun. Along the Way it's only a short stroll up to Little Dun Fell. The path crosses firm turf, well cropped by sheep and well decked with two plants which sheep do not find so much to their liking: round rosettes of hard rush with their flower or fruit heads poking up out of the middle, and mats of mat grasses with their one-sided flower heads, which look like miniature hayrakes. Then the tabletop summit of Cross Fell itself stands before you. On your right you will see the beginnings of a watercourse. It may not look much from up here, but that's the head of the great River Tees, beginning its long journey across to the other side of England, en route to the cold North Sea.

◀ Ashes to ashes on Muggleswick Moor: but the new heather is on the way up

▲ The rising of the Tees behind Little Dun Fell, with Great Dun Fell behind

The rockeries of angular stones that you can see scattered about, some tipped on their ends, are proof positive that at some time during a past Ice Age, glaciers overran even the highest fells, wiping out all life in the area. The many arctic and alpine plants still found here and on the lower altitudes of the Appleby and Teesdale fells are thought by scientists to have moved in from further south as the climate began to get warmer, melting away the glaciers and leaving behind the

11

type of soil upon which they could not only survive, but thrive.

Just a little farther, and maybe a little out of breath, you are up where we are now, on the summit of Cross Fell, sentinel of three great counties, Durham, Cumbria and Northumberland. Formerly known as 'Fiends Fell' this was the place where St Paulinus is said to have driven out the demons that lurked here, raising a cross to mark the coming of Christianity to the very top of this part of Britain. The cross is no longer there, and there's certainly no sign of any demons – unless of course you include the odd litter lout – but the vista is as magnificent as it was in St Paulinus' time, over fifteen centuries ago.

On a clear day you can see the land lie down before you: miniature people in their cars and houses, toy animals and trees in their fields. They are but pin-pricks in the distance, a sobering perspective from this height, for set against the ancient untamed shapes and folds of these hills, the affairs of men seem shallow, short-lived, tenuous things.

Even if you lose your human sense of perspective you are unlikely to lose your way or your sense of direction. For on a wet day, when the wind is driving force nine in the clouds, visibility is nil, and the rain pours down your face, it's still fairly easy, with the help of a compass, to establish your position. Turn to points north and the rain which drips off the end of your nose will take a northerly route into the Tyne and out into the great North Sea. Turn to face east and the rain which drips from the end of your nose will flow down the Tees, and eventually also into the North Sea. Turn west and the drips take you in the direction of the Eden and its eventual destination, the Irish Sea.

The best time to be here is when the sun is just up, or even better, before it's up. There are those who say that you have not lived until you've seen the dawn at Cross Fell. One visitor to the summit, the Reverend William Richardson, writing in the eighteenth century, described it thus: 'The most

delightful sight – the most noble spectacle I ever saw, was the sun rising when I was on the summit of Cross Fell.' All things must pass, but not sunrise on Cross Fell. And it's as glorious now as it was then, over 200 years ago.

Here with us, on the summit, join in a short reflection, back in time to when an ancient dawn spread its warming morning light on these magnificent hills. Then come with us on a new North Pennine Way, along roads, byways and riversides through the seven dales which lie below Cross Fell, on a journey of discovery in search of England's last wilderness: the North Pennines.

BLOODAXE COUNTRY . . . AND BEYOND

The North Pennines are less well known than the neighbouring National Park areas of Cumbria and North Yorkshire. Even for centuries before the invasions of travel writers and tour operators, the North Pennines were treated, like the European Alps, as a passing place, an obstacle in the progress from one side of England to another, not a journeying point in themselves.

Much of the area's history reflects this perception. But the people who have journeyed off the beaten paths through these hills, celebrated visitors like Turner, Sir Walter Scott and Dickens, have been enraptured and inspired with what they have seen. Other visitors have come, and like us, have stayed. History tells us too, that many more came, and failed to pass through! For the people who live, and have lived here, the hypnotic wild beauty of these hills and dales needs no interpretation: the North Pennines are, in the words of one old hillman, 'God's Own Country'.

However, even in God's Own Country the visitor needs some geographical bearings. The High Pennines are that northern stretch of the

Wainwright fans pause for a cuppa atop Cross Fell ▶

Pennine chain which lies between the east-west axes of the Pass of Stainmore to the south and the Tyne Gap to the north. On the west they are bounded by the western banks of the River Eden as it flows north to Carlisle. On the east the hills gradually slope into the lower moors and industrial coastal plains of Durham, Cleveland, and Tyne and Wear.

The two main passing places across the Pennines, the Tyne Gap and Stainmore, are in themselves places of historical interest and landscape importance, which have played their part in the shaping of the Pennines we know today. The Tyne Gap connects Newcastle to Carlisle and is the narrowest piece of Britain, coast to coast. It is also the location of Hadrian's Wall, the Roman Wall, one of the greatest relics of their Empire remaining in the northern world. The Gap is like a Pennine dale, rich and fertile, and it is important as a passing place for the migrating seabirds which traverse Britain's coasts every year, many of them pausing en route in the Pennines.

The Pass of Stainmore is more High Pennine in character, an untamed upland wilderness of moor and mire with here and there in the landscape patches of limestone pavement and of overgrown spoil. A major trunk road, the A66, traverses this wilderness, taking the route of the first Roman road through the area – the Maiden Way. At the side of the A66, on the boundary between Durham and Cumbria between Brough and Barnard Castle, there stands the stump of a cross, the Rey Cross, from the Norse word 'Hreyrr' meaning 'a boundary'. This is the remains of an old Wheel Cross which marked the division between the rival kingdoms of England and Scotland around the time of King William the Conqueror.

The Rey Cross has a darker association. It also marks the spot where King Eric Bloodaxe met his mortal end. According to the Norse saga, the *Eriksmal*, composed in his honour, it was from this lonely Pennine place that Eric set out on his last great journey – to Valhalla, hall of the gods

▲ The Rey Cross on Stainmore Pass: Eric Bloodaxe's solitary memorial

and of his Norse ancestors, his battle wounds in full display.

Eric Bloodaxe was the last of the Viking kings in England and the most famous Viking of his era. In a violent, chequered career in the years between 930 and 960 AD, Eric was at various times King of Norway, King of the Hebrides and pagan ruler of Jorvic (York).

A Dark Age lord true to his Dark Age times, Eric was described by his chroniclers as handsome but cruel, valiant but ruthless, a fitting king for the wild North Country at a time when few outsiders dared to enter without a personal army to defend them. In 952 the Northumbrians, in a last gesture of defiance against the southern kings, made him King of Northumbria, heir to a huge realm stretching from the Midlands to central Scotland. But this last great stand of the North against the South was short lived. Little more than two years after the Northumbrians had proclaimed this Norse lord as their king, they conspired against him and sided with the forces of the southern King Eadred.

A great battle was fought in which Eric Bloodaxe and a Norse army, which included five other kings (among them his son Haeric and his brother Ragnvald) met a bloody end. Eric himself was assassinated by one of his own stock, Maccus, agent for Oswulf, the English Earl of Bamburgh. *The Anglo-Saxon Chronicle* describes the setting as 'a certain lonely place called Stainmore'. The cross which marks the spot is our witness to Eric's treacherous end, as desolate and soulless a spot as you'll find anywhere in the wildest reaches of the Pennines. The ghost of Eric Bloodaxe, last of the great kings of Northumbria, is said to haunt these lonely hills, his long red hair and beard flowing in the breeze, his blood-red axe at the ready, lifted to avenge himself against his betrayers, his battle cry mingling with the desolate howling of a Pennine wind.

FROM ICE AGE TO PEAT BOG

These hills and dales were here long before Eric Bloodaxe, Oswulf and Maccus and their bands of merry men marched across the landscape. So we must go further back in time to find out how they came here and then retrace our steps through history back to today. Strange to some it may seem, but it was that great equaliser, the rain, which across the centuries has given the High Pennine fells so much of their character. Its

actions have given life to a brown blanket of living peat which has clothed their glacial contours. And within this peat, this partly decayed plant material, lies a record of the landscape history of the area since the time when the last great glaciers departed.

From the peat layers, a chronological sequence can be built up detailing exactly how the vegetation has changed with changing climates. Thus we know that if you had stood on the summit of Cross Fell a mere 12,000 years ago all around would have been ice and snow. Six thousand years later and this fell, as well as the vast bulk of the landscape of England, was covered with mixed forest of oak and elm. The boggy hollow at the back of Cross Fell, which still today gives birth to the Tees, was festooned with double dumplings, the local name for the beautiful but now less commonly found globe flower. What the Stone Age people called them we do not know, but they must have seen them as they crossed the open forests and way-marked the original Pennine Way. The peat record also tells us that it was their stone axes and a worsening climate that removed the trees, replacing them with blanket bog.

That multi-layered blanket bog is still with us to this day, and as long as we leave it in peace, in time it too will carry the record and relics of our civilisation well into the future; a puzzle for scientific generations to come. But within the time span of man's more recent past, from the Iron Age on, the peat of the Pennines only tells us part of the human story. The rest we must deduce from archaeological discoveries below the blanket bog altitudes and from patterns on the land.

Along the surfaces of successive historical layers of soil and peat there have walked, ridden and driven a succession of people since those early Stone Age pioneers. It is even possible that, as elsewhere in Britain and Ireland, another people walked before the Stone Age men and women. The peat is ambivalent about this, but a pre-Stone Age people may have also passed this way, hunter-gatherers who did not fell the trees but lived off the fruits and game of the ancient forests, leaving little to tell their tale.

After the Stone Age people came the Gaels, Celtic warriors of the Iron Age. But they were not just warriors, they were great cultivators and keepers of domestic animals. Remains of their settlements, fort-like encampments centring on a sacred hearth stone, have been found in various parts of the Pennines. One such settlement, above High Force waterfall in Upper Teesdale, proves that 3000 years ago, they liked a 'room with a view'!

More Celts followed, the Britons or Brythons, of varying origins and lifestyles. The hill tribes, that made the hills their own, we have come to know as the Brigantes. But even these tough hillmen gave way to new conquerors from the continent. As great Pennine eagles soared in the sky above, so a new generation of eagles, with silver wings, appeared moving on the land below – the Romans. The great legions marched in regimental columns across the Pennine passes, building roads like the Maiden Way, and opening up the lead and silver treasures which lay in the earth below the peat lines.

The Romans built Hadrian's Wall, placed their backs against the hills, and defended their empire of hill, fell peat and forest against the Picts from the north and insurgents from the south as best they could. The Empire fell, and the hill tribes again grew strong, living, fighting and dying under the direction of successive warrior rulers and kings, including one who roamed the length and breadth of Albion with his fearless band of knights – Arthur, the king whose legends still haunt the North Pennines.

In time, Saxons came to the Pennines, Vikings too, then Normans, and intermittently the Scots, in the shape of both wild armies and bands of raiders – the Border reivers. Kings, landlords and churchmen stole, traded and bought parts of the Pennines, right through the Middle Ages; while rebels plotted and hid in hill and dale. They all left their mark, in field systems and peat cuttings, in buildings built, strengthened or sacked, in ore workings and landforms, in forest plantings and cuttings, in peels and castles, moats and monasteries, stately houses and humble homes, courtyards and cottage gardens.

But the hand of man on the Pennines is most evident in more recent times, in the structures, landforms and relics of the mineral klondike, when it was discovered in the 1800s that 'them thar hills' were full, not of gold, but of commodities just as valuable in those days – silver and lead – and in large quantities too. The boom that followed, and then collapsed not long afterwards, created the industrial landmarks with which these hills are dotted today: chimneys and smelt mines, tunnels and reservoirs.

With the exploitation of the lead and the iron ores came the railways, the people and new housing. In the rapid expansion of the dales settlements, farmhouses became hamlets and hamlets, villages. Nowadays most of the railways are gone; one for industry and one for tourists remain. The great dale village populations are gone too; many an abandoned farmhouse, smallholding and hamlet dot the higher fells, the dwellings of sheep and ghosts. But the villages and the more financially viable farms live on, and the spirit of the Pennine people past and present, laced with character and colour, lives on with them.

THE LAST GREAT WILDERNESS

Celt, Roman, Saxon, Norman, warrior, farmer and lead miner: these in their time were the Pennine way-makers and way-farers, the conquistadors of the seven dales, their rivers and their moortops. They broke the back of a virgin wilderness and shaped it in the fashion that you can see from Cross Fell today, a man-made wilderness of moors, dykes and rivers, of bogs and birds, plants and pathways. Nowhere is nature pristine, untouched, but it is everywhere

▲ Falcon Clints: Long-gone golden eagles gave these rocks their name. One day the eagles may return

there. There are still hidden parts of these hills where few feet have ever trod.

The hidden parts are nature's best preserves, and the Pennines are covered in 'designations' intended to protect them and the wildlife within their borders. There are twenty-eight Sites of Special Scientific Interest, or SSSIs, in the North Pennines, a total of some 71,992 acres. Most of this land, some 68,000 acres, is in the adjoining high fells of Upper Teesdale and Appleby, Moor House and Cross Fell, Geltsdale and Glendue. Together these areas, with their unique complex of plant communities, spring gentians and yellow mountain saxifrage, represent an area of unparalleled biological richness in the uplands of England and Wales.

The North Pennines provide good terrain for birds too, attracting a concentration of rarities of international importance, particularly birds of prey. The area is host to nine breeding species, including hen harrier and goshawk, out of the seventy-nine which are given special protection at all times. Two more, the golden eagle and the red kite, are winter visitors and another great bird, the osprey, is a passage migrant. But most special of them all is the merlin, a bird present in numbers amounting to nearly half its English population.

The smallest of the British falcons, the merlin is little larger than a thrush. It feeds on small birds, pipits, larks and wheatears, nesting on the open moor, among the heather and the bilberries. It is a bold and solitary bird which appears suddenly on a rock or in low flight along a fellside, as if it had come by magic out of nowhere. From this bird, Merlin the magician received his name. It is a fitting association, for the Pennines, the home of the merlin, have an ancient wild magic all their own.

That magic of the North Pennines, their plants, animals and birds, sets the area apart from the other great upland landscapes of England and Wales. It is different in other respects too. The landforms may not be as rugged and spectacular as those of the Lake District to the west, and the Yorkshire Dales to the south, but the bleak rolling moors, sweeping down into lush green valleys, together with the rich heritage of the lead mining era, and some remarkable landforms like High Cup Nick and High Force, make it special – uniquely Pennine.

The magic is supplemented by a touch of mystery. Few have ever attempted to chronicle the area in any detail. Left out of the 'Domesday Book', and bypassed by Defoe in his great tour of Britain, it was not until the area opened up for lead mining in the seventeenth and eighteenth centuries that the first accounts appeared. Prior to this, the landscape was too wild, the passes too impenetrable, and the imagined wildness of the people a major disincentive.

Much of our knowledge of ancient life and custom in the North Pennines derives from the strong oral tradition which survives in parts still today – the stories of Arthur and of the last boar, of wolves and vampires, of tragic death and hauntings, stories and songs of work and toil. Many a legend lies too behind local place names. Only a 'magic' land could have a castle called Pendragon, landforms called Wallish Walls and Snods Edge, a hillside called The Hanging Walls of Mark Anthony and a waterfall called Cauldron Snout. There is mystery in some of the people too, in the stories of Walter the Molecatcher, the dialect of the last of the shepherds and the spar miners, and in the customs which survive, the horse fair at Appleby, the rushbearing at Warcop and the fire festival at Allendale. The North Pennines have long been a good tramping ground for the folklorist, the historian and the antiquarian.

These ancient hills have long attracted another breed of visitor, a species in little danger from extinction, the walker. For here lies the central section of the Pennine Way. Starting well to the south of Cross Fell, at Edale in Yorkshire, straddling England's central watershed for some 250 miles, it terminates at Kirk Yetholm north of the Tweed. But few would disagree that the North Pennine section is the most spectacular, the most definitively 'Pennine' of all the Way.

Such is the popularity of the route that originally two boots wide it is now braided across the fells skirting the wettest bits where constant traffic has cut deep into the peat blanket, revealing in places the stumps of trees which grew here 4000 years ago. This makes the North Pennines one of the few places on earth where you can walk on the tops of real trees!

Every year, thousands of new feet put pressure on the Way and the habitats it runs through. But there are other pressures too, new pressures for mineral 'winning' and open-cast coal mining, pressures from developers, and pressures from the people who live there, rightly anxious to ensure a viable economic future for themselves and their children. Recent plans for the area include a ski village in Weardale and the marketing of the remarkable Settle-Carlisle railway line for tourism, because it is no longer economic as a passenger service. Most surreal of all is the proposed construction of a wind park at Langdon Common in Teesdale, yielding the prospect of twenty-five great wind turbines, joining the golden plovers and the dunlins as new residents of the moortops.

None of these developments is bad for the area, if managed properly, along with the new visitors each will bring. But there has to be a balance between conservation and development, land-use and wilderness protection if

The pilgrimage to the highest point on the Pennine Way – the summit of Cross Fell ▶

the character of the North Pennines is to be preserved, if its natural beauty is to remain a key part of its biological and economic future.

With an eye to maintaining that balance, the North Pennines was considered for National Park status in 1945 by John Dower, the father of the National Park movement. However, by a slip of the pen or of concentration this, the most biologically important of all the areas under consideration for Park status, was left undesignated, and placed on a reserve list. The Pennines, England's backbone, land of seven great northern rivers, got left behind.

The situation has now been salvaged. In June 1988 the North Pennines was confirmed by Her Majesty's Government as an officially designated Area of Outstanding Natural Beauty, an AONB, Britain's largest. It is now a sort of National Park, officially on a par with the Lakes and the Yorkshire Moors, Exmoor and Snowdonia. The public inquiry that settled the issue took place in Durham in the glorious autumn of 1985. The natural beauty of the Pennines, visible to every enquiring eye, won the day.

A DIFFERENT KIND OF PENNINE WAY

This book is intended not for the specialist, the avid walker, the birdwatcher, or the historian of natural or human society alone, but for the general traveller. For the determined foot brigade there are some walks too – some of our favourites, in our favourite part of the world.

To introduce the visitor to the North Pennines we have devised a route by car through the hills: a new North Pennine Way. Follow this road-way precisely and in one go, and you'll have covered a lot of miles. You'll also have done something that, after over ten years in these parts, we've never done, at least not in one go.

Our new trail is not cast in Pennine stone, it's only a guide. We follow a route which

approaches the Pennines from the east, but you could just as easily approach from the west, from the corridor of the M6, the road to the Lakes and the Western Isles, though if you do that, you'll have done the best bits first. There are also hilltop routes from the Cheviots in the north and from the Yorkshire Dales in the south which our way crosses.

The route is best imagined in seven stages, one per dale, as set out in the schematic maps which introduce each chapter. And briefly, this is what it entails. Approaching north or south along the Old North Road, the A1, go left at Scotch Corner and follow the brown signs for the A66 and Teesdale. This, your passport to the High Pennines, can take you across the hills to Brough, but we suggest leaving that road to the lorry drivers. Come with us through Barnard Castle on the high road, the B6282, to Upper Teesdale and the other roads of the High Pennines . . . but do not do it all at once!

At the head of the Tees valley at Langdon Beck, you then turn right over the tops to meet the A689 going up and down Weardale. After seeing the sights of Killhope Wheel and Upper Weardale, travel east along the A689 to below Wolsingham where you will meet the A68, the famous High Road to Scotland. The A68 takes you into the higher tracts of the Derwent valley. At the curiously named Snods Edge turn west to Blanchland along some smaller roads, including one smaller than most, which points south to the little remote dale of Rookhope. After Rookhope your way west takes you up and over Killhope into the first of the Allen valleys.

Turn north again and you're downdale this time, heading for the meeting of the Allen waters. At Langley take the Alston road southwest and updale along the valley of the West Allen. This road winds across the back of Cross Fell and into the valleys of the Nent and the South Tyne. You are next on the A689 travelling north, and your route after this takes you out of the Pennines towards Haltwhistle in the Tyne Gap. Under the shadow of the Roman Wall you then have to skirt the Pennines, like many a good Roman before you, to reach the village of Brampton. You are now on the final, and some would say finest, leg of your Pennine journey, travelling south along the Pennine escarpment through the little villages of the glorious Eden valley.

So, armed with maps, lists of places to stay, a spare set of wellies or walking boots, camera, binoculars – for the bird life *is* good – and a bootful of Kendal Mint Cake, get ready to go. And if a soundtrack is required, stock up your Walkman or car cassette with music to go with just about every landscape echo in existence: classical, folk, jazz or popular, whatever your taste there's a hill, dale or hollow to suit. But keep an ear open for the natural sounds of the North Pennines, the sound of tinkling streams, the wind and the song of the birds, particularly the haunting cry of the curlew on the open moor. But above all, experience the great peace and tranquillity of England's last great wilderness. Let it inspire and calm you, and while journeying on these roads and in these hills take your time – and beware the ghost of Eric Bloodaxe!

1
TEESDALE
VALLEY OF THE ICE FLOWERS

To any botanist worth their salt, Teesdale is a magic word spoken with a sense of true reverence. It is a place of pilgrimage where memories of some 12,000 years of environmental change linger on in a bouquet of flowers. The valley is one of England's great historic landscapes, painted by Turner and immortalised in poems by Sir Walter Scott. There are castles and a ruined abbey, ghosts and a great grouse moor, Roman and Celtic remains, and through it all runs one of the best stretches of 'white' or fast river water in the country, fed by magnificent waterfalls, the most impressive being High Force.

But above, below and all around are Teesdale's flowers. Delicate blue gentians and pink primroses head a whole flowering of alpine and arctic plants which brighten each new spring as they have since the last Ice Age melted away.

Other plants in the Teesdale bouquet tell of warmer times. Hoary rockrose and horseshoe vetch, rejoicing in the warmth of south-facing knolls, hint of a struggle for space when a more temperate climate covered the whole dale in mixed forest. So too, the bog mosses and cotton grasses, which grow today in profusion, record another fact: that as the forest was removed by the first dalesfarmers the climate took a decided turn for the worse.

Other plants show yet another side to Teesdale's environmental history, for flowers like meadow cranesbill and yellow rattle are an indicator of the survival of age-old customs of ecologically sound farming which allowed the flowers to set seed before the haycrop was cut, while in parts the invasion of perennial ryegrass shows one sad side of twentieth-century 'aggroculture', the coming of monocrop.

Teesdale above all the other dales is the jewel in the botanical crown of the North Pennines, a floral tribute from ages past.

STANWICK-ST JOHN TO RABY CASTLE

Our route into the valley of the Tees, the A66, was in fact a way marked by the Romans, their route penetrating the Pennines. The road takes you past a remarkable monument to imperial times, the earthworks at

12,000 years on and still blooming: the haymeadows of Upper Teesdale ▶

Stanwick-St John. This is thought to have been the rallying point of the Celtic Brigantes, the people of the Pennine moors and dales, where they took their last stand against the invading Roman soldiers. To see the earthworks at close hand take the B6274 to Forcett off the A66. The earthworks lie on the right-hand side of the road before the village.

The fort covers about 750 acres and was built in three phases during the first century AD, a prehistoric feat of engineering unrivalled at the time. But it was not enough to keep the Romans at bay. The fortifications themselves may not have been at fault, for Venutius, the king of the Brigantes at the time, made one fateful error well known to the modern family: he allowed his work to interfere with his domestic life. Not only was Venutius fighting the Romans, he was also fighting his wife, Cartimandua. For reasons only known to the gossip columns of the time, she assigned her own personal militia to the cause of the invader.

Not just poor old Venutius but also Stanwick lost out. The fort was sacked, and thus it remains today, a great broken wedding ring of a monument. A circle of broken mounds enfolds a series of pleasant cow pastures draped with mixed woodland of oak and birch, with here and there, the odd sad, dead elm.

Beyond Stanwick, at a point where the old Roman road gives way to the upper dale route to Barnard Castle, there stands the great estate of Rokeby Park. Here, the road crosses the graceful curving arch of the Greta Bridge, one of two delightful spans across this tributary of the Tees. The waters of the Tees and its tributary, the Greta meets near the pretty Dairy Bridge. This is a place of charm and magic, the setting for paintings by Cotman and Turner no less, as well as many a local aspiring Turner. In a cave nearby, Sir Walter Scott is said to have drafted lines for his epic poem 'Rokeby', a work of poetic fiction, but drawing inspiration and storyline from local history, scenery, people and place names.

At the meeting of the waters sightings of a local ghost, the Maid of Rokeby, are not uncommon. An eighteenth-century legend relates that a cruel Lord Rokeby of an earlier, unspecified period of Rokeby Hall's history stabbed her to death in nearby Mortham Tower, so that he might inherit the estate. The bloodstains from this dastardly deed remained for years upon the staircase of the house, a grisly reminder and a stain for ever on the house of Rokeby. Eventually a local parson was called in to exorcise her spirit from the tower. She was cast out, but did not go far, still reappearing from time to time on the arch of the Dairy Bridge. A fine lady, she is heard wailing piteously, the train of her silk dress dragging behind her.

Barnard Castle is a pleasant market town and administrative centre for the dale. Known by the locals as 'Barney', it is perhaps best known in wider circles for its remarkable heritage of stone-built back alleys and its butter market, an eight-sided monument which now serves as a round-about for the roads which enter the town.

A day's cultural and architectural sightseeing in Barney will introduce you to some fine examples of Pennine heritage. Your itinerary should include the haunts of Charles Dickens, former woollen mills which overlook the river between the town and the village of Startforth, and the remains of the Castle, built in the twelfth century.

Some would argue that the most dramatic of the monuments which decorate the lower dale stand in fact outside the market town – Bowes Museum, Egglestone Abbey and Raby Castle. Bowes Museum to the south-east of the town is a monumental edifice. It is, by design, a French château, built by John Bowes, Earl of Strathmore, out of his profits from the coal industry. Bowes and his wife, a French actress, Josephine Benoite, used it to house a massive art collection including paintings by El Greco and Goya. Now a museum, it is well worth a visit as a truly remarkable piece of architectural whimsy. And if

Barnard Castle, mediaeval riverside real estate, a shimmering reflection of the dale's architectural glory ▶

you are lucky you may see a silver swan scoop up fish from a silver pool.

An altogether different experience can be had on a walk from Startforth through country lanes to Egglestone Abbey, above the turbulent Tees and its richly wooded banks. The best times are a summer's evening or early morning when the sun's red light shows up this Premonstratensian ruin at its best. At the click of a carefully set camera, doves will fly out from their nests on the Abbey's ruined high walls.

Like the doves which are the Abbey's only inhabitants today, the Premonstratensian monks wore white. An order modelled on the Cistercians and founded in France in the twelfth century, the monks' lives were not altogether as peaceful as their habit and the Abbey's gentle setting would suggest. For years they were subject to raids by parties of invading Scots – Teesdale was once Border country – and then to cap it all, when the northern barons were on their way with their armies to Durham to do battle with the Scots, they stayed at the Abbey, seriously depleting its meagre provisions. The monks did not lose out altogether. The Scots were trounced for good at the battle of Neville's Cross near Durham City in 1346 and the monks were spared further bagpipe, kilt and claymore sessions until the Reformation in 1540, when the monastery at Egglestone was dissolved.

A visit to Raby Castle requires a detour along the A688 to the village of Staindrop, with its Saxon church and village green overlooked on both sides by fine stone buildings. The Castle stands on its own in a stately deer park, overlooking moat and garden, and features some of the best stands of mature oak in the region. Home to a beautiful herd of fallow deer and a small, majestic herd of red deer, and to the Lord of the Manor for the upper dale, Lord Barnard, the Castle dates from the fourteenth century. It has been in the hands of the same family since 1616 and records show it to date from before 1031 when King Canute gave it to the Prior of Durham. It is not always open to the public, but

▲ The Bowes Museum by moonlight and floodlight

when it is, it is worth a long, cool look. Raby is one of the few castles in the Pennines still in active use. Keep an eye out for something truly unique: a doggy-skin fire rug, keeping odd company with a pair of albino moles.

After Raby Castle take the A688 back to Barnard Castle, go through the town, over the bridge, and past the ruins of Barnard Castle itself. Once over the bridge, take the B6277 for the villages of the middle dale, Cotherstone and Romaldkirk, eventually coming back across the river to the pretty village of Eggleston. If you want a good base from which to explore all three and perhaps to put yourself in the right frame of mind for the higher spots of the upper dale, the village of Romaldkirk is ideal.

▲ Egglestone Abbey: where once prayed white monks there now play white doves

FROM ROMALDKIRK TO MIDDLETON

If it is Sunday then one way of beginning the day is at the church of St Romald. Take a stroll around the village and its romantic graveyard before lunch at one of a malting of good pubs facing one another across the village green. If you miss Matins, the evening service is just as good a way of saying 'thank you' for another perfect Pennine day. Even if it is not Sunday the church is well worth a detour. Its interior dates from the twelfth to the fifteenth century, complete with statue of a mediaeval knight caught in the act of drawing his sword.

One of the best walks will take you to Eggleston along a series of narrow lanes, so walk or

▲ Romaldkirk

drive with care. It is here for the first time that you come face to face with the effects of the Ice Age, best seen on the left-hand side of the route. There the fields try to do their utmost to disguise a series of sculptured hummocks and hollows known in the geomorphological trade as 'kame' and 'kettle'.

The kames are made of rock debris, drift material ground down, scooped up and dumped by glacial action. The kettles are places where large lumps of ice were forced down into the drift. As the ice melted they first became closed lakes with no inflow and outflow streams, allowing their waters to become rich in all the minerals released from the rocks. Then as plants moved into the area the natural succession of swamp, marsh willow, carr and wet woodland gradually filled each lake with peat.

Peat is partially decayed plant material: leaves, stems, twigs, flowers, seeds and fruit, many of which even in their semi-decayed state can be identified by the expert. The bones and fur of animals, the skeletons of insects and the spores and pollen grains of plants are also perfectly preserved in the peat. The kettle hole thus filled up with a layered history book, a record of exactly what took place on that spot and its immediate surroundings, right back beyond the time when the first trees were felled and sheep were brought in to safely graze among the kames and kettles.

Peat borings taken down into two of the kettles have revealed the whole story right back to the glacial clay and ice-worked Shap granite which line the bottom. Shap granite? you may well ask. For Shap Fell is in the Lake District, miles away over the other side of the Pennines. How did that get there? The answer and the explanation, as for so much of Teesdale's natural heritage, lie in the ancient power of glaciation. It was right here between Romaldkirk and Eggleston that an unstoppable force met an immovable object: the one the local ice falling and spilling down from the upper dale, the other an enormous invading ice mass which poured over what is now the Bowes-Brough road, carting the debris of Shap Fell and many other local landmarks along with it and dumping them. Here millions of tons of ice met, were heaved up and pushed down. And when they melted around 12,000 years ago we got kame and kettle, and in the fullness of time a section of rock-encapsulated history.

Cotherstone village is a little lower down the dale, standing on the west bank of the Tees at its junction with the River Balder. In Celtic times, the confluences of rivers and streams were mysterious places, believed to be the haunts of spirits, both malevolent and benevolent. One famous legend concerns the last of the lords of Romaldkirk whose castle once looked down from high on the magical meeting of the Tees and the Balder. The castle no longer remains, but you can see the last of its foundations on the steep hill which overlooks the waters.

According to legend, the noble lord went hunting and on his way met Elspeth, an old woman who warned him against going out that day. However, the proud lord ignored the advice offered and headed with his hounds and horse to the wood. At twilight he became separated from the rest of the party, and entering a woodland glade saw a vision in the moonlight: a pure white hart. The rest of the story is best told in the anonymous local rhyme shown opposite.

The white hart was probably an albino red or roe deer, a rare phenomenon, though roes are the commonest of British deer. The woods around the Tees do provide good cover for these animals, but you have to be up early to catch sight of them. The crag where the hunting lord met his doom stands above a majestic bend in the River Tees, well beloved by kayak enthusiasts who tear round the bend and the old millhouse at a speed of knots. Oaks and elms hang above the waters, a glorious display in the autumn, a mourning veil for the passing of the lords of Romaldkirk.

In a beautiful building not far away – the Tudor High Shipley Lodge – there is a carving on a window panel which shows a stag being chased

▲ The River Tees near Cotherstone: resting place for the last of the lords of Romaldkirk

But night had fallen, and near by
Yawn'd a chasm dark and dread . . .
'Twas to the top of Percymere
The deer so swiftly sped;

The young Lord followed recklessly
Forgetting danger near;
His every thought was fixed upon
The slaying of the deer.

But now the dogs stopped suddenly,
A flash, as though of fire,
Revealed unto the luckless youth
The brink of Percymere.

And far below, in that dark dell,
Crept the river on its way,
Like some huge serpent coiling round
Its quivering, ghastly prey.

He checked his steed – but 'twas too late –
The tired beast reel'd and fell,
Roll'd on its rider, and both together
Were plunged in that awful dell.

And then, amid the dark, dim night,
Arose a fearful scream,
And horse and rider mangled lay:
Fulfill'd was Elspeth's dream!

by hounds, proof if any was needed that stag hunting has always been popular in these parts. The Lodge offers holiday accommodation, one of a number of country cottages marketed for the visitor by a group of enterprising farmers' wives and countrywomen in Teesdale. It was once the property of the hunchback king, Richard III, and given in 1484 to Miles Forest, one of the two men allegedly paid by Richard to murder the Princes in the Tower. The Lodge, an attractive and secluded retreat, was meant to buy his silence. He may not have been silent enough, for six months later his wife became a widow. Forest mysteriously disappeared, but the Lodge is still there to tell the tale.

The name for the River Balder comes from the Norse god of vegetation, the same god whose death is honoured in midwinter fires across Europe, and as we shall see later, even in the North Pennines. The Viking connection is strong in these parts, apparent in the names of local landforms and places, like Wodens Croft and Thorsgill. Scott's *Rokeby* contains rich references to the local mythology of place in one of the passages about the Tees:

> When Denmark's raven soared on high,
> Triumphant through Northumbrian sky,
> Till, hovering near, her fatal croak,
> Bade Reged's Britons dread the yoke;
> And the broad shadow of her wing,
> Blackened each cataract and spring,
> Where Tees in tumult leaves his source,
> Thundering o'er Caldron and High Force:
> Beneath the shade the North man came,
> Fixed on each vale a Runic name,
> Reared high their altar's rugged stone,
> And gave their Gods the land they won.
> Then, Balder, one bleak garth was thine,
> And one sweet brooklet's silver line;
> And Woden's croft did title gain
> From the stern Father of the Slain.

Passing up from Cotherstone through Romaldkirk to Eggleston, it is well worth stopping to look up the valley before you cross the bridge which takes you up to Eggleston village. Below the road a steep water-cut bank is still covered with woodland, complete with hazel which has grown hereabouts for at least 9000 years, and alder which arrived on a much warmer scene some 3000 years later. Each spring their catkins shed pollen in abundance, the same sort of pollen which, trapped in the core of the kettlehole, makes us so sure of our facts.

There amongst the trees are the great rhubarb-like leaves of butterbur, some belonging to male plants, others to female plants; but you must wait until they flower to sort out the sexes. Regardless of their gender, the leaves were used by farmers' wives to wrap fresh butter on its way to market.

The elegantly proportioned house by the bridge, complete with fully detached garage,

▼ Grey heron

30

must be everyone's idea of the perfect place to live in the country, but the narrow bridge itself is a nightmare for learner drivers. The view from the parapet, if you are lucky, may include a heron stalking the shadows, a dipper bobbing on a stone or swallows zipping back and forth feeding on the wing.

On the way up the hill you pass the elegance of Eggleston Hall, now a seat of floristry-and-cordon-bleu-business studies. Turn left, cross the main road and you're into the ancient village itself. Here in rougher times when the villagers were being attacked by raiders, their animals were herded on to the village green, while hay-cocks were used to fill up the spaces between the houses. Some security! The lower, more unkempt end of the green traversed by the

beck is however still a safe home for the meadow saxifrage. Heavy cream-white petals hint at the wealth of meadow plants whose abundance in the dales hangs in the scales of historical fact and modern conflict – flower-filled meadows versus monoculture.

The village is an opportune resting place, with good pubs and pub food . . . you'll have to try them both to find out which one is our favourite! While sampling the local produce – and your ploughman's lunch must include a bit of Cotherstone cheese – you could try debating with the landlord the origins of the name Eggleston. One story suggests that the village takes its name from a stone circle once located outside the village which was probably a monument to a Celtic chieftain felled in 603 AD at the battle of

▼ The tree-hung Tees: a living river

Egasan Stone. The stone circle though, like the origin of Eggleston, can no longer be clearly seen, though an intelligent bit of map reading will lead you to the spot where it once stood.

At Eggleston, take the lower road, the B6282 to Middleton, meander left, then up a long right-handed curve until a large layby on the right beckons you to stop. The view up the dale is truly magnificent. Middleton lies to the right, and Mickleton stands across the river set amongst a jumble of jewel-green fields appliquéd in dry-stone. Beyond lies unkempt brown-green 'inbye-land', the land 'in-by', or near to the steading. And beyond the highest walls you can make out dark fingers of 'outbye' – the land far from the steading – and moor, a tattered fetlock hanging about the hooves of the High Pennines.

In the foreground of your viewscape you may see a rabbit warren all a-hop with white bobtails and listening ears. And if the sun is out and shining you may, if your eyes are quick enough, see the flick of a common lizard on the wall. Unfortunately today they are no longer common anywhere in Britain and up here, unlike their more pampered cousins in the warmer south, they are viviparous. They lay babies ready before birth for life, not lazy eggs that must rely on lots of extra sun for incubation.

Middleton itself sleeps as if waiting for the next train or for John Betjeman to sing the praises of the wrought-iron drinking fountain. Sadly, neither will ever come to pass for the line was axed by Beeching and the Poet Laureate has gone where even yellow and black paint does not corrupt. Middleton, though less of a 'ton' and more of a large village, is the headquarters of the Raby estate. The tenant farmers still maintain the tradition of whitewashed homes and some, in active partnership with the Nature Conservancy Council, manage their land in time-honoured ways which leave room for the flowers and wildlife alike. A dearth of pseudo antique shops indicate this to be a working town and for further proof make your way down to the river on market day. There you will find exactly what the dale is

all about, a sense of neighbourhood and real hard graft, working on the margins of a sub-arctic climate which is always working against you.

For those with plenty of time and a keen interest in exploring Teesdale to its last detail the side valleys of Hudeshope, Lunedale and Baldersdale are all well worth visiting and provide a contrast to the landscapes in the upper dale. To get to Baldersdale you have to turn back down the valley and follow the signs from Romaldkirk to Hunderthwaite and Hury. Lunedale is best approached across the Tees from Middleton, up the B6276. Hudeshope is accessible on the B6277 on either the road to Snaisgill or Aukside. The landscapes of these three small valleys are in essence people-made but there the similarity stops.

Hudeshope, with its hamelts of Aukside and Snaisgill, is an industrial landscape, laid bare by picks, shovels and the enterprise of miners. The hills are marked with spoil heaps, drifts, adits, old mine shops and engine houses. No miners live there now, but sturdy ponies, the legacy from that era, still roam. They are perhaps descendants of the very stock which first supplied the Roman Army, and later the pack ponies of the lead miners. They graze amongst the mat grass tussocks on the bents and fescues which have grown there since before Roman times.

The landscapes of Lunedale and Baldersdale provide a glimpse of a more ordered period, an era of Victorian hydro-engineering, when big dams were the order of the day, and when stonework was made to last. Selset Reservoir has the longest dam in England, and the waters behind it provide some of the best sailing and windsurfing amenities in the North Pennines. There is fishing too, and space has been left for wildlife by the neat Victorians. Geese, ducks and lapwings take advantage of the water and its orderly edge.

Before leaving Middleton for the upper dale cast your eyes due south towards Lunedale and there in the hills above the town stands a solitary clump of ancient Scots pines. These dark trees

▲ A relic from Teesdale's Iron Age: Kirkcarrion, a chieftain's tomb

mark the site of a great tumulus, Kirkcarrion. This was excavated in 1804 and in it were found a cinerary urn and the bones of a Brigantine prince, Caryn, hence the name 'Kirkcarrion' – Caryn's Castle. It is a great romantic sight on a late summer evening when the sun slips down on the fells behind, or when the moon is full, shining an eerie light upon the sentinel trees and prehistoric mound lying below. When the moon is out, Caryn's unsettled spirit is believed to stalk the fells, no doubt lamenting the disturbance of his Celtic tomb.

FROM MIDDLETON TO HOLWICK

Back on the B6277 past Middleton-in-Teesdale, the river winds rather than wends its way across the flatness of the valley, still all in a rush as if trying to escape from the confines of the place before the next Ice Age freezes it in its tracks for another 50,000 years or more. On the other side of the valley can be seen the major outcrops of the Great Whin Sill, well scored by black, fluted, quarry-sized bites. These octagons of dolerite were laid down in a subterranean time when volcanic activity thrust a molten sheet of rock into the solid strata already there. The result was that the rocks on either side were baked into crystalline form. Metals like lead, silver and zinc melted and ran free through the cracks and crevices to form rich lodes and veins. They lay hidden until discovered and worked by miners who risked their lives to drag them into the new light of an industrialised age.

The size of the crystals produced tells the trained eye a lot about the process of their formation. The larger the crystals, the slower the molten rock will have cooled. So that whinstone with the larger crystals comes from the heart of the sill where heat escapes more slowly. Whinstone is very hard and so is in great demand for the 'metalling' of roads and motorways. The whinstones are the strong foundations of many 'outstanding' landscape features in the High Pennines.

The roadside verges in Teesdale are made of softer stuff, though like all soil it was rock once upon a time. From here on up both the soils and the verges take on a character of their own. Drifts of meadow cranesbill abound alongside the silver-backed leaves of melancholy thistle, which hang their heavy heads alongside water avens.

Just out of Middleton on the B6277 there is one magnificent view of the river in front of Park End Wood. You can see it as you pass or if you stop at the layby past the bend and walk back. Here the river uses the whole breadth of its flatlands, bumping against the steep bank beneath you and turning dog-leg fashion. On the far side it makes a great sweeping curve, the colours on the waters changing with the seasons: sparkling gold in the summer sun, grey-flecked silver under winter cloud, or a churning maelstrom of brown-white froth after rain. The woods represent one of the most extensive scraps of natural woodland left in the upper dale. There oak, ash, alder, hazel and even elm and pine still grow together as they have for far more than 6000 years. Red squirrels still nibble holes in the hazelnuts and strip out the winged fruits from pine cones.

The whole dale was once swathed in such forest, only the rush of melt water and flood (called 'freshets' locally) kept sections of its banks free from trees. These remained tiny, unstable places of refuge in which only the shade-shunning plants of open habitats could survive. And survive they did until stone, then bronze, then iron axes, along with the fire, helped remove the trees, replacing them with

pasture and meadows. All the flowers and grasses which had been held within the confines of the river, as if in protective custody, burst out to fill the new fields with a riot of colour.

Pastures are places in which animals are allowed to graze; their walls keep the animals in. Meadows have walls to keep animals out while they grow a crop of grass and flowers which is gathered in and stored for winter. Then and only then are the stock allowed in to graze on the stubble and regrowth. The meadows also provide cut pasture in the form of hay, which is baled for winter.

We know that this pattern of meadow management has been practised hereabouts since the year 1131 AD, when grazing of the unenclosed forest and beyond was banned between the eleventh of November and the first of April each year. Between these dates the farm animals have always been kept in the inbyeland near to the farmhouse and fed on hay. The plants of the meadowland were allowed to grow ungrazed and unchecked through the spring and early summer, encouraging the natural cycle of fruits and seeds. The animals then returned the goodness of the crop back into the fields from whence it came, fertilising, recycling, reseeding a self-perpetuating flower garden overflowing with a great variety of plants: yellow rattle, double dumplings, kingcups, lousewort, oxeye daisies, spotted orchids, twayblade, meadow vetchling, zig-zag clover and many, many more.

You can really see it all in closer perspective by walking up the other side of the valley, following the Pennine Way from Middleton to Holwick and above. In the old days, before the fouling of the lower reaches of the Tees, the Great North Salmon Run must have been a spectacular annual event, especially along this stretch of the river. Each year thousands of great silver fish splashed and thrashed their way through the freshets up and over the cataracts of Low Force, drawn by an inborn sense of direction and need of survival back to their spawning grounds. In those days tens of thousands of exhausted fish were scooped out, filled with the milk of salmon survival – sperm and spawn. Their fate was to be used as food for pigs, chickens and even fertiliser for the soil.

These were seasons of glut and seasons of plenty but yet they were also seasons of great hardship. In the interface of the seventeenth and eighteenth centuries the so-called Little Ice Age gripped the world and millions faced ruin as crops failed and starvation and death stalked even the good lands. Life in the upper dale became even harder. But for some, it became a Mecca for winter sports. Horse races were held on the frozen Tees at Barnard Castle. The great waterfall of High Force further up the dale became a major tourist attraction. It froze into a single hollow icicle over 20 yards in circumference and through the hollow the water roared. Luckily it didn't freeze completely solid. If the overall temperature of the world had dropped another couple of degrees the whole water cycle in the valley would have come to a complete standstill once again, and the whole 'advance' of civilisation come to nought.

HIGH FORCE WATERFALL AND THE JUNIPER

A focal point in everyone's progress through the dale must be Bowlees Visitor Centre. Bowlees is on a small tributary of the Tees, near the white village of Newbiggin. Thanks to the Durham Wildlife Trust and the local council the former Methodist chapel has been transformed into a real, live centre of information. Here you can find out about local evolution and all the processes of geology and human endeavour which have made Teesdale what it is today.

If you had come along the Pennine Way, you would have already crossed Wynch Bridge, one of the oldest suspension bridges in Europe. If you came by car then take a walk across the field, over the stile, through the wood and cross

the Tees the swinging chain-link way. Built around 1704, the first of its type in England, perhaps even in Europe, the bridge is at the heart of many local stories and poems:

My father was a miner, he lived down in the
    town
'Twas hard work and poverty that always
    kept him down
He aimed for us to go to school, but brass
    he could not pay
So we had to go to the washing rake for just
    fourpence a day.

Can you imagine what it was like to work in the middle of winter, half immersed in the part-frozen water of the Tees, washing lead ore, bare hands, bare feet, all to scrape a bare living? All the romance of Teesdale, the glories of the landscape and its pretty villages tend to cover up the sins and hardships of the past. Indeed the perceptions of Teesdale by the local people in times gone by are in a sense more in keeping with the culture of the working class than the musings of poets like Scott or the abstract representations of painters like Turner.

Even today, this part of the Pennines is a working landscape where people struggle against great odds to make a living, in farming and quarrying or a combination of both. Local landscapes do figure frequently in the songs and stories of local folk, but as places where minerals were 'won from the earth', where lives were tragically claimed, game was poached, ores were smelted and buildings, machinery, families and whole villages grew and declined. Teesdale balladeer, Richard Watson, wrote a rhyming Iliad out of his daily walk across the fell to work:

On my left hand Coldberry Mine appears;
The din of mills and jiggers strike the ears.
This sound does from the washing floors proceed
Where from the dross the mineral is freed.
Those interested in the dressing line
Should pay a visit to this busy mine;
Three chief points gained a skilled observer sees,
These are despatch, economy and ease.

▲ Coldberry Heights: a romantic ruin on an empty hill

Sadly, Coldberry mine is nowadays a ruin on an empty hill, the top of Hudeshope. If you don't get hypnotised by Gibson's metre and you listen closely to the sounds of the landscape, you may hear the cries of the old miners reverberate off the basalt, 'to the washing rake, rake, rake . . .' or you can imagine a thousand great fish trying to make it up Salmon Leap Falls just upriver. The old lead miners at least had that to look forward to every year and fourpence must have bought a lot of gourmet chicken food. They also knew all the local beauty spots and before you carry on up their hard-worked river take a look at Gibson's Cave, curtained by falling water gathered from the whole of Newbiggin Common.

At Holwick is the largest stand of juniper scrub in the British Isles. The pollen in the peat tells us that it has flourished here for some 11,000 years. Though nibbled by sheep, at least since Roman times and by rabbits since the Saxons brought them to these shores, these topiaried shapes are completely natural. Some are tall, like columnar cypresses; others almost flattened to the ground which is itself home to many mosses, liverworts, ferns and clubmosses. There are adders on the ground too, so tread carefully.

Above this ancient stand of juniper scrub, there is the great waterfall of High Force – a remarkable landscape monument. High Force has attracted people ever since Iron Age hunter-farmers came and set up encampments on the high ground above the waterfall, a place of great power and beauty. The remains of those Iron Age settlements can still be seen, on private land, at Force Garth Farm. The hearth stones still stand in the middle of the settlement's centre hut ring, where the fire used to burn at the heart of a once proud Celtic community.

The salmon of course cannot ascend the falls themselves, a dramatic cascade of water in the summer, water, icicles and mini-icebergs in the winter. If you cannot make it on a warm summer's day, then the next best time to go is on a cool winter's moonlit night, when there's frost on the rocks, moonlight on the water, and twinkling stars above. And for effect, see the falls when they are in spate, when the rain has saturated the fells around Cow Green, and water pours down both sides of High Force's central rock. This is the famous scene depicted in Turner's celebrated painting of the Force.

From High Force, our route takes us back up the path to the hotel. Here a force of another type is always with you. There's good food, great company, and beer well kept. This is also the very place from which the Backhouses, father and son, bankers and botanists set out in the summer of 1843 on a voyage of discovery. During a two days' walk across the head of the Tees they recorded for the first time so many of its botanical treasures. And perhaps it was these intrepid floral walks which gave them the inspiration for the cultivation, at their Weardale home, of the 400-plus varieties of daffodils which were once the stock-in-trade of the world's 'haute spring' – high class – horticulture.

Between the road and the river stand the white-painted settlements of Force Garth Farm, home to many a farmer from that first Iron Age settlement on. Thanks to the records of local

High Force: despite the idyllic impression, swimming here is very dangerous with several deaths in recent years ▶

births and baptisms, we know that there have normally been farm buildings at Force Garth since at least 1579. There is a story that several Charles I half-crown pieces were hidden at the farm. They came to light when it was rebuilt in 1838, and were probably buried when Oliver Cromwell was marching through the dale. Other records show that the old farmhouse was an oak-timbered building, with a thatched roof, high gables, low side walls and mullioned windows. Its outer door was of heavy oak studded with iron nails, strongly hinged and secured by a stout oaken beam slotted behind it into grooves in the wall on both sides of the doorway.

One can only wonder whether local girl Rebecca Robinson and her sister Margaret, who was baptised here on November 14th, 1641, happened to spy a Mr T. Willisel wandering the banks of the Tees. It was he who put Upper Teesdale on the botanical map by recording shrubby cinquefoil in the area and reporting the find to John Ray, the father of English botany.

Shrubby cinquefoil is perhaps one of the strangest of the Teesdale rarities, found naturally in Britain only along this stretch of the Tees and on Helvellyn, over in the Lakes. Although nowadays its abundant yellow flowers make it a favourite garden shrub and it's very easy to grow, why then is it so restricted in its natural haunts?

The hamlet of Forest-in-Teesdale is a wonderful place to stop and ponder on the fells in the distance. From left to right, the bumps visible on the skyline are Holwick Fell, Noon Hill, Cronkley Fell, Mickle Fell and Widdybank Fell – names to make the heart of every botanist beat a little faster. They are the high home of a mixture of plants drawn from the different climatic periods lost in prehistoric time: arctic alpine, warm boreal and wet oceanic, the great seasons which have held the High Pennines in their grip at various stages during their history.

As you look you can almost see that only 12,000 years ago all this was still covered with an age of ice that reshaped the upper valley, gouging out the softer bits, polishing the hardest rock,

bulldozing, scraping, shifting, dumping the detritus of drift and rock. As the climate took a turn for the better, melt waters took over the task, redistributing and re-sorting the drift, rolling the edges of the sharp, ice-scattered rock and reshaping the valley bottom once again.

In time the gentle power of plants gradually took over from the ice. Lush new growth, watered by mineral-rich, sweet water began to cover the freshly exposed drift. Roots penetrated and put out new, warm life below the surface in place of the cold ice that lay there before. The slow process of soil formation had been put in motion. At first the place must have resembled an all-over rockery of arctic alpine plants varied with patches of lichen and moss, basking in the clean, fresh, warming air of the upper dale.

Then, as the mean annual temperature rose to about 10°C above the Ice Age low, trees slowly but surely found their place. Juniper, birch, hazel, willow, pine, oak, elm and alder all found a home here. They came roughly in that order, drawing on the rich supplies of nutrients in the still young soil. However, these trees towered over the arctic alpines and other plants, taking away the abundant light they needed for their survival. But these plants of the open spaces were saved from local extinction by a scattering of places of refuge, steep cliffs, eroding river banks and flood plains, and by loose uncompacted soil on which the encroaching trees could gain no foothold.

Movement through any part of the dale at that time would have been very difficult, for the valley bottom and the more gentle slopes were swathed in impenetrable swamp forest. More open woodland only existed on the higher, upper slopes and it was along these more open areas of the High Pennine ridges that the first hunter-farmers came to discover the upper dale.

All this and more is contained in one view upwards from Forest-in-Teesdale towards the magical fells. It seems odd that the place is called Forest-in-Teesdale, for there is now no real forest anywhere to be seen!

FROM FOREST-IN-TEESDALE TO CAULDRON SNOUT

New human activity across the post-Ice Ages put another kind of pressure on the great green belt of the upper dale: building development. The first documentary evidence of a building within the area comes from the Saxon period with the giving of a grant allowing the building of a house 'at the head of Kevaset next to Ethergilebec'. The instructions were both detailed and clear as to the size of the building, 20 x 2 perches, with 5 acres of land enclosed by hedges and ditches for the winter pasturage of mares and their colts. The grant was to the Abbey of Rievaulx, and it supplemented rights granted at the same time to graze sixty mares and their offspring through the remaining forests of the upper dale.

This large house must have simply added to a scattering of farmhouses which had gradually developed since the days of the area's Iron Age pioneers. Each house and steading they created was an intake from the Pennine wilderness still pristine in parts, taken in from the remaining fell or forest. Hence the name of one such development, Intake Farm.

From the time of the Normans, written records are more numerous and more exact in their telling of overlordship, of mixed relations within church and state. In 1218 the first mention is made of demands from the lead and silver industries for fuel from the forest. Trees disappeared rapidly from the sylvan river banks and the fellsides.

In 1550, Edward VI granted the mining rights of the upper dale to the Bowes family. Their record of success shows that they put new pressure on the remaining forest resources of the upper dale. More wood was needed to smelt the ore. It was locally available and it was much cheaper than the coal which had to be hauled up, with difficulty, from the collieries near the coast. So the rest of the trees were felled.

So it was that in 1670 Roger Baynbrigg argued his claim to the rank of gentleman by citing that his ancestors, who had lived in the same house since at least 1519, had been rangers of the forest. The location of his house is in all probability the same as Kevaset, standing within a plot taken in from the forest 500 years before.

The old vicarage at Forest-in-Teesdale, in reality nearer to Langdon Beck, is now an adventure training centre for outward bounders. The Bible has been supplanted by boots and rucksacks, ropes and hip-flasks; the sermon from the pulpit has given up the ghost to be replaced by the new religion of the great outdoors. Until recently the old vicarage was home to one of the great characters of the dale – Hugh Proctor: vicar, local historian and botanist. He boasted some 20,000 sheep among his flock but few of them ever came to church. So he made a pact, not with the devil but with the warden of the Youth Hostel. If any hostellers wanted to attend morning service, then the warden would hang a sheet from his window, clearly visible from the vicarage below. No sheet meant that Evensong was the order of that day.

A walk across the fells with the Reverend Hugh was a walk in praise of the theory of creative evolution, for this man of both god and science could name each and every plant that you'd come across. Hugh could even tell the genealogy of the willow hybrids along the becks. Family lines were recorded in his notebooks as assiduously as those in the baptismal records.

You can, of course, stay at the hostel or a number of B-and-Bs in Upper Teesdale, and if you do, how about a little genealogical research? A flick through the local telephone book and you should find the names Dowson, Tallentire, Anderson, Bainbridge, Scott, Watson, Walton, Teward, Beadle, Bell, Hutchinson, Tarn, Allinson, Rumeney, Collinson, Garrett, Robinson, Horn, Howard and Cousin. The top twenty families in the upper dale, well, they were in 1751 – are they still?

From Langdon Beck there are roads which lead up into the heart of sugar limestone country, the hills from which the Tees rises and where the landforms and flower life begin to get really interesting. The keen botanist can find spring gentian, alpine rue, Teesdale violet and another 136 plants of phytogeographical interest. Phytogeography is the discipline which seeks answers to the whys and wherefores of plant distribution – why some plants for example only grow in the Arctic while others favour the Alps. The fact that 139 different species drawn from many different backgrounds all grow together in Teesdale is of great interest and work still goes on to find out just why this should be so, and is one reason why much of the area was made a National Nature Reserve.

▼ Alpine bistort: one of the special Teesdale plants

Local farmer Alan Scott who lives at Intake Farm remembers when his family discovered that they had for years being ploughing up a patch of botanical heaven – without knowing it. When his father took over the neighbouring Widdy Bank Farm in the fifties Alan recalls, 'it was full of plants that we didn't know anything about in those days . . . From a little toddler I knew about th' blue gentian, but I didn't know anything about the alpine vartsias or bird's eye primroses or anythin' like this. We raked a lot of it, an' we fertilised it, even. Then, about the late fifties, the Nature Conservancy Council had a look at it an' decided we were going too far. Ah was vurry green an' vurry young, and I knew nothin' about business, like. An' it was just when father died. He jes dropped down dead at th' auction mart for sucklin' calves at Middleton-in-Teesdale. He went off one mornin' quite all right . . . an' came back dead . . . So bein' th' only one, I had tae set to work, and follow in his footsteps. Just at that time we were told that it was goin' tae be National Nature Reserve, the first in the area. I was astounded really. The powers that be were tellin' me what the restrictions were goin' tae be. Ah was worried. But I set tae work. Later in th' day the Nature Conservancy Council said they were as green in what they were doin' as ah was. It was the first management agreement of this type, that took a total farm into consideration.'

Over the years the NCC and Alan Scott have grown up together, guided by the need to maintain the rich alpine flora of Upper Teesdale, guided by nature and the life-cycle of plants like the hair sedge and spring cinquefoil.

In local farming circles it's still all a bit odd. 'I occasionally get asked to go to various farming groups in the winter, to talk to them about farming. And when I tell th' other farmers that one of my farms is a National Nature Reserve, th' other farm is an Environmentally Sensitive Area, and overall we've got an Area of Outstanding Natural Beauty, they wonder how on earth we move to do anythin' at all. In their infancy, these

▲ Cow Green Reservoir: wall-to-wall fitted water, a mirror to the seasons of the Upper Dale

things always set off a little bit daft, but after a little bit o' knockin' off the corners from both sides the job comes around. Some o' the things we do, to a neighbour over th' wall looks a bit silly, an' they'll say things, ye know. Me man that lives at Widdy Bank will come over to me an' he's been in th' pub an' the others will have been askin' what we're been up to: because you know, we've left a field late for cuttin', or done some wallin' and left a big dog-leg to miss a patch of a wet area where th' plants are, or somethin'. A bit of teasin' goes on. But when we explain it to people an' they realise what it's all about, *we* think it's worthwhile.'

Another scientific reason why Upper Teesdale is such an important heritage area is its archaeology. James Backhouse started research in 1887

in a cave at Moking Hurth near Langdon Beck. Detailed excavation revealed the bones of thirty animals including wolf and lynx, plus the skeleton of a prehistoric person. Further up the valley lie dramatic landform features like Falcon Clints, Cronkley Scar, Cauldron Snout and Cow Green but only Cow Green can be seen from the road. If you want to really see the others, and they are well worth the effort, follow the walk on page 43.

The Cow Green Reservoir route goes past Intake Farm over a dog-leg bridge complete with concrete flume and recorder put there to gauge the flow of the beck, then over a series of noisy cattle grids and across Widdybank Fell. In winter it can be a treacherous, ice-clad road, in summer it's a-dance with rain, or all of a shimmer with heat. On the left, the peat blanket laps down as if

▲ Cauldron Snout

to engulf the tarmacadam while on the right old mine workings gape in the hillside.

Then, there it is – Cow Green – a great upland lake, looking as natural as the Ice Age was long, a fell-to-fell fitted mirror, reflecting all the changes which the seasons ring on this land-scape. But it's a man-made affair. The truth of the matter is that the real Cow Green, an intermix of mines and grazing land, lies hidden beneath its iron-grey waters. Hidden too is one of the great features of the river which was, in the past, the subject of many postcards, the fabled Wheel of the Tees. Back in the pre-reservoir days the river made one great curve, or 'wheel', almost half a meander, before leaping down the cataracts of Cauldron Snout.

In the 1960s a scheme was put forward to dam the Tees at Cow Green in order to even out the flow of the river and thus ensure a summer supply of water for Teesside's thirsty industries: chemical and steel. Battle lines were drawn between pro- and anti-reservoir factions, and the lions of conservation and the unicorns of the water authority slogged it out in press, media and in a public inquiry. In the end the reservoir got the approval of a parliamentary bill and the world lost Cow Green and some of the High Pennines' unique plant communities. The Tees lost its 'wheel' but it gained a lake, the margin of which is a favourite haunt for lapwings and curlews. Cow Green is a good place to sit and reflect on all the other sacred Cow Greens in the world today and on the wise management of the resources of this earth.

A WALK AMONG THE ICE FLOWERS
CAULDRON SNOUT AND FALCON CLINTS

Teesdale has its secret places, places not signposted from the B6277, but accessible by car and foot. One such place, ideal for walkers, is the route to Wheeldale Sike and Cauldron Snout in the upper dale. This is rare flower country, a natural reserve of international acclaim, and a place of dramatic landscapes created by the Great Ice Age, with equally dramatic names. The total length of this walk is about 8 miles, taking about 4–5 hours. If you prefer something slightly shorter, you could retrace your steps from the Snout to where we suggest you leave your car. On both walks, it is important to remember you are in a National Nature Reserve, and to walk carefully.

From the B6277 take the turning for Langdon Beck north of Forest-in-Teesdale. The road goes past the Langdon Beck Hotel with its tiny bar, frequented by the local farmers. Known as 'the Warden's road', it rises and falls on its lonely way into the fells. Always on the horizon are a back view of the three peaks, Little Dun Fell, Great Dun Fell and, large and dominant, Cross Fell itself. After a gradual descent up and over the brow of the hill you come to Cow Green Reservoir.

From the car park follow the gravel path along the Nature Trail, lying above Cow Green Reservoir and leading to the big dam at its eastern end. Keep an eye

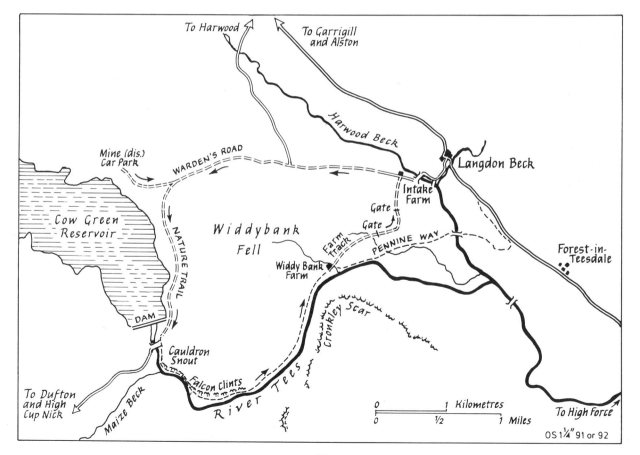

out for the birds; lapwing, curlew and the red grouse are resident here, the dunlin and oystercatcher are visitors. Before the reservoir, birds and flowers became an attraction to people, there were other riches, most notably mineral deposits. Near the car park from where you start your walk, there lies the opening to Cow Green mine. The mine now sleeps, but there are still minerals there, lead, barytes, silver and purple crystal fluorspar.

Follow the black tarmacadam road wending its way along the reservoir and look out for the patches of sugar limestone by the side of the road. Trees never found firm footholds in these places, nor did blanket-bog – the water just drained away. So the sugar limestone has remained open to the sky. It provided a safe retreat for arctic alpine and all other plants of open spaces during the thousands of years when the rest of the fells were covered with tall trees and acid bog. That is why one area of sugar limestone near the road has been fenced off to prevent the sheep from eating all the flowers.

On the fell beside the reservoir you will see, only in May or June, gentians which only open their trumpets on sunny days, blue moor grass, the first to flower in the year, hair sedge, alpine cinquefoil and sea plantain. Sea plantain? No, you didn't read us wrong, both sea plantain and sea thrift, which provide a floral welcome by the sea, are among the special plants of Upper Teesdale. Not just cliff ledges and sand dunes washed by salt spray, but also mountain pastures grazed hard by sheep, provide them with perfect habitats.

The little road dips and dips again and here you may need to brace yourself against the cool air pouring down from the distant High Pennine peaks and pounding against the slopes of Widdybank Fell. Despite the fact that this is a south-facing slope the temperature stays cool even on the warmest of days.

Near the stone pile on the south-west side of the reservoir you can stand and imagine where the great Wheel of the Tees used to turn and turn again. This was not however a man-made wheel but a crescent of golden water where the river turned in a great loop, as if savouring the magic and delight of the place before plunging headlong over Cauldron Snout. Old post-cards still turn up in farm kitchens and local sales showing crinolined ladies crossing the former bridge above the falls with the Wheel in the background.

The 'slap-slap' of the reservoir waves empounded by the strait-jacket of the dam suggests that the Tees is impatient to get on with its journey. After heavy rain when the reservoir is full, curtains of water spill over the top and within minutes build up to the awesome roar of the Tees in full flood cataracting over Cauldron Snout. Here it is swollen even more by the strength of Maize Beck before crashing further downriver over the rocks of High Force. It is an amazing sight.

It is at this point, at Cauldron Snout, that the trekkers on the Pennine Way heading north usually find themselves directed westwards to Dufton and High Cup Nick overlooking the glorious vale of Eden on the other side of the Pennines. It is a diversion well worth taking if you have the time – a full day and a friend with another car to get you back. You'll also need equipment: boots, waterproofs, food, hot drink, compass, maps, whistle, and spare warm clothing. Is all this equipment necessary? you may ask. The answer is an emphatic yes. Snow can lie up here even in June, and the first flurries of winter appear in September. And when it rains, it doesn't just rain, it 'tanks' it down, as they say locally. If you take this route you will see the Lakeland hills appear in the distance. The walk draws to an end over smooth limestone sward, until suddenly the ground drops away, and the full spectacle of High Cup Nick lies before you. This is the most dramatic approach to it, but a shorter route is described in another walk (page 186).

Continuing with our Teesdale walk back at Cauldron Snout, you have to scramble down beside the falls. If you continue the walk, rather than retrace your steps, you would be well advised to wear stout footwear and waterproofs. The whinstone provides a good pathway of flat steps and stairs. But it can be slippery, and precious plants grow between the rocks, enjoying an equal right to be there. Most of them won't survive a trip down the foamy Tees any better than us.

At the bottom there is time to stand and take in a marvellous panorama, an amphitheatre of sheer wonder, the living heart of Upper Teesdale complete with pulsing water. Behind to the north, tower the rock bastions of Falcon Clints. As the name suggests, golden eagles used to wheel over these great cliffs. Perhaps one day they will be back to enjoy lost eyries, still full of ferns and heather. Cowberry and crowberry cling to the cliffs with the odd gnarled mountain ash hinting of the forest that once did its best to cover the whole terrain.

The path skirts along the base of the cliffs, nearly becoming lost in the gigantic rockery. The boulders themselves provide firm footholds for a mass of mosses and lichens including the mustard-yellow spotty one that paints maps across the rock surface – hence one of its names, *geographicum*. Down among the boulders is the home of the chasmophytes – not dwarfs and gnomes, but plants like broad buckler, lady fern, wood anemone and wood horsetail; plants left over from forest times but, having no trees to provide shelter and shade, they now hide away among the fallen rocks.

In places duckboards have been installed to stop too many feet damaging the wettest parts. It certainly has become wetter in recent times. Possibly, the water pounding behind that high level dam is leaking through the joints in the rock, perhaps even finding its way through the galleries of old lead mines, in the maze of 't'auld men's workings', as these are locally known.

Across the river there is the gradual swell of Cronkley Fell. Beside one of the many becks draining you can see a few of the gaunt junipers which lead in a great dark green tattered arc back to their stronghold near High Force. Further along lies Cronkley Scar, a superb example of Teesdale landscape and once the location of the Widdy Bank Pencil Mill. A small outcrop of pre-Devonian shale in the rocks proved ideal for the manufacture of slate – or more correctly shale – pencils. At one time these were a must for every schoolchild when slates and not paper were the tools of the classroom.

Beyond Cronkley Scar, the valley opens out and the going gets easier, welcoming you into the green fields of Widdy Bank Farm, and one of the most fantastic settings for a house anywhere within the Pennines. If you are in luck you may get to meet Harold and his family, and you will certainly hear his dogs, chickens and cows. The difficulties of farming in this high and remote corner of England can be surmised when you see one of Harold's preferred animal breeds – Highland cattle. In summertime you may be able to buy a welcome cup of tea and hear at first hand the problems of farming within a flower-decked National Nature Reserve.

From here you follow the farm track, away from the river and the Pennine Way towards Langdon Beck. You'll soon see the road come into view as well as the farms and hamlet of Langdon Beck. You've then got a 2½-mile walk back along the unfenced moorland road to the car park at Cow Green, and home base.

2
WEARDALE
LAND OF THE LEAD MEN

Over the hills, but not so far away from Langdon Beck, along a small, unclassified mountain road signposted for St John's Chapel lies Weardale, a 'working' landscape pocked with lead hills and abandoned quarries. Weardale is a wide valley which may lack the landscape qualities of Teesdale or the Eden valley, but more than makes up for them with its industrial heritage, its stone villages, its rich haymeadows, flower-decked wooded tracts and the little 'linns' or waterfalls which pour from the hills into the Wear. The caves are said to be frequented by little folk, and there are the remains of a forest where the Prince Bishops of Durham once sported for venison, and a network of the pathways where once ran local railway lines.

Beyond the cattle grids on the road over from Teesdale you're into wild, high, open country. This route reaches the dizzy height of 2056 feet as it crosses the flank of Harthope Moor, giving good access for each winter's supply of cross-country skiers. On the fellside there are ski tows and a club which meets in the bright white of winter. But the presence of skiers in these parts is no modern phenomenon. In *Walks in Weardale* (1885) Hubert Smith recounts:

When the fells are covered with snow, the hardy dalesmen indulge in the favourite exercise of skeeing; skees are large wooden skates or snow shoes. The skee is about 6 feet long, from 4 to 6 inches wide, about half an inch thick and slightly curved upwards at the toe. About six inches back from the middle of the skee is a wood upright against which the heel rests, the foot is further secured by a strap. A six foot pole, called a skee pleeat, is used with the skees, for steering and for leaping over walls . . . The skees are utilised for travelling over the fells in a snowstorm to rescue overblown sheep; the treacherous drifts of snow, that make the fellsides inaccessible to the ordinary pedestrian are safely traversed by aid of the skees.

On the watershed between dales there used to be a notice warning of the dangers of blasting, and iron pillboxes for the flag people to hid in. The notice, the boxes and the red flag are no longer there. Yet the quarry somehow keeps getting larger. In ten years of crossing this road neither of us has ever seen machines or explosives in action. It is a mystery.

Weardale: a dale for all seasons ▶

There is one good thing though: the activities of quarrymen have provided a splendid nesting area for black-headed gulls. These seabirds seem to like the peace and quiet of the fells and the watery places of the deserted quarries. Every spring, between the piles of stones and the diggers, their eggs are laid in little piles amidst circles of tufty grass.

Though the shortest, the Langdon road is just one of many routes between the two dales. Another runs from just below Ashgill Head in Teesdale skirting Coldberry End at 2212 feet to Ireshopeburn. It is not an advisable route to try in winter! Even in the summer it is little more than a track with gates to open and close, a challenge to anyone's perseverance with the country code.

A third route between the two dales is the B6278 from Middleton-in-Teesdale and though it only touches 1678 feet, it leads you on to the ford at Stanhope which is great fun to cross, but dangerous in flood.

FROM ST JOHN'S CHAPEL TO THE KILLHOPE WHEEL

The Langdon road drops like a roller-coaster ride into the vale of Weardale and St John's Chapel, home of the annual Pennine sheep auctions which bring in farmers with an eye for a bargain from far and wide. Though modest in its general landscape, Weardale is dramatic enough country. Both river and road lead eventually downdale to one of Britain's World Heritage Sites – the great cathedral church of Durham.

Back up the valley stands another World Heritage Site, Killhope Wheel. A simple turn left through Ireshopeburn past Cromptons, the stylish wool weavers and its shop which sells 'fresh milk, plain or flavoured' brings you to Cowshill with its bull-size 'boot hill', a long graveyard on the far side of the river stretching from the church. Fork left at the Allendale Turn and there in the distance the great wheel of the Wear

▲ Retired quarry: yet there's wildlife amidst the rubbish

Weardale's golden fleeces ▶
(Inset) Sheep talk at St John's Chapel mart

comes into view. Unlike the 'wheel' of the Tees which was natural but ultimately destroyed to make way for industry, this one was specially constructed, formed by industry.

Near 40 feet in diameter, this tremendous water wheel, wrought in iron, was mobilised by the energy of moving water flowing on to the top of the wheel and filling its buckets – a process known as the overshot system. The power it

▲ Killhope, the great wheel of the Wear

cheaper ores were found elsewhere. The wheel stopped, and for nearly a century the great wheel of Weardale and its outhouses have stood derelict. During the last war it was scheduled to be cut up for scrap but fortunately the man with the cutting apparatus simply failed to turn up!

Happily in 1968 Durham County Council took a lease on the site and opened it up as a picnic area. Then twelve years later, they began major restoration works on the wheel and buildings, making the site the largest employer of labour in the upper dale. The restoration was financed by the European Development Fund and various UK organisations, including the Countryside Commission and English Heritage, with help from two local firms, Blue Circle Industries of Eastgate and Weardale Mineral Holdings. The 'Friends of Killhope' have provided volunteers, collected material and helped in research. They also organise fund-raising events. Their annual quoits match is one of the highlights of the year.

Another Killhope friend is the poet Jon Silkin, whose visit to the ruin in the late 1960s filled him with a mixture of feelings of romance and terror:

> The earth comes moist looking and
>   blackens;
> a trickle of earth where the feet pressed,
> twice a day, wearing off the grass.
> Where the miners
> were seen; a letter blown damply
> into the corner of a hut: "Oh dear love,
>   come to me"
> and nothing else.
> Where are they?
> The sheep bleat back to the mist balding
> with terror; where
> are they? The miners
> are under the ground.

generated was used to crush the galena or lead ore brought up from the mines, or 'levels' which puncture the hillsides all around.

The water, led by a large wooden aqueduct from stream-fed reservoirs on the moor above, drove the wheel and was then collected and used again and again to wash the ore clean of unwanted dirt and stone, and to drive smaller water wheels on the washing floor.

The wheel made its final turn at the end of the nineteenth century, probably crushing the last ore mined in the upper dale. Lead mining died –

Since Silkin wrote those lines things have changed. For the wheel of Weardale is now a heritage centre, explaining all the aspects of the lead mining industry, from extracting the rock, or 'bouse' dressing, to recovering the lead and silver ore. In the reconstructed 'mine shop' you can see where the miners spent their off-duty time away from their homes. You can also see the washing floor, where the galena was extracted from out of the 'bouse', and the buildings where further refinement of the 'bouse' took place.

Wilf Swindle Brown of Rookhope, one of the few of the original Weardale lead miners still alive in the 1980s to tell his tale, remembers starting work in a now long gone mine yard not far from Killhope:

'Ah was fourteen years old in 1913. An' ah finished school on the Friday an' ah started work on th' Monday, for a penny an hour on th' pickin' table. The lead was put out of a hopper into this movin' table. You picked the stones off, that's all ye did, ye let go th' ones that had lead ore in, an' you let them go, and ye let them goa inte th' crusher. Then there used to be a little gauge railway line thet ran all th' way up inta th' smelt mill, an' the lead ores wuz roasted, an' when it came out o' thar, they put it into anuther furnace, an' they got the lead out, what we called the pigs, or ingots o' lead. After that it went to Castleside for lead sheeting and piping an' that.'

The system of labour carried out at Killhope and the other mines by Wilf Swindle Brown and his fellows is interesting. The miners did not work for the company – but for themselves, in partnerships of any number from three to ten. This was part of a 'bargain' struck with the London Lead Company to work a part of the mine. They were paid for ore produced, a bonus system without a wage. Their output of 'bouse' was brought out of the mine in mine cars, or trams, and tipped into 'bousesteads'. There are ten of these at Killhope, one for each of the partnerships.

At the 'bousesteads', the material was washed by running water to clear away dirt and to make it possible to pick out the large pieces of shining silvery galena, which were then taken straight to the 'bingstead'. There the ore was weighed, put into carts and taken down the valley on the road built by the Quaker-owned London Lead Company, to the smelt mill. Here it was turned into lead, to be used as sheet for roofing, or pipes for water, or lead shot for sport and war – an odd end use for a Quaker and therefore peace-loving company.

The larger pieces of stone and lead were broken by hand using a hammer with a flat-iron head. The work was done by women and girls as well as washer boys. Regardless of age, sex, health or temperament, they all had to face the rigours of the long hours and inclement weather on the washing floor. Washing the ore must have had its moments though – like panning for gold. Galena is heavier than the surrounding rock and other minerals. It was extracted by simply washing away the lighter material and leaving behind the lead ore, 'Killhope gold'. Other more sophisticated methods were also used. In fact the washing floor at Killhope has been excavated by archaeologists to reveal a network of water channels or 'buddles' which used running water at various speeds to sort out the ore.

The Wear is a hard-working river and its valley a hard-worked dale. At the very top you can see how the scars of industry are healing as old spoil heaps turn into flower-rich grassland and short heath. Steep sides rich in minerals and limestone make the valley of the Wear ideal for mining and for quarrying. A railway line down the dale still serves the mineral extractions and, on odd occasions, the more general public, as a way to and from the rich pastures. There are plans for it to be opened up as a regular passenger line once more.

At the heart of every landscape is a river, and every river is made up of its tributaries, each in its time-worn place. Those of the Tees are called 'becks' reminiscent of the Lake District and all Pennine stations south. But those of the Wear are called 'burns' – possibly a hangover from the era of the Border reivers! You can even do a 'burns' tour!

Killhope, Wellhope, and Burnhope burns are ideal starting points. A walk along the rim of their catchments is a muddy challenge even on the driest day. Their rim makes up the furthest boundary of the Durham County Palatine, taking in such high spots as Burnhope Seat, Dead Stones, Nag's Head and Knoutberry Hill, all well above 2000 feet. 'Knout' is a local common name for the succulent fruit of the cloudberry, now a rarity, especially in flower. The cloudberry was once so common it was on sale in High Pennine markets.

There are no points for guessing how Wear-head got its name. Below the village which straggles along the A689, the trinity of headwaters are swollen in turn by the burns of Burnhope, Ireshope, Middlehope, Westernhope and Rookhope. 'Hope' stands for 'valley', clipped by local accent to 'up' – ups down which the waters flow. But 'ups' were also 'hopes' like the hope from those families of the past who scraped a dual existence from the dale: families who hoped beyond hope some day to strike it rich from mineral winnings. And hopes were rekindled each Sunday at each one of the many Methodist chapels which dot the dale.

The lead days in Weardale were hard times and no doubt religion provided a necessary balance against the hardship and the wilderness. But somehow in the old culture of the dale all these worldly and pious aspirations got jumbled up together. Rookhope miner, Wilf Swindle Brown, remembers the curious religiousness of one of the old families in his story of Jim, Jack and the horse and trap on which their survival depended:

'There were two young fellows, Jim and Jack, and they'd lived on a farmstead with the old man, and the mother and then the old man had died. When he died, ye see, he hadn't much tae leave, but anyway he had a little Galloway [horse] an' cart, so he left it between them. An' they had te share that Galloway an' cart for takin' one thing or t'other out, like. Then Jim fell bad, an' Jack used to go, an' sit down by the bedside an' pray with him. At the finish, he wuz ill. An' Jack clasped his hands an' sat down by the bedside, an' he said:

> *"O Jesus Christ my heavenly king*
> *Look down upon my brother Jim*
> *And take him to thy heavenly home*
> *An then th'Galloway an' cart'll be*
> *   my own".*

You can catch more than a glimpse of the way of life of the dale's mining community at the Weardale Museum in Ireshopeburn. The old

▼ Flush with rushes and wet grasses: Knoutberry Hill

minister's house adjoining High House Chapel has been converted on one side for new seekers of dale spirit, where the events of bygone dale days are woven into a colourful back-parlour tapestry. A moment in the chapel itself is a good excuse for a rest and the opportunity to gather tranquil strength from the prayers, music and hope that has reverberated around these galleried walls in the past.

Parking is in the Rancho Del Rio, now the 'Rancho'. Here music of another sort, complete with a wrap-round wild west experience, links you with the many who, finding few 'ups' and too many 'downs', left the dale to make new-world lives in the wild west of America. If you book in advance at the 'Ranch' you can enjoy all the home comforts of a good western evening, with tacos, coffee, horse liquor and beans. At one time the Rancho organised cowboy evenings in full regalia, complete with spurs and six-guns, shoot-outs and bar bowls. A little excessive, you might think, but appropriate in another way – for Weardale was once a haven for cattle rustlers who stole from the lowlands by night. Nowadays the odd bit of rustling still goes on in these parts. So watch you tether your car!

Down the dale there are roads on both sides of the river, port and starboard, except through Stanhope where there is but one. So there are various permutations and combinations of route, of loop and flailing figures of eight to add spice to your journey. Each bridge you cross holds out the chance of seeing trout or even salmon swimming against the current. On the dry banks and above on the fellsides stand lone farmhouses in the corner of their very own jumble of sloping fields.

ROOKHOPE AND THE BACK ROAD

Rookhope is one of our favourite places in the whole of the Pennines. The burn which runs through it from head to foot is associated in history with Border broils, and with a foray by moss-troopers in 1569, during the Rising of the North. According to a ballad of the time, the 'Rookhope Ryde', the invading moss-troopers were intent on lamb for supper:

> Then in at Rookhope head they came;
> They ran the forest but a mile.
> They gathered together in four hours
> Six hundred sheep within a while.

But the pillagers were seen by the watch, and were chased off by the Bailiff of Eastgate, one George Emerson, and his men.

▼ One of the arches that bore the Rookhope Chimney

The wild beauty of Rookhope incorporates some great 'small' landscape features, rolling moors, bracken banks and wooded glens, abandoned quarries and hillside haymeadows, as well as old lime kilns and lead workings. Beyond the last of the farmsteadings where the road winds ever on up to the pass of Allenheads, you will see the iron tower of Groverake, until recently a working fluorspar mine, now an overground shelter for owls and sheep. Working or not, Groverake is still a great sight from the road, a little winding column and wheel from a once working dale. There's a nursery specialising in arctic alpines, a wealth of industrial archaeology, lead and iron and some really bracing walks. Perhaps most famous of the dale's archaeological relics are the Rookhope Borehole, the Rookhope Chimney – still there to be seen – and the famous Redburn Skulls.

The Bore-hole was the brainchild of Sir Kingsley Dunham, a former Professor of Geology at Durham University. He cored deep beneath the Pennine moors to discover solid granite. The Rookhope Chimney ran up to the hill over the road, a stone smoke-o-duct. The remains of the chimney are still there and the course of the flue can be followed up the hillside by foot or by eye. Part of it can be seen at the junction of the Allendale-Blanchland road, then up on the valley side, where it once discharged its noxious fumes high above the village. The chimney's enormous length not only provided the draft necessary to keep the smelters roaring but also served as a depository for the valuable particles of lead and silver swept out of the smelt mill by the draught – and which would have been lost in the clean moorland air along with the sulphurous fumes. They were not wanted, but the metals were, and teams of boys used to sweep out the chimney at weekends.

All those with a real interest in industrial archaeology could spend a lifetime around Rookhope probing into the past of a village which has been in existence at least since Roman times. The diligent could well unearth new skeletons from Weardale's historical cupboard. Not so long ago workmen in the Gannister quarry discovered eight complete and one battered human skull all bearing terrible teeth marks. No other remains of bodies were found and the Redburn Skulls mystery remains unsolved. As those fingers of mist creep down the old back of the chimney, what, you might well ask, still lurks up there on the fells?

Rookhope is not all old relics and chilling tales. The dale is alive with flowers and romance too. If you look closely, you'll see roadsides, haymeadows and old quarry floors stacked with the colours that wild pansies and early purple orchids bring in spring and summer. Rookhope has inspired romantic poetry too. Sir Walter Scott based his epic poem 'Harold the Dauntless' on a visit to Rookhope: in the poem, Rookhope is home to an outlaw forest archer, a Robin Hood of sorts, Wulfstane, married to a witch, the

▼ An early purple orchid, flourishing on Weardale's lead wasteground

notorious Jutta. They had a daughter Metelill, who:

> One morn in kirtle green array'd
> Deep in the wood the maiden stray'd
> And where a fountain sprung
> She sate her down, unseen, to thread
> The scarlet berry's mimic braid,
> And while the beads she strung
> Like the blithe lark, whose carol gay
> Gives a good morrow to the day,
> So lightsomely she sung.

Then Harold the Dauntless chanced upon her. And if you want to know what happens from there, you'll have to read the poem. It is stirring stuff, as befits the romance and power of the scene in which it is cast, down by the Rookhope Burn.

To pick up our route, travel up the dale via the A689 from Eastgate, at the foot of Rookhope, to Daddry Shield. If you have a sense of adventure you may like to travel the next stage down the dale via its infamous 'Bak Rood', the back road. At one time this was the main road through the dale. It is narrow, it runs between stone walls, twists and turns and invariably somewhere en route you will meet a farm tractor. However it has many compensations, chiefly scenery and tranquillity. For there is very little through traffic, and the farms and buildings along the route are charming. This is Weardale at its best.

At Daddry Shield the back road is on the left after you cross the Wear. It can also be reached either from the centre of the village of Westgate, by crossing the Wear, or further down the dale at Eastgate, about a quarter of a mile east of the road junction.

Travelling now on the south side of the river, you can clearly see the height to which the cultivated fields, the 'intake' fields taken in from the surrounding moorland, reach up the south-facing side of the dale, the highest extending up to 1200 feet above sea level. This is hill farming country, the pattern of the land and the farming year shaped and dictated by the breeding habits of sheep. Lambing comes much later up the dale: even as late as the month of May, for snow can linger until then, and longer too, in the higher fells and the north-facing gullies. Haymaking can be as late as July or August. In the days when the dale was busy with lead mining, the miners were also smallholders with small fields of oats harvested before the hay for the horses. Lead ore and ironstone were carried around the dale by packhorse and cart to the smelt mills and railheads until the arrival of the steam wagon in the early part of this century. Horses were kept in the dale for farming purposes well after the demise of the lead mine.

Down the road, away from Westgate lies Eastgate. The area in between the two gates, a 'garden' of trees and fields, used to be known as the Forest Quarter. This is prime visitor country, complete with camping and caravanning facilities and village shops. Time was when this area served the Bishops of Durham with venison, and it was also known as the Bishops' Park. Described in 1540 as 'rudley enclosed with stone of a twelve or fourteen miles in compass', it was not all trees at the time (a forest was as much an area of jurisdiction as a description of the vegetation cover): there were farms and pastures as well. The 'branches' moving in the middle distance were antlers not trees. A poem from the time of the Bishops recalls 'the antlered monarch of the waste' springing 'from his heathery couch in haste', as the hunting horn echoed from hill to hill. The Bishops took their toll on the game forest. And during the sixteenth century it was reported that deer were becoming scarce in the forest. Yet it was not hunting that sounded their ultimate death knell. Like the trees which gave them shelter and cover from the huntsman's eye, they were victims to the predations of cultivation and their historic stamping ground was taken over for the new mineral enterprises of the dalesmen.

The Durham Prince Bishops have suddenly enjoyed a revival in County Durham, now known as the 'Land of the Prince Bishops' after the County's tourist planners realised in the 1980s their historical uniqueness. They reigned from Roman times to the 1800s. Their castle was a palace at Bishop Auckland further down the Wear valley, their church the tremendous cathedral at Durham, and their estates included land in Northumberland, North Yorkshire and the hunting park in Weardale. At one time in 1302 they were regarded as the second kings of England, wearing mitres instead of crowns as their symbols of regality. To all intents and purposes they behaved like kings, with independent powers of 'kingship' vested by the Norman king, William Rufus. The Prince Bishops administered civil and criminal law and had the power of pardon, the right to mint money, charter markets, create barons and raise their own army.

The English kings saw the Prince Bishops as an important buffer against the Scots. The Bishops and their men fought against the Scots at Falkirk and at the famous battle of Otterburn in 1388. But the relationship between crown and mitre wasn't always so friendly. At various times in the Middle Ages the crown temporarily took back the helm. In the seventeenth century the Bishops' power began to decline and they came under severe general criticism for their feudal ways, power and political excesses. Then in 1836 with the founding of Durham University by Bishop Van Mildert, the rights and privileges of the Palatinate were reinstated with those of the crown.

Westgate village was a railhead from about the middle of the nineteenth century when the Weardale Iron Company built its remarkable railway from Rookhope contouring the northern rim of the dale into the Middlehope valley. They engineered the way down into Westgate, the famous Scutterhill incline, to collect the ironstone being brought down from Wearhead and Ireshopeburn.

The back road twists and turns through Brotherlee up to the edge of the moorland. Following the road here gives a good opportunity to look across the valley to the ancient field system behind Old Park Farm, and to see the platform site of the Prince Bishops' mediaeval hunting lodge, set in the centre of a mediaeval park carved out of the wild uncultivated area of the upper dale. There were very few settlements, if any, in the park, with perhaps only the faint remains of the clearings for summer pastures with their hut, or 'schele', as at Daddry Shields. The park was enclosed with a stone wall and had an Eastgate and a Westgate, and way up on the fell a Northgate, where there is a farm with that name.

Once through all the 'gates' our own Weardale way dips past Westernhopeburn, where there are two delightful seventeenth-century buildings. One of these, a farmhouse with an unaltered facade, has the date 1606 inscribed on the door lintel. The building next door has been altered, though not too recently. It has the date 1671 inscribed. Both houses have steep stone slate roofs and attached farm buildings which are of a similar age.

▼ One of the Westernhopeburn farmhouses

Horsley Hall, now a hotel, was at one time the home of the Hildyards. This grand stone building occupies an imposing position on the hillside between the fell and the river. The new owner of the Hall has tastefully renovated its crumbling exterior, though the addition of the stone horses at the front and the giant piranha beside the bar is more indicative of his sense of humour!

The last of the line of the original occupants of Horsley Hall was E. J. W. Hildyard. He was a notable local amateur archaeologist, whose work and own discoveries persuaded many a dales shepherd and farmer to pass on to him all their casual finds. Between 1945 and 1952 he wrote up a summary of his collection in six whole volumes, an encyclopaedia of archaeological dale riches. Hildyard established a grand Weardale tradition. In 1985 Dr Robert Young of Lampeter College, another local man, produced a three-volume thesis on the archaeology of Weardale describing the great wealth of remains in the dale, from the Bronze Age hut circles on Bollihope Common to the lead mining remains scattered throughout. It was at Eastgate, in the Rookhope Burn, that the schoolmaster and innkeeper Thomas Moore found the Roman altar stone dedicated to the god Silvanus, giving thanks for a successful hunt. A replica has been made of the altar and is neatly displayed beside the telephone kiosk on the main road at Eastgate.

Between Eastgate and Stanhope the dale is narrow and the roads, railway and river are in close proximity to one another, weaving through farms with such delightful names as Snow Field, Howl John, Hag Gate and Golden Lands. From Aller Gill for the next mile or two the roadside verge is crowded with beautiful fronds of sweet cicely. This northern plant gives off a strong fragrance of aniseed when any part of its leaf or stem is crushed. During the last war it was used by the local housewives as a sweetener for jams and pies. The sweet cicely jostles for roadside space with the exquisite flowers of the meadow cranesbill which paint the dale blue from May to October.

STANHOPE, THE QUEEN OF THE DALE

The back road joins the B6278 after crossing the railway line. A left turn brings you over the river via the mediaeval Stanhope Bridge and on to the main dales road at Stanhope. The centre of the dale, Stanhope stands on a crossroads, the main dales road running east and west. The B6278 north from Stanhope to Derwentside climbs the notorious Crawleyside Bank with its essential escape lane.

This is old railway country, where the Iron Horse served the industry of the dale. Despite the steepness of the gradients a railway used to run alongside the road. Its route tunnelled under the road and reappeared at the site of Crawley Engine, where a stationary engine once hauled up the trucks of lime, ironstone and lead ore. The line of the Stanhope and Tyne Railroad ran alongside the road on a green sward to the higher site of another stationary winding engine, known as the Weatherhill. Removed after the closure of the line in 1951, this winding engine was re-erected in the National Railway Museum at York.

The original railroad was first opened in 1834, a project unique for its time. It ran across bare moorland, and had to run up and down the sides of a ravine on an elaborate cradle, but did not work too well, being replaced in the end by a viaduct. The line from Stanhope to South Shields ran into financial difficulties, and had to be rescued and divided into two sections. The eastern half became the profitable coal-carrying Pontop and Jarrow Railway. The western half became part of the Stockton and Darlington Railway, hauling limestone and ironstone to the ironworks at Consett, Tow Law and Tudhoe.

Stanhope, with its air of Victorian regality, became known as 'the queen of the dale'. The main road leads into a small square, the Market Square, under the back wall of Stanhope Castle which was built in 1798 on the site of an ancient ruined castle, at a cost so high it ruined its builder. From then on it had a chequered history, beginning as a county seat and becoming amongst other things a museum to house stuffed birds and mineral displays, a shooting lodge and an approved school – a fortress for keeping hooligans in rather than invading armies out! Its

▲ Stanhope Castle

future is now uncertain, but it may become a hotel.

More impressive is the massively built fortified manor house of Stanhope Hall on a small rise above the Stanhope Burn. Surrounded by old outbuildings it has a brew house, a cornmill and some good examples of typical dale farm buildings, including byres, cattle pens and a threshing floor. From about the middle of the twelfth century it was the home of the Featherstonehaughs; pronounced the Weardale way 'Featherstunhaff'. The house grew with the family. It is part mediaeval, part Elizabethan and part Jacobean and was theirs until the last male member of the line died during Marlborough's campaign in Austria in 1704.

On the same side of the road stands what used to be the Stanhope Castle Gardens, a nursery garden with a heated wall for warmth-loving creepers, and for figs and grapes, a gazebo and tower. The tower is still there: old gardeners had the luxury of a two-storey crenellated building overlooking their gardens in which to draw up their plans and keep an eye out for the gaffer. Fortified potting sheds – what next! There are plans in the dale to use the site for generating different types of products within a brand new Dales Centre, a multi-purpose enterprise which will provide information and facilities for the visitor and training in lost dales skills and crafts for the young people of Weardale and the wider Pennines.

On the south side of Stanhope's Front Street, hiding behind a high garden wall and a line of lime trees and showing its back to the town, is the Rectory. This grand mansion, now the parish hall, a house and flats, was built ' . . . anno pacis evangelii 1697 Ryswicii' as recorded on its shield of arms above the door. It was rebuilt in 1821 as a faithful copy of the original building by the Durham architect Ignatius Bonomi, for the then Rector, one Dr Philpotts, at a cost of £12,000. Expensive for the times, but then the Rectorship of Stanhope was one of the richest church livings in England, if not the richest.

Its income was derived from the lead tithes paid by the miners from days of lead mining dating back to the Elizabethan era. The attraction of such a large income often led to the Rectorship being held by a non-resident priest, more often than not a bishop. This fact is revealed on the roll-call of the priests from 1200 onwards on the tower wall of the church. In 1835 the Rector received a gross income of £4,875 but because he was absent he had to delegate all his parish work to two curates. Together their total pay amounted to little more than £279 out of the £4,875.

In 1646 the Rector was Dr Isaac Basire, who was chaplain to Charles I. After his imprisonment in Stockton Castle during the Civil War, Basire fled the country to preach to and to convert Greeks and Arabs from their 'heathen' ways. He returned to Stanhope on the restoration of Charles II, and demanded the outstanding tithes of lead ore from the miners. They rightly refused to pay. Basire responded by threatening to excommunicate them. He took the case to law and to the House of Commons. Parliament decided that the tithe had to be paid 'for all time'. However, in 1837 a more enlightened Rector proposed that it should be abolished. It was no wonder that when Wesley came to preach there in the late 1740s he attracted huge crowds of lead miners disillusioned with the greed of the established Church. Following Wesley, Methodism spread quickly in the dale.

St Thomas's Church with its Norman tower stands on the north side of the Market Square. At

▲ The Frosterley marble coffin

▲ Stanhope's 250-million-year-old tree

the base of the tower beside the porch lie some thirteenth-century grave covers and a fine example of a stone coffin of Frosterley marble. In front of the churchyard wall stands the market cross, and on the church wall the 250-million-year-old fossil tree, discovered in 1962 in a local quarry and carefully extracted and rebuilt on this site. There is a plaque which reads:

This great tree grew in a forest of the carboniferous period about two hundred and fifty million years ago near Edmundbyers Cross now 1,556 feet above sea level. As the vegetable matter decayed it was replaced by sand which has formed a perfect cast in hard ganister. The roots' stigmaria show their characteristic form. The tree was brought to Stanhope and erected here in 1962 by Mr J. Beaston.

The structure is a reminder written in ancient stone that although the Rector of Stanhope earned his keep from lead mining the majority of his local male parishioners earned their meagre income from quarrying. They could not live on lead alone.

Quarries lie across the landscape in both the north and south of the town. Work in them finished long ago. They are now deserted and stand empty, forlorn, but grand with their sheer cliff walls and damp stony floors. They are viewed with envious eyes by the waste disposal industry, calculating how many tons of waste and how many years they would take to fill. The steep and precipitous sides, stabilised now after years of weathering, serve a much better purpose as nesting sites for kestrels and ravens which live there. Where the quarry floor is grass covered, cropped short by sheep, there are spring-fed ponds of clear, sweet water abundant with insect and amphibian life. On grass-covered ledges inaccessible to the sheep, lime-loving plants are becoming established. Drier grazing slopes are purpled by patches of wild mountain thyme.

Stanhope is a town for walks. There is a simple stroll around the town, the church, the castle and the castle park which takes you into quiet corners, and on sunny days, into some busy ones. If you are keen on the built environment there are some good historic buildings to admire, like the Methodist Chapel first opened in 1851 to keep pace with the rising popularity of Methodism in the dale, and the more humble school which goes with it. Across the road from the Market Place stands the former Phoenix Hotel, renamed the Bonny Moor Hen. This was once known as the Black Bull Inn and was the scene of the notorious 'Battle of Stanhope'. It, however, was more of a popular insurrection than a 'battle', an insurrection fought for the rights to the 'bonny moor hen' and the pub's new name.

Life for the lead miner was hard and food expensive, yet all round on the moors flew free breakfast, dinner and tea in the shape of the 'bonny moor hen' – the red grouse. This local game bird was however strictly reserved for the Bishop of Durham and his guests, a privilege closely protected by his keepers. If the miners wanted to eat grouse, and to provide for their families when times were hard, they had to poach it. But one day in 1818 a group of them were caught in the act by a bevy of gamekeepers who put the miners under arrest. They were marched off to Stanhope and locked in a room in the Black Bull awaiting transportation to Durham Gaol. Their fellow miners formed a rescue party and burst into the inn, and fought fiercely with the hated keepers, working men like themselves. In the fracas all the prisoners got away and the keepers were thrashed to within an inch of their lives. Strangely, no one was ever charged nor brought to book. The event is marked as a resounding victory for the miners in a desperate age, and is remembered in these anonymous lines:

> You brave lads of Weardale, I pray lend an
>   ear,
> The account of a battle you quickly shall
>   hear,
> That was fought by the miners, so well you
>   may ken,
> By claiming a right to their bonny moor
>   hen.
> Oh, this bonny moor hen, as it plainly
>   appears,
> She belongs to their fathers some hundreds
>   of years;
> But the miners of Weardale are all valiant
>   men,
> They will fight till they die for the bonny
>   moor hen.

An ironic twist to this tale is that on one of the moors near Stanhope there is a 'gin palace', a deluxe shooting box for wealthy visitors to Weardale who come in hot pursuit of the 'bonny moor hen'. They come in by helicopter, apply eye to gun barrel and do one-sided battle with the bonny bird of the moors!

THE HEATHERY BURN CAVES

The limestone around Stanhope is famous for its caves. The one south of Ludwell, known as Fairy Holes, which is a designated Site of Special Scientific Interest, developed along a major fault in the great limestone layers. Another important cave in the system is on the Shittlehope Burn (across the fields from Jollybody Farm, just below Hill Crest), where traces of early habitation by people have been found. The entrance has now unfortunately caved in.

The dark holes in the ground were at one time regarded as the homes of the little people – the fairies. For, it is said, Weardale is full of fairies and of tall stories. Here's one. Sitting comfortably?

Long, long ago, one moonlit night, the young daughter of a Stanhope farmer caught sight of a group of fairies dancing by the side of the river. At the end of their festivities they retired into a cave. Entranced and curious, she followed them and saw them feasting. She rushed home and told her father of her adventure. He was afraid that the little people would come for her, for it was known that they guard their secrets well. Distraught, he sought the advice of a local soothsayer. She told him that if he could keep an absolute silence when they came at midnight they would not be able to find the power to abduct the child. But, she warned, even the slightest noise would break the spell, and the child would be taken from him.

He went home with an anxious heart and frantically began preparations for their coming. The hens were banished to a hutch in a far field, the cows were turned out along with the sheep and goats to a distant pasture. In the house the clocks were stopped so that their ticking would not break the silence. And the fire was doused so that the wood would not crackle or splutter. The dogs and cats were fed an enormous meal so that they slept soundly. He then sat down to wait.

They came at midnight; the jingling of the harnesses of their little ponies was all he heard. There was a pause and then he heard them ride away. But, the little girl's pet spaniel had heard the noise too and whimpered and barked. There was a whoosh and they were completely gone, and so too had his little daughter.

Being a good and determined father he vowed that he would get his daughter back from the fairies. He went again to the wise old woman who told him he had to take three gifts to the fairy king in exchange for his child: a light that would not burn; a chicken with no bone; and an animal that would yield part of its body without shedding blood. But to understand these he would need to perform three acts of charity.

He had his opportunity. On his way home he gave a coin to a beggar, saved a thrush from a kestrel and released a rabbit from a snare. The beggar in return told him that a glow-worm would light his way to the fairies. The thrush he saved from the kestrel told him that an egg from under a hen would be a chicken with no bones. And the rabbit whom he saved from the snare said that a lizard when grasped by the tail would run away, leaving the tail behind without shedding one drop of blood.

Armed with these three gifts and a sprig of rowan in his hat he entered the cave and challenged the fairy king. The rowan gave him a charm they could not overcome and when he presented his gifts they were forced into granting him a favour. He asked for his daughter to be returned, and together they left the cave, the home of the little people, and so both lived happily ever after.

In the early nineteenth century local people were frequent visitors to the cave system high up at Stanhope Burn, where the Heathery Burn joined the main stream. In 1843 the cave system was progressively entered into and destroyed by quarrying. The quarrymen were working underneath the cave in 1850 when they unearthed from below the mud floor the finest collection of Bronze Age relics ever found in the U.K. The find of bronze and gold ornaments and artifacts is one of the richest and most important ever. They found amber necklaces, bronze spearheads, fragments of pottery, animal bones, two gold articles, an armlet and a pot and the symbol of rank of a chieftain. Other items showed that this Late Bronze Age group had used horses and carts or chariots, for among the pieces uncovered were part of the bridle of a horse, sections from the hub of a wheel and its circular rim. The hoard, known as the Heathery Burn Collection, is now in the British Museum. Sadly the cave is no longer there, lost to extensive quarrying.

FROSTERLEY AND WOLSINGHAM

Down the road from Stanhope lies the village of Frosterley, formerly 'Forest Lea'. There are not as many trees about as once there were, but you can see what this whole area must have looked like from the wonderful sweep of mature beeches which drape the bends on the roadside as you enter the village on the road from Stanhope. The forest around Frosterley was once prime deer hunting country, and the hunters used to meet in a hostel now called The Forester's Arms. When it was rebuilt, mediaeval bows and arrows, the belongings of local hunting men, were found in the earth of the old buildings.

The contribution Frosterley has made to Britain's mineral wealth and industrial heritage must have been enormous, judging by the huge holes in the ground which surround it. To the south are the vast limestone quarries exploited by the Teesside ironmasters to feed their blast furnaces spewing out iron railway lines. Countless bridge spans which wrap the world in an iron embrace have their origins in Frosterley.

There were also quarries around the village which produced another limestone, the so-called Frosterley marble. A black heavily fossilised stone, it has been used since mediaeval times as a decorative material in churches, for fonts and grave covers. It was used extensively in the Chapel of the Nine Altars in Durham Cathedral as slender vertical polished shafts. The marble has been described as Durham's substitute for Purbeck marble, and was used as such right through the Middle Ages. You can see the marble in its full fossilised splendour at Durham or in its raw state in the rocks near Bollihope Burn.

The railway arrived in Frosterley in 1847 under the title of the Bishop Auckland and Weardale Railway. It was planned as an extension of the historic Stockton and Darlington Railway, intended to reach the 'mountain limestone', as the hills around here were then called. As soon as new quarries were opened up, so too was the extensive rail network. One branch climbed up under the village street to the Rogerley quarry which lies discreetly hidden alongside the Stanhope road. Another toiled up the Bollihope Burn to White Kirkley, then on ledges cut in the side of

White Kirkley's lime kilns ▼

the valley, and over wooden trestle bridges across streams to reach the quarries and lead mines at Whitfield Brow. Like the Weardale railways, these were bold, adventurous undertakings. Most of the route can actually be walked. Only by doing so can one discover the difficulties which were overcome by the unique engineering skills and sheer tenacity of these railway pioneers.

At White Kirkley the railway company erected a lengthy range of stone-built lime kilns for the burning of limestone into agricultural and industrial lime. The lime was carried away by rail to the farms in the lower Tees valley and the North Yorkshire plain. The remains of these kilns are still standing, four-square to the elements. A less obtrusive block of ivy-covered lime kilns with three 'eyes' stands by the roadside above Rogerley Hall. Used in the past to produce and supply the local farmers with agricultural lime, it is now a scheduled monument.

There's a detour at Frosterley which many local visitors to Weardale regularly take: the road to Eggleston in Teesdale. It joins on to the main Stanhope-Teesdale road along a route over the moors first worked out by the Romans, and is a drive of staggering views. However, as we're doing a Weardale Way we suggest a short stop at Bollihope quarries near White Kirkley. Here you'll find a little piece of Pennine magic, of wild Pennine tranquillity crafted not by nature but by man. A short distance from where the cars are parked beside Bollihope Burn you'll find yourself lost in a world of mounds and water, screened at

▼ Man-made moonscapes at Bollihope Burn

the back by a great cliff edge. When the sun sets red in the west on a warm summer evening you'll swear you're on the edge of the Arizona Desert. The brown, thin-soiled mounds of quarry spoil are like little mesas, and the water beneath the rock canyon of the quarry face is like an oasis in the sand and rock. It is a great site for playing cowboys and indians, if your childhood is still with you, and a wonderful place for picnics.

Wolsingham itself is perhaps best viewed from the B6296, the Tow Law road which drops down into the town from Redgate Hall on the northern ridge of the valley. The stone buildings of the steelworks at Stanners Garth, established in 1862, are prominent at the east end of the town. They are surrounded by the neat rows of Victorian streets and new council estates which sharply contrast with the jumble of roofs, pan-tiled and stone-slated, of the old village at the bottom of the hill.

Two roads, one from Tow Law, the other from modest Crook, meet in the middle of a traffic island at the Market Place, in the centre of which stands the modest Town Hall (in the middle of a traffic island!). It is only when Wolsingham Show, England's oldest agricultural show, is held on the first Saturday in September that the small space of the Market Place shows its limits, when the whole area is full of carousels and hoop-la-stalls.

One of the buildings along Front Street is Peel Cottage, the town's first police station, named after Sir Robert, the founder of the English police service. The original complement of officers was a sergeant and three constables. Their first task appears not to have been the apprehending of villains but the rounding up of the itinerant pig population, roaming freely and destructively through the town's gardens. When the police officers had the pigs successfully confined to their styes, the number of policemen required in Wolsingham suddenly reduced. Not only did the local 'oink' count go down, but also the 'hello hellos'!

Another outstanding building stands by the side of Peel Cottage: Whitfield House. Built in the 1700s with three storeys and a high parapet, it remains hidden behind two unusual trees for this part of the country, both evergreen holm oaks. Next door are the carefully restored Whitfield Cottages, dated MDCXXVII, at one time the Pack Horse Inn which used to provide essential refreshment for man and horse in times gone by.

The ironworks at the eastern end of the town were built by a Worcestershire-born glass maker, Charles Attwood. He moved to the North in 1809 at the age of eighteen to work for a glass manufacturer in Gateshead. After a long, wrangling law suit over some patents he had invented he left Gateshead and secured a lease of the ironstone in the manors of Stanhope and Wolsingham. He then went into partnership with Baring Brothers, the bankers, set up the Weardale Iron Company and established in 1845 an ironworks at Tow Law, about two miles to the north-east. When he retired Attwood began his search for the ironmaster's 'philosopher's stone': the secret of turning iron not into gold but into a material just as wondrous, and much more useful – steel. He made it, and, with a patent to rival the famous one by his friend Bessemer, he opened the ironworks at Stanners Close to turn iron into steel.

Since those heady days, the plant has had its changes of ownership and its ups and downs, but it still manufactures solid steel, for the sternframes and rudders of ships, and heavy steel castings for industry. One of the surprises – and frustrations – of the dale is to meet, or follow, a slow-moving lorry loaded with one of their enormous castings heading for Europe, or America or India, for the firm exports worldwide.

FROM TUNSTALL RESERVOIR TO HAMSTERLEY FOREST

Waskerley Beck flows down into Wolsingham town from the north. The valley of the beck is full of interesting natural history, including the ancient oakwood at Backstone Bank, known for its woodland birds and adders. Wolsingham Park, in which the Tunstall valley lies, dates from 1274 and has been maintained under the guardianship of the Bishop of Durham's Master Forester and Parkers – in the accounts for 1500 we find that Backstone Bank was deliberately planted or replanted. In later years, wood from here was a principal source of timber for major construction works by the Bishop in various parts of the county. The value of Backstone Bank wood is enriched by knowing that it is one of the few mediaeval woods in the county for which we have documentary evidence and from which we can reconstruct lost woodland management techniques.

There are also the ancient oak woodlands of Baal Hill and Bishop Oak, now under the custodianship of the Durham Wildlife Trust. Tunstall Reservoir is a must for natural historians, landscape enthusiasts, and anglers. But there's something of interest for historic building enthusiasts too: the eighteenth-century farms at Bishop Oak and Fawnlees Hall. Perched above the valley on the south side is the mediaeval peel or tower house of Baal Hill House with its very thick walls, originally built as a defensive home against marauders and freebooters, and once the home of the Bailiff of Wolsingham Park.

The gem at the top of the valley is the Tunstall Reservoir itself. It was built in the middle of the nineteenth century for the collection and conveyance of lime-free water for the locomotives of the Stockton and Darlington Railway. The Weardale and Shildon Water Company, which had been formed to carry out this project, had the local Pease family as its main shareholders. It was later used to supply the mining communities of south-west Durham. The moorland water was described by one sceptic as being 'the colour of Indian Pale Ale, with a slight taste of pond', and because of the presence of unfiltered peaty material was known as 'Pease soup'.

Back in the main valley, to the south of Wolsingham town, a road leads up the fellside

and over the hill to the hamlet of Bedburn and the entrance point to the Bedburn valley. Here, between Pikeston Fell, Eggleston Common and Woodland Fell, rises Bedburn Beck, a babbling, winding river which eats away at the millstone grit, creating some dramatic small landscape features, hidden away in the cloak of dark green and shadow of Hamsterley Forest.

Originally, Hamsterley was an agricultural and sporting estate belonging to the Surtees family. The centre of the estate, The Grove, still stands in an idyllic spot at the bottom of the beck, described in glowing terms in an early guide book to Weardale by Herbert Smith (first published in 1885):

. . . snugly ensconced in the bottom of a deep valley surrounded on all sides by steep acclivities, and embowered in woods, so that it is invisible on every side. In summer or autumn, when the fragrant heather is in bloom and the woods gay with the innumerable rowan trees laden with their bright coral berries, a wearied harassed citizen could scarcely find a more congenial retreat to recruit his exhausted energies "the world forgetting, by the world forgot".

The estate was purchased by the Forestry Commission in 1927 and has been almost totally transformed. A well-managed forest though is like a well-managed coppice woodland, for it contains stands of timber of all ages. The trees are mainly sitka spruce, Scots pine, hybrid larch and Norway spruce and provide cover for a diversity of wildlife. There are adders, badgers, roe deer, red squirrels, and forty different species of birds including heron, sparrowhawk, woodcock, green and spotted woodpeckers, redstart, redwing, fieldfare and goldfinch.

If you get lost in either the ecology or the darker stretches of these vast backwoods, Chief Forester Gordon Simpson and Forest Ranger Brian Walker are at hand to help out. They know these woods, the tracks of its animals, the flights of its birds, like they know the backs of their hands. Apart from noisier wildlife, like jays and magpies, the forest is a peaceful and pleasant

place. But you will hear the odd chainsaw, and catch the smell of freshly cut logs. It is a good reminder of the fact that as you walk through the trees you are in fact walking through nothing less than a gigantic three-dimensional crop. It is a magical place, well worth many a visit; a show-place of good forest practice; a template for all our futures.

The trees and bracken of Hamsterley Forest disguise a previous incarnation of this part of the Pennines as a centre of industrial activity, much like the rest of Weardale and the adjacent parts of Teesdale. Iron smelting started officially in these parts as early as 1408, using charcoal from the indigenous forest to fuel the fires. Bits and pieces of the old processes dating from this and earlier times can still be found: traces of slag and parts of smelting implements lie hidden in the deepest pools.

There is a rich and diverse undergrowth in the gaps between the trees, profuse where there is light and dampness. Blackberries and bilberries, cowberries and strawberries abound beneath hazelnuts and acorns. In the very deepest recesses of the forest the ground yields fruit in the shape of a large variety of fungi and toad-stools and mushrooms living off the damp decay of the forest floor. Among them is the fly agaric. It was used in olden times as a fly killer, and by Siberian medicine men as an intoxicant! – not to be tampered with.

Badgers abound in the forest, as do roe deer and red squirrels. Otters were here once, their place usurped by mink. These ferocious pred-ators share the waters of the Old Mill Pond in Bedburn village, at the eastern end of the forest, along with wriggly eels and ducks and Welling-ton the swan.

▲ The lowlife of the forest floor
◄ Hamsterley Forest

▲ Beware the spectacular fly agaric: it's beautiful but it's also deadly!

In the main valley, the A689 continues through Wolsingham and goes out of the upper dale, to the industrial heartland of the lower Wear valley, Durham and Wearside. The valley is wider here; neither the railway nor the river can be seen from the road. The farms are much larger too. Prominent among them is Bradley Hall with its three-storied Georgian facade. Standing behind the tree-covered ruins of its mediaeval foundations can be seen the high earthworks of a long-disused moat. Sadly however, for the purists, this romantic dwelling is now dominated by those great symbols of agricultural industrialisation, the silo tower and asbestos barn. But it remains one of the oldest farms in the dale, for we know that in 1431 the de Eure family was granted permission to crenellate their house by Cardinal Langley, Bishop of Durham.

Just beyond Bradley Hall, where the land rises up on the left behind Helme Park Wood, we leave Weardale to join the A68 and the entrance to the Derwent valley. Later, by a moorland route, we re-enter Weardale at its Rookhope end and take the high road into the Allendales.

A LEAD AND SILVER WALK
FROM WESTGATE TO MIDDLEHOPE

Running north from Westgate in Weardale is the Middlehope, or 'Middle-up' valley, as they say in these parts. A 'hope' or an 'up' is a side valley, and this is easily the most interesting side valley in the dale. It is also the most accessible, with a footpath running its full length. On this walk you're likely to encounter a rattle of ramblers – rattle from the flasks and sandwich boxes they all take with them – and the odd guided walk complete with expert guide, archaeologist, botanist, geologist or historian. This is Pennine countryside at its best, revealing the industrial heritage of the North Pennines at its richest. It covers approximately 4 miles and takes about 2 hours.

The layby opposite the caravan park on the A689 in Westgate is an ideal starting place. The Middlehope Burn flows under the main road to the east, and to the west is a chapel with a footpath sign pointing north. Take this lane up to Weeds, the farm buildings ahead. If you are in the right season, and do not suffer too much from hay fever, you will see on either side of the path haymeadows typical of the dale. These are fortunately not cut until all the wild flowers and herbs have seeded. So you are likely to see yellow rattle, early purple orchid, maybe even northern marsh orchid and many, many more.

At Weeds turn right and head towards Westgate village, crossing the burn in the process. At one time, somewhere near here stood Westgate Castle, not a castle in the usual sense, more of a defendable house similar to a bastle-house or peel tower. This was probably the home of the gamekeepers for the mediaeval Prince Bishops of Durham, for here we are on the western edge of the large mediaeval deer park between Eastgate and Westgate, in which the Bishops hunted. Northgate Farm marks another of the old boundaries.

At the end of the path, where you meet the road, turn left and there before you is a very large building engraved with the date 1791. This was once the Wesleyan Methodist Chapel. It was enlarged in 1878 and closed in 1938 when the Wesleyan and Methodist societies were merged. Follow the path to the west of

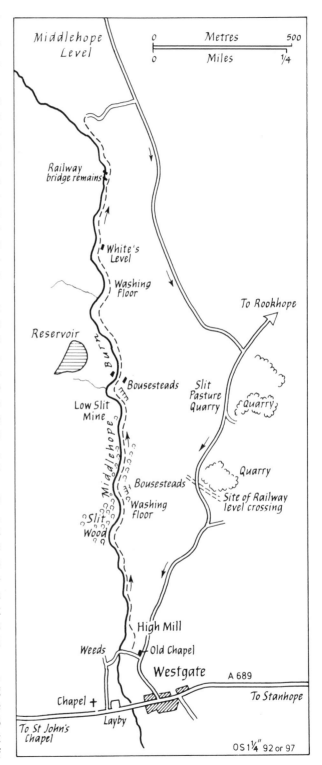

the old chapel building around two old houses with large lintels and a blind window until you come to a farm gate. In the wall beside the gate grows an uncommon variety of cranesbill, the shining cranesbill. The house is High Mill, a one-time flour mill. At the rear is the recently uncovered wheel pit for a huge 16-foot-diameter water wheel. The water which turned it was led off the stream from above the waterfall.

It is the siting of the many waterfalls in the stream which indicate the geological complexity of this valley. As you walk up the stream you pass through a succession of rock strata: limestones, shales and sandstones. The harder rocks, limestones and sandstones, are resistant to wear by the water and form the waterfalls. Where these rocks occur, the valley is narrow and the sides steep. Where the softer shales occur, the valley opens out and the stream bed becomes level and full of deposited debris. The lead miners drove their levels or 'adits' into the shales because they were easier to work. The first such level appears on the right, gushing water and practically filled with debris. This may have been driven as a water level to drain the higher levels.

The stream flows through one of the last remnants of ancient woodland in the dale, Slit Wood, a Site of Special Scientific Interest, or SSSI, and a favourite dales picnic spot. Who says that nature conservation and tourism cannot be compatible? Slit Wood contains the flowers indicative of old woodland – bluebells, dog's mercury and wood anemone. Other woodland plants include the two strawberries, the wild and the barren, wood-sorrel and strong-smelling ransoms with their wonderful cluster flowers, looking, when in flower, like stars on the ground.

Taking the path further upstream, the valley suddenly opens out near the lead mining remains of the Low Slit mine. One of the old lead miners who worked here must have been fond of London pride and must have grown it in his garden, bringing a seed or two with him to work one day, for it now festoons the mine entrance. Further along the path are the stone walls of a 'bousestead' or storage bay for the mixture of galena and waste rock or bouse, obtained from the mine by the miners working in partnerships. You can even see the remains of a washing floor, the area beside the stream, where the ore was processed.

One of the waste minerals was fluorspar, and if you search around the stream and floor – 'fossicking' as it is called – you will almost certainly find small purple crystals of this mineral. If you search in the stream above the bridges, you may find pebbles with the shining silvery-grey cubes of galena. It is not often that a walk includes a treasure hunt for silver or spar. And if you do not find any of these, you can content yourself with a sighting of the delicate spring sandwort, a plant which grows on lead waste grounds.

The small bridges you see were built to cover over the stream for this was a busy working area, and the beck needed to be culverted. On the left bank, under the metal plates, is the Slit mine shaft, at 585 feet one of the deepest in Weardale. It was sunk to work the Slit lead vein, at nearly 14 miles in length the longest single vein in the ore field. On the eastern bank opposite you will see a deep gully where this vein was opened out from the surface. Beside this lies the stone base of the hydraulic engine used to wind materials out of the shaft. The engine is somewhat similar to a steam engine with a cylinder but utilises high-pressure water, fed to it through large diameter iron pipes from the West Slit Dam high up on the western side of the valley.

The walk continues upstream where more and yet more remains of the busy lead mining industry are revealed. The level path was once the tramway down which full tubs of lead ore were hauled to the crushing mill. There was an earlier mill in the next tumble of stones, probably driven by a waterwheel. The water used to drive the wheel was carried by wooden troughs through holes in supporting walls. Further up the valley are a series of reservoirs and a complex of water channels, some open, others covered and completely hidden.

Another lead mine level, White's Level, gushes water across a bed of watercress and globe flowers. There has been a roof fall inside the level and you can hear the waterfall which has taken its place. Near by lie the ruins of a mine shop where the miners changed clothing and kept their tool stands beside the entrance.

The remains of the stone abutments of the railway bridge lie across the burn. The Rookhope and Middlehope Railway was built by the Weardale Iron Company to carry iron ore from the mines and quarries in the area to their ironworks at Tow Law on the ridge above Wolsingham. But to reach the works the line had to contour around the rim of the dale into the Rookhope valley, and then climb again to the top of the ridge, before following the contours round again. The line was opened at some time before 1854 and closed at this end in the 1880s.

Middlehope Level has had its entrance renewed and a tramway laid down, in the search for fluorspar, but without success. The route we follow turns right and climbs out of this area to an intake track. Turn right and follow the track up to the metalled country road above the huge ironstone quarry of Slit Pasture. The quarry on the east side of the road, your left as you travel the mile back to Westgate, is an SSSI because of its geology.

Further along the road, on the left-hand (east) side is another quarry. This was a limestone quarry and is noted for its display of spring flowers. The road levels out – but briefly – to allow the Rookhope and Middlehope Railway to cross it; the gateposts carried level crossing gates, one of which remained until the mid-1960s. It is at this point on the road that the stone boundary walls leap forward to edge the road. There are no wide verges. This was where the Elizabethan enclosure ended on the edge of the moor. Note how much has been taken in since then. Some of the cottages you pass on the way back to the village are unfortunately in a sad state of dereliction. They date from the sixteenth century when the original enclosure took place.

You will find that the Ordnance Survey map Outdoor Leisure 31, Teesdale, will be especially useful on this walk.

3
DERWENTDALE
VALLEY OF THE BLACK MOOR

The face of the Derwent valley is to the north and east, and in some senses it is the most north-eastern or 'Geordie'-like of the Pennine dales. The conurbation of Consett, until recently home of one of the major iron and steel foundries in the whole of England, has given the lower dale a distinctive Tyneside character. This is a place where industry and open country have always competed for space, where the people have had hard working lives, a taste for the extremes of prosperity and poverty, of work and unemployment in equal measure. Fittingly, alone of all the Pennine rivers, the Derwent flows directly into the Tyne itself, racing in past the former site of Blaydon racecourse and out into the North Sea.

The rugged edge is also a characteristic of the upper dale, and of the moorland tracts around it. There are two main routes to the Derwent Pennines, along the A68, the High Road to Scotland, or along the A694 from Tyneside. Our preferred route is the Scottish one, a great road which carries us across open, hilly, farm-strewn country from Wolsingham in Weardale to Castleside and above the sprawl of Consett.

But before we pick up on the attractions of the upper dale it is worth a detour downriver, as far as Gibside and back, for a little taste of Derwent Geordie life. If you're up to a bit of urban wilderness on the north-eastern edge of the Pennines then we suggest taking a right turn on the A68 at Castleside on to the A692. This takes you through the sprawling settlements of Leadgate and Dipton, to Burnopfield. Turn north-west here on to the B6314 for Rowland's Gill and the entrance to Gibside Chapel.

FROM GIBSIDE TO SHOTLEY BRIDGE

As you round the bend of the road which crosses the River Derwent and enters Rowland's Gill you can see down the valley to the point where the concrete jungle rises in earnest, where the tower blocks and city smoke of Gateshead rise into a greyer sky. At night it is a different sight; it glows fluorescent orange with a passion undimmed by the distance. At one

Heather in bloom on Muggleswick Moor, upper Derwent valley ▶

time from this vantage point you could see a fluorescent glow in the other direction too, emanating from the forges of Consett ironworks, but that is long gone.

Gone too is another local legacy of the lower Derwent, Gibside House, a manor built during the seventeenth century and for many generations the home of the Bowes family, one of the most powerful of the great northern landowning dynasties. The remains are clearly visible from the hillside on the opposite side of the river, just up from the Derwent bridge. Nature has truly taken over, aided and abetted by the Forestry Commission. For tall trees grow through the roof of the hall, and behind and around can be clearly seen the famous landscape stamp of the Commission – banks of exotic conifers . . .

The public is denied access to the ruins of Gibside, its serpentine drives, fish pond and Gothic banqueting hall, but the National Trust has taken over the chapel and some of the grounds, and in the season the glories of Gibside are there to be seen and enjoyed. A prominent landmark is a 140-foot stone column, topped by a statue of British Liberty, placed there by George Bowes in 1757 to overlook the meanderings of the Derwent and the Tyne. If you can measure the liberty of the North Country, the freedom of the Derwent waters in column inches, then that statue serves a useful purpose: it shows there's room for every reasonable whim in these parts.

The chapel, designed by James Paine in the 1760s, is a National Trust monument. Built as a mausoleum for the Bowes family, it is like an Italian villa with tall Ionic columns, arches and a central dome above the chapel. The Bowes family were originally Whigs and coal owners, part of the later Bowes-Lyon line, perhaps better known as the Lords of Strathmore, who are still one of the largest landowning families in the North Pennines, and are connected by blood to the present British royal family.

There's a story about one of the last of the direct Bowes line which we could not bypass in our tour of the Derwent, a tale which has given rise to many a wry smile in working-class Derwentside, but is none the less a North Country tragedy with a far from humorous history. Mary Eleanor Bowes, the only child of John Bowes, who died in 1760, was married to John the ninth Earl of Strathmore. But nine years into the marriage, her husband died, and the Unhappy Countess, as she became known, fell prey to the advances of a military adventurer, a Captain Andrew Robinson Stoney.

It seemed that Captain Stoney engineered a duel between himself and the editor of a newspaper *The Morning Star*, a friend of one of the Countess's admirers, in order to impress the lady. Stoney feigned mortal injury at the hands of the press man and won over the Countess's sympathy and passion. It is said that after the duel, the Countess even kissed Stoney's bloody sword and hung it over her bed. Stoney recovered fully and the two married but the union was bloodied from the beginning.

In a remarkable chain of events, which proved a great scandal of its time and was the inspiration for Thackeray's celebrated novel *Barry Lyndon*, the life of the Countess turned to ruin. 'Stoney' Bowes, as he was locally known, set about dissipating his wife's fortune in every manner possible, gambling and drinking and investing in dubious enterprises, while at the same time mistreating her savagely, privately and publicly. The extent of his depravations seemed truly horrendous, even for the time. His character was described by an acquaintance in Ralph Arnold's chronicle, *The Unhappy Countess:*

His mind was treacherous and inconstant even to itself. He was a villain to the backbone! In every turn of his affairs, his passion indicated all the sufferings of a coward, without the smallest show of fortitude. He was cowardly, insidious, hypocritical, tyrannical, mean, violent, selfish, jealous, revengeful, inhuman and savage, without a single countervailing quality.

None of this stopped Captain Stoney from standing for Parliament in 1780, as one of the representatives for Newcastle. In order to pay for the election he felled and sold off a stand of magnificent beech trees at Gibside. And elected he was, despite his local notoriety as a despot who horsewhipped his tenants and closed down the local free schools. But Stoney had little interest in politics and did little for those who elected him.

In time the Countess herself ran away, seeking the refuge of the law and bringing legal actions against her dissolute spouse. Stoney, however, put together a band of brigands and abducted her. There followed a chase the length and breadth of the country, until Stoney was caught and imprisoned. There he remained, in considerable comfort, keeping alive a series of legal actions in order to recover his former grip on Gibside and his wife's remaining inheritance. The Countess, a broken woman, died before him, leaving her estates to her son by Strathmore, John Bowes, who attempted Gibside's final restoration, but did not live there, preferring the life of Paris and the happier atmosphere of another estate holding, Streatlam Castle.

Looking now at the ruin of Gibside House, eventually abandoned by the Bowes-Lyons, it is not hard to imagine the ghosts of the tormented Countess and her savage suitor, Stoney Bowes, flitting among the stones.

Leaving the Countess and the ghosts of Gibside to the sands of history, and going back up the Derwent valley south-west on the A694 towards Consett, you can see pine forest on all sides of the dale. The evergreens vastly outnumber the deciduous woods which at one time wholly clothed the valley floor. But it is not all bad for wildlife; some of the forest is Scots pine, part of the indigenous forest cover which once cloaked these northern dales. Most of today's specimens have been planted for timber, but no matter, for these stately pines allow some light through, and the result is a fairly healthy woodland floor, with bracken, bramble and a dense undercover of woodland shrubs.

At one time, some of the original trees in these park-like plantations were used to make paper, to feed the mill at Lintzford. This is one of a number of mills on the Derwent, built on the various river bends to take advantage of the power that lies within its swiftly flowing watercourses. Some mills were of the traditional type, where corn was ground into flour. But Lintzford did a bit of both, hence its old description in 1840 as a 'water-corne mill'. But most of the paper made at Lintzford and its sister mill at Shotley Bridge came from abroad, and by far the major part of the raw material consisted of rags. Rags now may be the cast-offs of a consumer society, but in those days, there was wealth in recycling, and jobs too – over 300 in the 1880s.

The mill at Lintzford remains a pretty spot, with a huge chimney, the last of its type in the whole of the Pennines, and is the only surviving paper mill on the Derwent. Entrance is over a graceful bridge, and a cobbled yard separates a group of brick buildings and an important Georgian residence from which the mill owner used to crack the whip and keep an eye on his race. This building and the bridge are listed, protected from damage by Act of Parliament. And so too is the mill race, with its stone steps and sluices and its cast-iron wheels and tackle on which you can

▼ Lintzford Mill: it's gone from paper processing to ink making. But what of its future?

clearly see the name of the foundry, Parson's, where this gear was solidly cast. The wheels have clearly stood the test of time, and withstood the ravages of the Derwent in all its moods: a paper empire built solidly on wheels of iron used to tame the wild waters of the River Derwent.

In recent years Lintzford Mill has been used as an ink works. But the market for ink, as for the old types of recycled paper, has now declined. As we went to press Lintzford was up for sale, a remarkable monument, like so much waste paper, dying for a good use.

Chopwell Wood is one of the pleasantest stretches on our route. The woods are there for commercial timber, as the name Chop-well suggests, but at one time this area was covered in oak – a mini Sherwood that must have provided a refuge for many an outlaw. Over 2000 of those original oaks ended up going to sea: they were felled in the seventeenth century to provide timber for the first of Britain's three great battleships, the *Royal Sovereign.*

There are deep burns in the wood with ample vegetation providing a good cover for badgers and deer. And as with so many parts of the Pennine dales, in various places you can see remnants of old mine workings, small tunnels and gadgets of iron and concrete sticking out from the undergrowth.

One apparition that's been known to stick its nose out of the undergrowth in these woods is a black fox, seen from time to time haunting the fields and farms around. Foxes are usually red with a white-tipped tail. But from time to time colour variations do appear. These genetic mutations are very desirable in domestic species of dog, cat, horse and cow, allowing breeders to produce attractive variations on the basic animal, and a new selling line! And there's even a strain of captive fox – the North American Silver Fox – which is all black. The Derwent black fox could be an escapee from a fur farm, but that seems unlikely. He's either just a genetic freak, or a figment of a powerful local imagination. In any event he's been around for a long time, so

he's managed to keep his head well down and out of sight of the barrel of a keeper's shotgun or a poacher's snare.

For, make no mistake, this is true poaching country, a subject to which we will return. But Chopwell is famous for something else too. The village on the side road going north past Blackhall Mill, lying behind the wood, at one time acquired the name of 'Little Moscow'. In 1926 during the national General Strike, when feelings of revolution ran high, the miners of Chopwell pulled down the union jack on the council offices and replaced it with the hammer and sickle. They took the Bible from the church and replaced it with one of the works of Karl Marx. Streets were even re-named after heroes of the Russian Revolution: Lenin, Engels and Marx. The names have now been changed but you can still walk down them and dream the dreams of freedom of the miners of 'Little Moscow'.

As with all revolutions, the status quo was quickly reasserted, with one of the imprisoned miners' leaders going on to become a pillar of Chopwell society and a knight of the realm! The militancy has disappeared along with the coal mines. Work can only be sought elsewhere, in Tyneside and beyond. But militant or not, the views across the Derwent valley from 'Little Moscow', while maybe not on anything like the same scale as the steppes of the Ukraine, are quite special.

Continuing back along the A694 past Chopwell Wood and a plantation known as 'Make me Rich', consisting of what else but quick-growing conifers, you will bypass two other mill-based Derwent villages, Blackhall Mill and Hamsterley. The river takes a sharp bend away from the road at Ebchester, the site of a Roman fort, Vindomora. An encampment on the famous Roman road through the Pennines, Dere Street, Vindomora stands for 'The Edge of the Black Moor', which is obviously how the Romans thought of the Pennine felltops: black and dangerous. This can be interpreted not quite like the children's joke, a crow with a machine gun, but the next best thing, a wild and gloomy place filled with dangerous peat bogs and even more dangerous Pennine and Brigantine rebels against the rule of Rome.

The Ebchester fort against the black moor dates from the first century, during the time of the Emperor Agricola. It was home to the sixth legion, a home of wood, clay and stone, with bathhouses, dormitories and sacrificial altars. Not much of Ebchester remains. A few of the more interesting parts can still be seen outside the door of Ebchester church, including an altar with an eagle and a sacrificial knife sculpted on one side, and a stone with the mark of a dolphin, though clearly not of the Derwent variety!

To appreciate the rest of this archaeological relic, large parts of which were excavated in 1936 and again in 1962, you would have to make a real nuisance of yourself, and go poking in amongst the gardens, roads and cottages of modern-day Ebchester, for there are bits of the fort everywhere. It's not really worth it.

Try instead a calming walk by the riverside at Ebchester, under the old waggoners' bridge, which though a hundred years older than its modern equivalent a few hundred yards downriver is in a better state of repair than its newer brother! It has got more style too, and it overlooks a smithy, the last on the Derwent. A footpath along the south-west bank of the river takes you through some fine mature National Trust oak and beech woodland, marching up the hillsides. The willow and alder droop over the silent waters of the Derwent, traditionally known hereabouts as 'The Smiling River'. The best time to come is in the spring when catkins of alder, willow and hazel hang pendulously over the water, swaying in the breeze, while at the water's sandy edge, clumps of spring snowflake and poet's narcissus peer out at the sun. These two plants pass at first glance for snowdrops and daffodils, to which they are related, but look more closely, for they're not!

On the lower Derwent is the attractive village of Shotley Bridge, now almost a suburb of Consett. The bridge of Shotley spans the Derwent beside an inn called The Crown and Crossed Swords, a name which refers to the remarkable history of Shotley Bridge. At one time it was the centre of the entire country's swordmaking industry. That industry has long since gone, there being a slight shortage of markets for blades these days! On an old swordmakers' house, Cutlers Hall (now cottages numbers 22 and 23 on the road to Blackhill), there is an inscription:

$$O$$
$$W \qquad A$$
$$1787$$

This stands for W. and A. Oley, one of the swordmaking families who used to live and work here. They came originally from Solingen in Germany, a leading world centre for the manufacture of crafted steel blades. A group of craft families was enticed over by a small consortium of English businessmen anxious to tap into the booming armaments business of the 1680s.

The Solingen swordmakers were willing emigrés. The cut and thrust industry was then in decline in Germany, there was acute rivalry between guildsmen over methods and patents, and as Lutherans the swordsmen were liable to religious persecution. Perhaps because of this, or because they carried with them a secret formula for the manufacture of prized 'hollow swords', they were sneaked into the country, shipped via Rotterdam to Tyneside and brought up the Derwent to Shotley. So precious was the secret formula that Solingen guildsmen were required to vow never to give it up, under pain of death. So serious was the vow that, according to one story, one of the chosen immigrants, Hermann Mohll, was imported in 1687 in a tub.

But why Shotley and the Derwent, you may well ask? A combination of factors: locally available iron ore for smelting; 'chop-well' wood for burning; millstone grit stones for grinding; and nearby ports for shipping. But the two most important factors were closely related to the character of the place: its remoteness – out of the way of industrial espionage – and the Derwent itself. Not only did the swift river current ensure power to the mills, grist to the enterprise, but the water also had certain unknown qualities and as yet undiscovered properties which, according to some old documents, were ideal for tempering steel.

▼ Swordmaker's house and mill: all that's left of the industry that gave birth to Derwentside's age of iron and steel

In short, only the Derwent could produce the Rolls-Royce product the customer wanted. And there was something in this, for although sword-making at Shotley is a thing of the past, among its descendants are the Wilkinson's Sword company, now one of the world's leading manufacturers of disposable razor blades!

The Shotley swordsmen had a royal charter too, and they were very busy for over a hundred years, producing high quality swords which had one characteristic that put them in a class above all others: some were engraved by the then unknown engraver, Thomas Bewick.

With markets guaranteed in the world of war and of fashion, the swordsmen lived by the riverside in Shotley in a group of stone cottages called Wood Street, fine buildings for their time, and contrasting with the wood, wattle and plaster shanties in which the local poor lived and died. Despite their lowly circumstances in Shotley Bridge, this mysterious band of immigrant artisans had powerful connections in England. At the time of the Jacobite rebellion one of them was arrested for smuggling hollow blades from Germany into Britain, but he was mysteriously set free after a brief spell in gaol. And there were dubious financial operations at a high level, including a Sword Blade bank, fire office and coffee house in London, all linked to the financial crash of the South Sea Company in 1720. At Shotley Bridge the industry went into recession towards the end of the 1700s. Some of the families continued to live there until recent times, but you will find the grave of the last of the swordmakers, Joseph Oley, suitably inscribed and dated in Ebchester churchyard.

Walking along the river banks at Shotley or picnicking beside the swift Derwent waters it's not hard to imagine the presence of an ancient band of craftsmen smelting and forging steel on the site of the ghostly mill ruins across the way. You can almost smell the burning metal, the crackle of wood on the fire and the hiss of steam from the cooling casts. In later times, Shotley Bridge became a major tourist attraction for its spa. Two low stone buildings beside the cricket ground were the site of a diversion of water from the Derwent, its qualities apparently rendering it an ideal cure for scrofula and cancer. Fashionable visitors of the times included Charles Dickens who dropped in, we must suppose for a quick cure, in 1839.

FROM CONSETT TO CROOKED OAK

On the A691 up the valley from Shotley turn left before Blackhill on the Pemberton road for Allensford. Here we rejoin the famous High Road across the Pennines to Scotland, bypassing the town of Consett. This is not a particularly pretty place, but one with a rich and remarkable past. Its origins lie with those Shotley swordmakers, for it was their local presence which led to the opening up of the iron ore veins in the hillside for the first time on a large scale in the early 1830s.

In fact there was nothing there until 1840, when the Consett Iron Company first appeared on the scene. Originally the place was called Berry Edge, and at the time it must have resembled something out of an Alaskan gold-field, an array of mine workings, holes in the ground and ramshackle dwellings, with no water supply or sanitation. Among the first real buildings of any substance were public houses, and inevitably the local lock-up. For these were wild times, witnessed among others by Mr John Calvert, who wrote that in 1844 he stood in his doorway and counted a dozen fights going on at the same time.

By the late nineteenth century, iron had been supplanted by steel, a requirement for ships and railway lines the world over. And the Consett Iron Company, by now a multi-million pound affair, became famous as having the best steel plate rolling mills in the world. But merely a hundred years later, there are few signs of this great industry. The plant closed in the early 1980s and the site has now been landscaped.

After many bleak years when unemployment reached the highest levels in the country, there is recovery. Jobs and manufacturing are returning, as Consett turns its face towards the end of the century and embraces a new world of high-technology and service industry. One successful new industry is the manufacture of savouries from around the world, going under the name 'Phileas Fogg'. From world fame with steel-forging to world renown for crisp-making: you can almost hear the great ironmasters slavering in their graves!

One Consett story which must be told concerns that sad period in the area's history when the steelworks were first closed and 2000 men were put out of work. The direct and knock-on effects on the local economy, as well as on the local society, had some very strange repercussions. Chief amongst these was the sudden rise in the early 1980s of the incidence of poaching and badger-baiting in the area around, and beyond, well into the North Country and extending even into the game-rich lowlands and uplands of Scotland to the north. The A68 provided the route through which gangs of poachers traversed the country in search of game and in search of new markets for their produce.

There is a long history in the pit villages of Durham and Northumberland of men with terriers and whippets sporting their dogs on the creatures of the wild, chasing deer and foxes, and even digging out badgers for baiting or as a sport in itself, known as 'Badger Busting'. As unemployment climbed, these sports and the poaching that traditionally went with them got right out of hand. A blood sport fraternity developed, mostly young men denied work and a role in life, but with the time and the opportunity to invest in dogs, guns, crossbows, gaff sticks, traps, radio collars and all the old-tech and new-tech paraphernalia of hunting and shooting. In one village near Consett with a population of over 800, an estimated eighty people became involved in these bloody sports.

Some members of this fraternity, with its totemic displays of camouflage jackets, snakeskin belts and home displays of animal pelts and tails, had gone even further. They became involved in the trapping, selling and even stuffing of endangered species. Anything was fair game, from whole red deer to ospreys and merlins, golden eagles from Scotland and peregrines from the Lake District. These men were hunters, professionals, hardened to life in an iron foundry but now hardened to a new life which was just as dangerous, just as fulfilling in one way, but hard on the wildlife and a disaster for Derwentside and for Britain's natural heritage.

Poaching had in these times taken on a more sinister aspect. 'The Badger Men' were a new breed, an anarchic menace let loose in the countryside. In time many of them were caught by the police and the RSPB inspectors, but not before much damage had been done to rare species of birds and animals. The national press furore which followed the reports of the rise in poaching and badger-baiting did some good, leading to a change in the legislation, a stiffening of fines and a heightening of public consciousness about the problem.

The Badger Men themselves saw a lot of this as hypocrisy. They saw their activities as legitimate sports, as legitimate as farmers gassing badgers, as gamekeepers trapping 'vermin', as landowners shooting grouse and pheasants, or as the Forestry Commission culling deer. And they saw themselves as hunters, as part of an old tradition. Their being branded as dangerous criminals was for them simply an illustration of the different attitude society takes to its fortunate rich and its unfortunate poor. And as always in the history of modern times, unemployment lay at the heart of it. Men with nothing to do and with limited opportunities discovered a rich economic and recreational resource in the countryside nearby.

The Pemberton road joins the A68 at Allensford – a very pretty place, almost hard to imagine being so close to Consett. There's a riverside picnic spot with walks along the Derwent and a compelling view uphill and north-east towards Blackhill in Consett. You don't see Consett though, just the fairy castle spires of St Mary's Church at the back of the hill, seeming to rise up from out of the reclaimed steelworks site like an elven castle from *The Lord of the Rings*.

The magic does not stop there. There is a footpath walk on the other side of the Allensford bridge from the visitors' car park which goes west following the Derwent part of the way on its tortuous route up to the great Derwent Reservoir at the valley head. Here the traveller is entering the beginnings of a mini hidden wilderness paradise rich in wildlife interest and close-knit scenery. Accessible only from the bridge at Allensford, it is hidden away. You just cannot see it from the road. It is a secret, magical place.

To really appreciate the gorge you have to walk it. But if you're content with our description you need only do the short riverbank walk from Allensford to Wharnley Burn waterfall, then rejoin the A68. Travelling north-west by car, once you are round the bend and over the hill you can drive on a minor unclassified farm road through Wallish Walls to Crooked Oak, and from there get another glimpse of the Derwent Gorge lying below. There follows another short walk down to the river's edge before rejoining the A69 road past Durhamfield.

Local naturalist Ken Hopper, born, brought up and working in the Derwent Gorge, knew all its secrets. In his unpublished wildlife diaries he describes it thus:

Heading up river from Allensford, the first point of interest we reach is the picturesque waterfall on the Wharnley Burn, just before it runs into the Derwent. Depending on the time of year and on the weather, the fall can be a trickle, or after heavy rain or a thaw it

Horsleyhope Ravine: an earthly Avalon, 'where falls not hail, or rain or any snows, nor ever wind blows loudly' ▶

can become a raging torrent of brown-coloured water which can be heard long before it can be seen, as it thunders over the rock ledge and onto the boulders below, before eventually rushing down to swell the by now already swollen Derwent. Leaving the Wharnley Burn behind, we come upon an impressive cliff and rock fall known as the Craggs, and we can clearly see where the river has worn, and undercut the cliff to cause the rock falls that have made the river turn and run almost at right angles.

Ken's favourite walk leaves the riverside not long after, and the visitor must be content with spectacular views up the gorge and up Horsleyhope Ravine. On this stretch of the walk the sitka spruce merchants have been busy, overplanting the old birch and alder woods and old tracts of heather moor with antiseptic invaders. In parts the wood is quiet as only a pine forest can be. But there is lots of life and noise from the river itself, its bubbling passing at times for human conversation, and from the hazel, birch and beech woods opposite.

The stretch of valley woodland which follows both sides of the river upwards from here is designated SSSI and the southern part, owned by the Nature Conservancy Council, is regarded as a place of great national wildlife importance. The primary or ancient woodland, with species like sessile oak on the higher ground and wych elm below, have grown there without human interference for centuries, and the lack of disturbance and grazing has also encouraged a rich ground flora. You can tell the woodland is truly old because of the presence of indigenous air plants, epiphytic lichens, living off the clean air, firm-footed on the bark of tree trunks.

In spring and high summer the meadows are yellow with cowslips, and the riverside blue with bells and sweet smelling from the rich growth of water mint that thrives beside the crystal-clean waters of the Derwent. Other local plants include the pink valerian, woodsage, dog's mercury, early purple orchid and the herb-Paris. A posset of herbal remedies but among them can also be found one that's not so remedial, enchanter's nightshade, a pretty white-flowered plant.

There are a couple of stories about this part of the Smiling River which deal with the two extremes of enchantment, the black and the white, the sinister and the sacred. The first concerns Crooked Oak Farm, an old building which can be dated by the lintel above the door to the year 1684. There has been a farm here since the fourteenth century, and in the seventeenth century, when witches were said to be common in these parts, someone lived here called Jane Frizzle. According to an old account she 'followed the usual life of a witch, nightly rode in the air on a broomstick, and cast curses on the bodies and possessions of all who offended her'.

The other story of enchantment involves none other than the legendary King Arthur, for on this part of the River Derwent there is a secret inaccessible place near to Crooked Oak Farm called the Sneep. Near a deep pool before the river rounds a sharp bend the land rises up suddenly. At the top there is a ridge overhung by an old oak and a very twisted birch. Beneath are a couple of small cavern-like openings in the rock face, overhung with ivy, ferns and wild flowers of the season. According to local legend this is Avalon, a place of mythological enchantment where the legendary King Arthur lies asleep with his horses and knights waiting for the clarion call that will rouse them from their slumbers to reclaim Albion.

The horseshoe tongue of land that is the Sneep is but one of a number of places in Old England where Arthur, according to local legend, is said to be lying sleeping, but the quiet seclusion of the place puts it, in our view, well near the top of the list. For, near the confluence of the Hisehope and the Horsleyhope burns which feed the river near this spot, can be found the remains of an ancient British road, the old

Deep-flowered meadows where King Arthur sleeps; the Sneep's dreamy pastures ▶

82

road to Penrith where the Round Table once stood. The woods themselves in those times would have been alive with game – deer, boar and wolf – for Arthur to indulge his favourite pastime . . . the royal hunt. So, according to the story, when mortally wounded by his nephew Mordred, Arthur was carried away by Morgan le Faye to a cavern beneath the Sneep, there to sleep in a subterranean place, a cavern below the waters.

According to the legend the hero lies on a couch formed of many sorts and manners of good herbs and flowers which send out a delicate odour like the pure balsam. His terrible sword, Excalibur, is hung up in its sheath close beside him, and near it a huge brazen trumpet. His horsemen and their horses, all equipped and ready to march, lie entranced on the floor of the hall. When the appointed hour comes, they will start to their feet and follow their old leader. In Tennyson's famous 'Morte D'Arthur', as indeed in the legend, Arthur's departure is for a healing:

> For so the whole round earth is every way
> Bound by gold chains about the feet of God
> But now farewell. I am going a long way
> With these thou seest – if indeed I go . . .
> . . . to the island-valley of Avilion;
> Where falls not hail, or rain or any snow,
> Nor ever wind blows loudly; but it lies
> Deep-meadow'd, happy, fair with orchard-
>   lawns
> And bowery hollows crown'd with summer
>   sea
> Where I will heal me of my grievous wound.

Meanwhile, lulled by the gentle waters of the Derwent, Arthur in his Sneep sleeps the peace of a hero.

There is not much chance of Arthur's slumber being broken by any of us, as public access to the Sneep is on a very steep bank, subject to erosion and in the caring hands of the Nature Conservancy Council. But no matter, we have the legend.

On your route up the valley from Crooked Oak, or along the A68 above the gorge, you may get to spy some natural magic too. If you are lucky you'll see a heron flap by this corner of Albion, or a dipper darting on rocks across the water. Ken Hopper, who worked for eight years for the farmer who owns this land, knew its birdlife well, spotting rare birds like merlin, buzzard, montagu's and hen harriers, peregrines and even drop-and-dive-in visitations from ospreys. There are also the remains of an old silver mine in the woods, a wind-pump, a rare sight on farmland these days, and the odd very exotic visitor has been seen by the riverside; minks and even an otter which once came, but, sadly, went away again.

FROM MUGGLESWICK TO DERWENT RESERVOIR

The other way to catch a glimpse of this enchanting section of Pennine countryside is to turn south-west off the A68 at Carterway Heads, on to the B6278 and make a slight detour down the small winding roads to Muggleswick and Eddy's Bridge and from there back on to the B6306 to Derwent Reservoir. Take care not to miss Muggleswick altogether, for it is now only a scattering of houses without a stopping-off point except for the nineteenth-century church. In a nearby farmyard you can see the ruins of a manor house and grange which date back to before the twelfth century.

They were part of a huge parkland known as 'Moclyngeswick' (the original Muggleswick), named after the descendants of Mocla, a Celtic chief. The park was enclosed by one of the Bishops of Durham for a priory and convent, complete with grass pastures, over 800 acres of mature woodland and a section of open fell. The enclosure was so complete that the monks and nuns had the liberty of 'free chase' and the sole game rights on the 'eyries of sylvan birds' throughout the park. To keep their animal inheritance in, the residents were empowered to build high fences. The park is long gone and so

▲ Smiddy Shaw Reservoir: caledonian pines, from the ancient forest's past

▲ Mr Grey of Muggleswick, with dog and grouse

too is much of the original woodland, but there are still religious orders owning parkland in this section of the Pennines, with Minsteracres Monastery visible standing in parkland to the east of Slaley Forest on the other side of the Derwent valley.

Once a forest of indigenous British conifers, a unique area of ancient Caledonian pine, grew where Slaley Forest is today. Only in Scotland's Cairngorms can you find now the still-living descendants of Britain's native pines, so conditions on the Derwent at the time of the trees must have been a lot like those on the higher latitudes of the Cairngorms today. The stumps of trees which have long been visible in the eroded blanket peat of the Hisehope, Eudon and Burn-

hope burns have been identified as pines from the old forest, as chips off the old post-glacial pine block. In the dry summers of 1976 and 1977, an entire forest of stumps was clearly exposed on the floor of the Smiddy Shaw Reservoir high up on Muggleswick Common.

Some of these stumps are now in permanent public view on the banks of the reservoir, near the village of Waskerley where a railway line once crossed the common connecting the Derwent and Wear valleys. If you peer over the water's edge you might still see the odd submerged tree trunk. The wood has been well preserved, as gnarled and knotted as when its upper branches were felled so many thousands of years ago. But look closely, for you're looking

▲ Green grows the bog moss above Edmundbyers

at not just a piece of wood, but a piece of the Derwent valley's unique prehistoric past.

The other old story from Muggleswick's dim and misty past is more frivolous. In 1662 word arrived in Durham that a large party of Covenanters had gathered at Muggleswick Park to plot treason. It would seem that the Covenanters were planning the overthrow of Parliament, the Government and the Church of the day, because they had outlawed 'liberty of conscience', the freedom to worship in whatever manner you chose. It was said that bands of thousands of Anabaptists, Independents and Quakers were drilling on the fell by night and amassing armaments for the big fight. When the time was right they were apparently going to murder all bishops, deans and chapters, and all ministers of the Church, and to break all organs in pieces, to destroy the common prayer books, and to pull down all churches and further to kill the gentry that should either oppose them, or not join with them in their design.

The Bishop of Durham and his High Sheriffs reacted by amassing an army, armed to the hilt, to quell the Muggleswick plot. But the joke was on them, for on reaching the Derwent the Bishop's men discovered no rebel army. Had they sneaked away into the night, or were they biding their time in a distant Pennine copse, waiting for the 'polis' to pass by? Had they outwitted their enemy, and taken Durham Castle while the Bishop's army was out enjoying a breath of fresh fellside air?

Investigations by the Bishop's men in the cold

▲ The old drovers' road goes ever on

light of day discovered an astonishing fact. There was not, nor ever had been, a rebel army. But the whole affair was not a ruse, cunningly worked out to embarrass the establishment. Legend has it that the terrific array of mounted Anabaptists seen mustering on the fell turned out to be nothing more than the chance sighting of local man, Joe Hopper, coming back on horseback across the moor at the end of a brief holiday jaunt across to Ireland and back!

The army was an army of rumour and imagination, with its size increasing as the story got passed from place to place until it reached Durham. The Bishop's army returned to Durham with their tails between their legs. The people of Muggleswick must have split their sides for days with stories about the re-conquest

of their village green by the Bishop of Durham.

At Eddy's Bridge the Muggleswick road rejoins the B6278 which takes the traveller to Edmundbyers and the B6306 to the top of the Derwent valley. Here you can follow a circular route through Edmundbyers to Blanchland and then back around the north side of the Derwent Reservoir to Carterway Heads. The circuit continues along the B6306 and then turns east on the edge of Slaley Forest, allowing you to rejoin the A68 for routes north to Scotland, and some views of living Caledonian pines, or you can venture south to 'civilisation'.

If, however, you are following the complete North Pennines trail, you will have to turn around after visiting the north shore of the reservoir and continue further up the valley past

Blanchland, Baybridge and Hunstanworth. From there the road takes you over the top, across Hunstanworth Moor, into Rookhope and the back entrance to the Northumbrian Pennine valleys of Allendale and South Tynedale.

The Derwent Reservoir is the largest body of standing water in the North Pennines and one of the largest artificially created lakes in Britain. It is outshadowed only by Kielder to the north, but for scenic views, wildlife and recreation it is a prime development. Its 11,000 million gallons of water fills from a catchment area of over 42 square miles of rough fell. And through its 3000-foot dam trickles the last of the Derwent that is allowed to get through. There's a sailing club and reserves for boats, anglers and birds, and when the wind is high and the sun strong, the Derwent is the ideal venue for the British Windsurfing Championships. The rushing water and the colourful sails of this new breed of water-folk contrast well with the austere moors and green fields around. And if you're on the water with dancing sun and flying waves, time and life just seem to pass on by.

The great white Derwent water is a paradise for anglers too, stocked full of brown and rainbow trout, but it is also important for anglers of a different type . . . the birds. Since the very early days of its construction the reservoir provided rich feeding grounds for large numbers of waders and wildfowl. If you get out there with your binoculars at the best time for birds, the middle of winter, you can check the following species off your list of sightings: redshank, golden plover, curlew, pochard and wigeon. Do watch out for the spectacular swoop and splash of passing ospreys as they lift brown trout out of the water to keep them going on the long haul north to their breeding grounds in Scotland. You may be able to fasten your binoculars on hen harrier, ring-necked duck and even, wait for it, a Chilean flamingo. From the Andes to the Derwent, now there's a migration to write home about!

These birds are not just passing fancies. There is a fair quota of breeding species present too. Among those that have made their homes in the woods and water's edge of the Derwent Reservoir are mallard, teal and tufted duck, woodcock, oystercatcher, common sandpiper and little ringed plover.

Part of the reservoir and its shoreline have been partitioned off as a wildlife sanctuary, with access only possible by permit. The sailing boats are kept at a distance to prevent disturbance of the birds at roost, but there are ample viewing places, a nature trail and a hide to witness their comings and goings. Best times are early morning and late evening but you have to be quiet if you are to see anything other than a distant flurry of feathers and a rapid-fire 'quack, quack'!

FROM BLANCHLAND TO ROOKHOPE

Away from the ducks and back up the B6306 to the furthest reaches of the Derwent valley a pretty sight awaits the traveller: the village of Blanchland. The name means simply 'white land', an apt description for its winter setting at 1000 feet-high in the Pennine hills. The name also recalls the white waters of the Derwent which foam under its picturesque bridge, and the white monks which at one time walked the Derwent's banks. Its overall aspect is one of purity and grace, a pretty English village in a splendid setting. But not all of Blanchland's history is so clean and cosy, and not far away on the western edge of Bulbeck's enclosed moor, there runs a torrent with a celebrated name, Devil's Water. This is a small tributary of the Tyne, creating a small Pennine valley in itself, rejoining the mother river near the ruin of Dilston Castle.

Dilston, at the head of the 'eighth' Pennine dale, was the family home of the Radcliffe family, the famous Earls of Derwentwater. The last Earl rode forth in 1715, the subject of many a romantic ballad. For he was a Jacobite, a supporter of the Pretender to the throne of England, who was beheaded in 1716 on Tower Hill for his part in the ill-fated 'Rising of the North'. One ballad related the Earl's parting from his beloved wife Anna as he rallied to the Jacobite cause, and as he so correctly foresaw, to his doom:

> Farewell, farewell, my lady dear,
> Ill, ill thou counsell'dst me.
> I never more may see the babe
> That smiles upon thy knee.

The last Laird was well liked locally, and his death was marked by much local mourning and not a few tall stories. Apparently, on the night of his execution, the red fingers of the aurora borealis could be clearly seen playing in the sky above Dilston Castle's towers. Locals watching saw in it the portent of their Laird's passing, and since then have referred to sightings of them not as the northern, but as Lord Derwentwater's lights!

The village of Blanchland was built around a now ruined Abbey of the Premonstratensian Order, an order of Cistercian canons founded in France in the twelfth century by St Norbert.

▼ Still shrouded in mist and mystery: but spirits of a different kind frequent Blanchland's ancient abbey walls

The Abbey at Blanchland was founded in 1214 by the local landowner, a Norman Walter de Bolbec. The monks had a quiet life over the centuries: never more than twelve in number including the abbot, they worked closely with the local people, as much as the constraints of a monastic life and the periods of silence would allow them. But their white-robed purity failed to protect them from the two great predatory forces of the Middle Ages, the Scots and Henry Tudor.

According to one old legend, a band of Border raiders intent on sacking the Abbey got lost on the fell in a mist near a place now called Grey Friars Hill. The monks, overjoyed that they had escaped the attentions of the Scots, rang the Abbey bells to celebrate. But unfortunately for the incautious, ill-witted monks, the chiming of the bells, much magnified by the stillness of the night, boomed through the mist. The sound was a siren to the fog-bound reivers, bringing them straight to the door of the Abbey. Their visit was not a courteous affair, and the place name Dead Friars below Bell's Hill on the common reveals as much as needs to be said of their fate.

The Abbey and its Order was closed by Henry in 1539. The monks were given pensions and the buildings and estate passed eventually to the Earls of Derwentwater. Through time and marriage Blanchland became the property of Lord Crewe, the Bishop of Durham around the time of the Jacobite Rebellion. Most of the Abbey building itself has followed the Scots raiders, Henry Tudor and Lord Crewe into the mists of time, but part of the monks' cloisters now forms a splendid hotel and public bar, the Lord Crewe Arms. Here you can eat and drink in luxurious surroundings, in a crypt or cellar bar, or in an ante-room complete with mediaeval chimney, embroidered wall hangings and Arthurian armour sculpture. And if you're suitably accompanied you can enjoy a four-poster bed, preceded by a romantic walk in the old monastery gardens, following pleasant paths once trod by white monks.

Here we must take our leave of the Derwent

valley, the most urban and in some ways the most unusual of the Pennine dales. The unnumbered hilltop road south from Baybridge above Blanchland passes Hunstanworth and a series of ruins from the era of lead mining. Here there are vistas of the Pennines at their most open and at their wildest, across Hunstanworth Moor and Stanhope Common, until we reach the Weardale village of Rookhope en route to the Allen valley. Except for the sheep and the moor birds, the grouse and the curlew, when you're out here, you're well and truly on your own. If the sun is shining, enjoy it. It may be empty, a no-man's-land reserved for game and the casual visitor, but there are few more tranquil spots on the face of England.

THE WALKS OF THE MONKS
AROUND BLANCHLAND

One of the most attractive settings in the North Country, the pretty village of Blanchland in the Derwent valley is also an excellent centre for walks, short and long. The walks here will give you an idea of what life was like for the monks of Blanchland Abbey whose activities played such an important role in Pennine mediaeval land use.

To get to Blanchland take the A68 Corbridge road going north. Take the turning marked Blanchland/ Derwent Reservoir at Carterway Heads and you are on the B6278 which takes you to Edmundbyers. Then take the B6306 from there around the Derwent Reservoir to Blanchland. The road crosses the stone bridge across the Derwent with its wonderful views of the village and the brown moors beyond. Welcome to Blanchland, as the sign says, where there are plenty of places to leave your car.

At Blanchland we suggest a sojourn at the Lord Crewe Arms, built out of the remains of the Abbey, for breakfast, a barsnack, dinner or even a four-poster night, to be followed by one or more of three short leisurely walks from the village, following in the paths of the white-robed Premonstratensian monks who founded an abbey here in the thirteenth century.

Walk 1
The first walk, which covers a distance of approximately 4 miles, is a simple one downstream, alongside the Derwent, to the Carrick picnic area. The walk begins alongside the B6306 river bridge to the south of the village. Take the left-hand, or downstream side, and walk east for about 2 miles to Carrick bridge, then across into the picnic area. To return, you just retrace your route. The path is quite easy but can be muddy – or 'clarty', to use the local expression – after rain. Although the opposite bank appears to be covered by the ubiquitous pine, there is in fact more than one

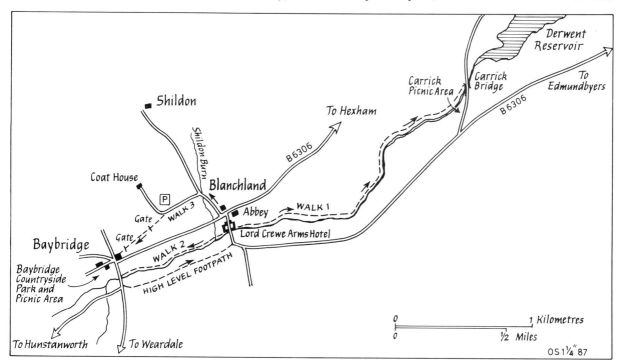

91

sort of conifer, for all discerning species spotters to test their expertise on.

Among the gravel beds beside the river you may find the purple or mauve pebbles of fluorspar. These have been thrown away as waste material from the lead mines higher up the valley and the river has carried them down, rounding them into pebbles. Today it is no longer regarded as waste but is being mined in the Boltsburn valley near Blanchland to the south. Fluorspar is used as a flux in steel making, as an ingredient in your toothpaste, and a means of making cooking and frying pans non-stick.

Walk 2

There is an easy circular walk from Blanchland which covers a distance of about 4 miles. This goes west from the village to the Baybridge picnic area, and returns on the other bank – the Durham side – of the river. It starts from the upstream side of the bridge. Clamber through the gap in the stone wall and across the footbridge over the Shildon Burn. On this path there are two occasions when you have to cross ladder stiles to get over the cattle-watering areas. There is a very good indicator board which tells you more about the area, erected in the Baybridge picnic site by Durham County Council. Blanchland exists in a sort of no-man's land between Durham and Northumberland, Derwent District and Tynedale District. All would like to lay claim to all or part of the village and its surrounds. As a result it is unevenly partitioned. While the main village itself is all in Northumberland – it tells you as you cross the bridge from the south – by some odd quirk of boundary marking, the small area where the board is situated is in County Durham!

Crossing the bridge on to the Durham side puts you on the high level path back to Blanchland. This route takes you high above the river, and at the end of the walk provides you with a very good view of the village of Blanchland. On quiet days you may have the good fortune to catch a glimpse of the roe deer in the woodlands. In winter, when the frost lies hard on the ground, icicles play patterns with the pure air lichens on the stone walls, and there is white all around; it is not hard to see how 'Blanchland' or 'White-Land', got its name.

Walk 3

An alternative circular route to Baybridge and back to Blanchland (total distance about 4 miles) is to leave the village in the opposite direction to the river bridge, walking up through the village, past the car park on the left. About 200 yards further on turn left through the gate to Coat House Farm and follow the track as it climbs to the top of the hill. Here there is a wonderful view of the Abbey, the village, and the surrounding countryside. Where the farm road turns right up to the house, head straight ahead towards the metal gate beside a small pylon. Go through the gate, not forgetting to close it carefully, and follow the faint grassy track down the hillside towards the road.

The gash you can see in the wooded hillside on the other side of the river is the scar left when a pipeline was put through from England into Scotland. You may even be able to spot where it crosses the path. At the road please go carefully, for it can be very busy on a summer weekend. Ahead is the tiny hamlet of Baybridge, where the first stone-built house you will see was at one time an inn. The road leads to the Baybridge picnic area. The path back to Blanchland is the one described for Walk 2.

These walks are where the monks of Blanchland will once have strolled too, on their meditations, or in search of firewood or game for the monastery pot. So it is fitting to end your walks in the heart of what remains of the monks' sanctuary, their church, rebuilt in 1752 out of those parts of the old abbey church that had survived. The church is easy to locate, set back at the side of the Lord Crewe Arms in a traditional English churchyard complete with yew trees and lichen-draped grey gravestones.

All that remained of the original abbey church was the tower, the north transept, the crossing and the sanctuary. These were made into one by eighteenth-century restorers by filling in the gaps with new walls. As you enter the churchyard keep an eye out for the grave of farmer Robert Snowball of Hunstanworth who was murdered and is buried here. His housekeeper was accused of the crime, but was later set free. Watch out also for the mediaeval cross used as a roadside shrine by travellers, joined to its base with molten lead, no doubt taken from the lead smelt mill up the road.

Once inside the church, admire the graceful archway over the nave and notice the window arches on the left, filled with stones. This indicates the room of the old village school. There's a colourful church guide for schoolchildren to be picked up at the entrance. Amongst a number of other leading questions, it asks how the children got up into the room where the window arches are? The church schoolroom was in constant use before the new village school was built in the 1850s. Sadly the village is not provided with enough young Blanchlanders to keep it going. It closed in 1982 after an all time low of eight pupils was reached.

While gazing around you in the chapel, watch you do not trip over the sculpted tombstones; three carved with the croziers of past abbots, two with bows, arrows and hunting horns, symbols of the foresters, and the last one belonging to a fine lady. In fact the church is full of treasures to look out for, though not all of them from the time of the monks. There's a pelican window, an iron fireback showing the coat of arms of King James, the first of the Stuart monarchs, a shepherd's crook and an ancient piece of glass complete with an image of a very fat monk! Clearly they ate well in Blanchland even before the founding of the Lord Crewe Arms.

Back in the village square you will not be able to miss the mediaeval gatehouse, formerly the workman's entrance to the Abbey. At one time the village road used to pass through this archway, but it is not big enough for the four-wheel-drive jeeps that are all the rage in these country parts. However, the building itself has not become completely redundant. It houses a post office and gift shop. You can still see the shelter with fireplace inside the gatehouse where poor travellers took refuge in mediaeval times.

The cellar bar and the lounge at the Lord Crewe Arms were once store rooms for the Abbey. Look up the chimney and you will see the remains of an old priests' hidey-hole. The graceful lawn at the back of the hotel was once the Abbey's cloister. Behind and to the south-east stood the monks' living quarters and former estate offices. The cottages now overlooking the south-eastern miniature square further down the street towards the bridge, at the back of the garden, include some of the walls of the monks' refectory.

4
ALLENDALE
VALLEY OF THE SHINING WATER

Allen-a-Dale is known to most schoolboys above the age of thirty-five as the name of one of the leading members of the original Robin Hood's Band of Merry Men. Perhaps Allendale was his place of origin, an origin fitting for an outlaw and a solid opponent of the rigid regime of the Sheriff of Nottingham. For historically, Allendale is wild country, a home for generations of non-conformists and for itinerant mineral workers, for smallholding pioneers, freethinkers and the odd Border raider.

The landscape somehow says it all: a mix of open moor and lush grassy green dale, where mine workings and cottages lie overgrown with fell grasses and mosses, where sheep and curlew now outnumber the human inhabitants, where a wilderness of nature and empty sky reign supreme. But the wilderness of Upper Allendale is none the less romantic for it. The wind, as it moans past the hearth stones of empty cottages, whistles with the warmth of the lives that once dwelt there: giving rise to many a ghost story. And on a full moon the water-logged fellsides and the dale burns shine like silver.

There are traces of silver within the river from which the dale takes its name. Deposits of galena, lead and silver ore, formed when volcanic rock of the Whin Sill intruded into the limestone above, can still be panned from the water. Though – in case you fancy making your fortune from it – not in the quantities which made the old mine at the top of the dale once the richest silver mine in the world. Even the name of the river reflects this ancient treasure. According to one source, it comes from the Celtic 'aln', meaning foaming and sometimes shining. Another source, local historian George Dickinson, writing in 1884, maintains that Allen can be traced to the Celtic words 'al', white, and 'aon', water; to which has been added by the Saxons, or Danes, 'del', a dale or valley. Allendale is then 'The Valley of the White or Shining Water'.

Either way, the dale is a precious treasure, a visual treat to the visitor, a hidden and magical place. There are other treasures too, hidden like Allenheads village itself, from the world outside but awaiting discovery by the discerning eye, the keen walker and even by the passing motorist.

The shining water: the sapphire-silver River Allen, captured by moonlight ▶

ALLENHEADS VILLAGE

There are two ways into the head of the valley from Weardale, via Killhope Wheel and Cowshill and on to the B6295, or through the Rookhope valley. The road from Rookhope drops you down from the top of the fells into the heart of Allenheads village. But this is no normal road and Allenheads is no ordinary village. In the middle of winter, when the snow is piled high on the roadside, the entrance to Allenheads is like a mini Glencoe. There are skiers tearing down the hillside along the side of the road, careering over the ice-capped depths of Risegreen Reservoir and down towards the bottom of the slope.

The road itself is just as precipitous, snaking round at an angle of 45 degrees, while as often as not a torrent of water and ice pours across the surface. It is a brave soul that enters the Allen pass in the winter, but the rewards are considerable. Tucked away in the trees at the foot of the fell sleeps Allenheads. Towered over on three sides by high rising heather moor, it is a place to retreat from the world, to have a quiet drink at the inn and pass an afternoon treading the tracks of villagers past and present through the woods and hills around.

Time was when Allenheads was invisible from the top of the fell, hidden by a forest of conifers on all sides. But those days, and that forest, are gone. The trees were felled for timber and only the broadleaves remain, a reminder of a stately past, when Allenheads was once the summer

▼ Allenheads village, at sunrise

quarters of the Beaumont family, the landowners in this neck of the woods. The conifers were planted by the head of the family, Lord Allendale, in the early part of this century, in place of an earlier crop. But when the trees came down for the second time in a century, the thin layer of soil which remained was washed away. It is unlikely that there will be successful tree regrowth after the rain and the rabbits have taken their share and in any case three generations of acid-loving and acid-producing conifers are more than even the best of already acid upland soils can really bear.

The Allendale family now live in another part of Hexhamshire, but they still retain an active presence in the area, owning the tenant farms at the head of the valley and using Allenheads Hall as a shooting lodge for wealthy Americans who come here for the grouse and no doubt also for the upland experience, for a day out on the heather moors, washed down with whisky. They get a good deal at Allenheads, for the moors around offer some of the best shooting in the country, with record numbers of this uniquely British bird having been bred and brought down in the past.

Allenheads itself belongs to another era, an era of lead mining and estate work. The village overlooks a mineyard, now a storage place for equipment belonging to the Weardale Minerals Company. The yard is now a tidy and, at times, a busy place. But for years it was a forgotten corner, a place where in the days of the great lead rush between the sixteenth and nineteenth centuries, it housed a huge mining enterprise. This was an enterprise so important to the economy of England's North Country that the little village of Allenheads had electricity before the great conurbation of Newcastle!

Allenheads was the epicentre of the great northern lead and iron ore fields. The mine at its heart yielded over 300,000 tons of lead and silver from 1780 until its closure in 1896. In that period, the mine made the mine owners, the Blackett-Beaumonts, an extremely wealthy family. Over 52,000 ounces of silver were struck in one glorious year in 1869, and a solid lump of the metal weighing 12,162 ounces, worth some £3,344 – a fortune at the time – was recovered.

The glitter did not last. In the 1880s the British lead industry collapsed, like so much heavy metal. The village of Allenheads suffered a spectacular decline in activity and in population. From an all-time population high of 1089 in 1880, the population of Allenheads now is just over 160.

There was a small recovery to the village's mining fortunes in 1972, when the mine was re-opened for the production of fluorspar, a mineral associated with lead, and in great demand for its role as a flux in the smelting of steel. After seven years of digging and a considerable investment of time and money, the well was shown to be dry: the fluorspar was just not there in sufficient quantities to be mined. Imagine the desolation felt by some when everything went quiet, yet again. Of this lean time Sarah Goodfellow, a local widow reminisced:

'All day it used to be clang and a clatter in that yard the whole time, you know, and stuff was coming out of the mine. And now it's all silent except for the pumps . . . It's been awful since they closed it down, for silence . . .'

A few years afterwards, the pumps stopped too, the mine was declared unworkable, and all work was abandoned. The mine is closed but the mine entrance is still there, though water swishes around inside, covering over the tracks left by men across the centuries, and rusting the rails along which lead-filled buggies used to run. Deep down below, the once busy heart of Allenheads is silent.

Up above, life goes on. Allenheads is used to these dramatic changes in fortune. Even at the very height of its success as a mining centre there was much coming and going of the local people. A flush of departures followed the Great Strike in 1849 when the celebrated mine agent and engineer, Sir Thomas Sopwith, introduced a time and motion study on the miners' working practices. The walk-out against the new regime lasted for 18 weeks and involved 350 men and boys. Feelings ran so high that in one speech against those who did not back the strike, one strike leader called down the wrath of hell upon the 'blacklegs', invoking the strikers to 'torment them while on earth, and when they die may the devil torment them to all eternity'. The strike collapsed in the end, and the striking families, their labour replaced by men brought in from the outside, were banished for all time from work down the Allendale mines.

The families had no choice but to leave the area. Many packed their belongings and a sad, defeated army of men, women and children took to the road and headed for the coast and a passage to America. It is said that there are now thriving communities of old Allendonians in America, though none of the locals knows quite where. But if you're American, and your name is Dixon, Shield, Dargue, Rutherford, Hewitson or Phillipson – all the local names – the chances are there's a bit of the Silver River running through your veins!

After the strike had ended Allenheads bounced back; so too after the first collapse of the lead industry, and again after the spar forays down the new mine in the 1970s. A village trust has been set up which is converting old buildings in the centre of the village, and is planning to open up a museum and a shop, an interpretation centre, craft workshops to encourage new businesses, and a place to display the unique Armstrong Hydraulic Engine which used to be at work down the shafts but was found, having languished in obscurity in a workshed for the last hundred years. Soon, Allenheads will be open for business to the outside world again, but tapping a different and hopefully longer lasting source of wealth – tourism. Already in 1988, the trust struck gold, with a royal visit, a tour of the village by the next in line to the throne of England.

One of Allenhead's unexpected heritages from those klondike days of yore is an awful lot of subterranean space, a maze of passages and caverns, great cavities in the earth, worked out by the old miners, and formerly a treasure house of sparkling spar clusters, called 'bonny bits' by the miners, and lead heavy with silver and with dead weight. In one of these great cavities, the mine owner's family used to hold parties. Bits of broken china and torn petticoat were still being brought up as souvenirs until recently, detritus of the odd wild night in the shafts.

In recent years the villagers of Allenheads have encountered problems with these underground holes. They've been creeping to the surface. Liz Maddison of Dirt Pot recalls hanging out her washing one day when the ground suddenly gave way, and she found herself staring into a cavernous hole, a lead 'level' or drainage tunnel below ground, where the level roof had collapsed from waterlogging. For Liz, washing days have never been the same since.

Between pints of his home brew, her husband Bob Maddison is the local artist, a large friendly man, who paints large friendly pictures of the surrounding landscape and has a gallery in his garage on the bridge at Dirt Pot. His favourite haunt for painting and inspiration is up behind Allenheads, in a lonely romantic spot called Byerhope.

BY BYERHOPE BANK

At the time of the lead klondike Byerhope was a thriving community of miners who supplemented their lead winnings with smallholding: an acre of inbyeland on which they grazed a horse, a few milch cattle, some chickens and a parcel of outbye or fell land on which they kept a few sheep. While father was exploring the bowels of the earth, mother kept it all together out on the holding, and reared the children. There were gangs of these. Even today, Allenheads' older villagers remember the days when the hill which separated Allenheads from Byerhope used to ring with the laughter of little Byerhope children as they swarmed over the hillside to the school each morning.

That sound has long since been taken over by the wind. The school at Allenheads is closed, and of the Byerhope community nothing remains but a long line of abandoned dwellings, built at the height of the lead boom from stone ground at Byerhope Head. You can still see the old quarries at the side of the Allenheads-Rookhope road. It was good solid stone: these buildings were made to last. Some of them are in good condition still, and if you look through the window, you can still see the kitchen ranges where the mother cooked and the life of the household revolved. Most of the cottages were

▼ Byerhope: abandoned smallholdings in a large landscape, but still standing after all these years

empty by the early part of this century, but one was more recently inhabited, taken over by an ambitious 'offcomer', who even brought in an electricity supply.

The locals recall with a touch of amusement that the poor chap had grand ideas of living off the land. He hadn't, however, reckoned on the fell winter, and his enterprise quickly foundered, with money owing. One night he disappeared without a word, presumed returned to the city from where he came. You can still see the electricity cables, dangling in the wind, a perch for spring swallows and the Byerhope kestrels, but the supply has long been cut off.

Byerhope's like that, a place of ghosts, of sad memories, where people disappear overnight without trace, and nature reclaims her own. As Sarah Goodfellow said, these once proud small-holdings, where a living was once 'won' from the fell have 'gone back to it, back to the wilderness'.

If you are lucky, and the hawk-like eyes of the Allendale gamekeepers don't alight on you, you might get a close look at Byerhope Reservoir, as grand a body of water as anywhere else in the North Pennines. This was constructed by Thomas Sopwith, the Blackett-Beaumonts' globetrotting engineer, in order to create a constant supply of water for lead washing operations at the bottom of the valley. It is one of a number of man-made reservoirs which dot the hills around the head of the valley, and which in recent years the estate has been trying to drain, for reasons of public safety, they say.

They should tell that to the birds, the plants and the fishes which now inhabit these wonderful water creations. Byerhope is the best. At certain times of the year it is a critical stopping-off point for Pennine-weary ducks, geese and the odd swan. The water has found its own level through leakage through the dam wall, and this has encouraged the growth of wonderful water plant species like water horsetail and lesser pond sedge. Foxes breed in the woods at the back, and for years a pair of kestrels has made a comfortable home in a clump of Scots pine which towers over the reservoir waters. In the early morning they can be seen hovering over the edge of the water, eyes trained on the ground for the flurry of a small mammal, a shrew or mouse, or for the hop of an unwary frog.

Byerhope is a place for lovers, for romantic walks on soft summer evenings, a place for assignations where at one time many a village match was made . . . and unmade. There are stories of unclothed couples cavorting in the woods and in the water by moonlight, though how they coped with Byerhope's infamous summer midges is a mystery to all! But there are other stories too. One year a miner, an old man, went missing from the village. His body was recovered from the shallow waters of Byerhope. No one knows how he met his end, but it must have been a curious one. When they pulled his body out of the water, his pipe was still in his mouth. Such was the power of the old 'baccy pipe', beloved of the Dales miners, inseparable from them, and in this poor chap's case, even after death.

FROM BYERHOPE BRIDGE UP TO KILLHOPE LAW

Leaving Byerhope to the wind and to the swish of Bob Maddison's brush strokes, the B6295 takes you down past an abandoned farm building on the left before Byerhope bridge. This is known locally as Burnfoot, a place of local scandal from times remote to times present. For here in the 1800s was located one of the Allen valley's many inns, where miners and farmers used to gather to drink and occasionally fight the long winter nights away. These inns were as often as not just the front room of someone's smallholding – an extra way of making a penny – but the rowdiness associated with them led eventually to them all being closed down in the early nineteenth century when Methodism and temperance gained a grip on the valley of the white water.

Now, at the foot of Middlehope Burn, Burnfoot

is a quiet, pretty place, a cottage by a footbridge over a tributary of the Allen which is overhung by trees and sheltered from the blasts that scour Killhope above. However, if your eye is good and your mind mischievous you can make out a ring of earth on a piece of ground between Burnfoot and the river which once served as a cockpit. This is where the miners used to gather at night, well armed with bevvies and betting money, following the fortunes of fighting cocks which they threw into the ring.

The Burnfoot cockpit is strategically placed, just a bit out of sight of the B6295 to Allendale Town, but within shouting distance, in case the lookout posted on the roadside spied the town 'polis' on the road. For the cruel sport of cock-fighting was banned at the turn of the century. Among North Country gaming circles it still goes on today, though fortunately not in Allendale.

From the small bridge at Byerhope, the B6295 takes you down to the hamlet of Spartylea, called after the 'sparts' or fell grasses which dominate the steep-sided sheep pastures hereabouts. 'The grund's varra sparty aboot here,' is one recorded local saying. It's a good description of the land above the road, where good grass is sparse and the sheep have that lean spartan look of creatures that have spent a large part of their lives on a permanent diet of Outward Bound breakfast. But the landscape below the road is a lot richer, and the names get better too: it's a day out for the etymologists among you. See how quickly you can figure out the origins of place names like Hammershield, Brekonholme, Peasmeadows, Coatenhill and Blacklot. Some of them are pretty straightforward though, like White Ridge and Huntwell.

One of these place names has always aroused a lot of local controversy. There is a large vicarage-style building on the roadside corner

▼ Grasses at sunset, on the fell above Spartylea

▲ Shepherd's watch at the head of the Allen valley

which used to be called Elia House. At one time there were disputes about the precise pronunciation of 'Elia', about whether it was 'Ee-eelya', or 'Ee-eeleea', or the more Biblical 'Eelaeya'. Who cares, you might think? But in these hills there's a lot in a name: names connect people to the landscape, expressing an almost totemic affinity with the soil upon which generations have laboured. It's common for fields or fellsides to be named after particular members of the family, like Dan's Lot, Varty's Sike, or Graham's Moss. Place-naming is a serious business: you will not find a Kate's Bottom in these parts!

Imagine then the local consternation when one day in 1978 the sign 'Elia House' was removed from the gateside post where it had lain undisturbed for decades, attracting only local disputes and the attention of passing idle etymologists . . . and no doubt the odd visitor. This was sacrilege enough, but the new name was extraordinary – Kailash Bawan. For those of you not well versed in Sanskrit or steeped in the Everyman translation of the Hindu Mahabharata, this means 'seat of the gods' or more specifically 'throne of Siva', Siva being the Hindu god of creation and destruction, Lord of the Overworld and Lord of the Underworld.

Elia House had become a retreat, home to a Buddhist meditation centre, where Sunday prayers after chapel were replaced overnight with mantras. Where once the kitchen savoured strongly of the smell of farmhouse cooking – of game pie, egg and chips – it became strongly scented with Tassajara bread, zen brownies, tarragon and that most mysterious of macrobiotic concoctions, miso. The funny smells were a talking point in Spartylea for years to come, but nothing aroused local tongues more than the

▲ Kailash Bawan, footsteps to another heaven?

the Roman Wall and the Cheviots, over 50 miles distant at the far end of the Pennine chain. On Killhope top there is a stone beacon erected long ago. Great fires would be lit there to warn the Allendonians of flying visits from Border Scotsmen, or to celebrate great events like the turning of the year, the coronation of a king or the glorious victory of the Slag Hill dominoes team over their great rivals from Sinderhope in the 1920 grand final at Byerhope Inn.

On Killhope's highest point there also stands the remains of a great smelt chimney where the fumes from the lead smelting processes in Allenheads mine were channelled through a flue tunnel dug deep into the hillside and reaching from the bottom of the dale to its very top. If you brave the excellent walk past Killhope Law along the old Carriers Way from the Killhope Museum in Weardale over to Allenheads, you will see beneath the Killhope Chimney an area of wasteground, where the 'fall-out' from melted lead laid waste the heather and bog grasses. Even after a hundred years, long since the mines stopped operating, the ground has never recovered – a testament to the true toxicity of lead. What it must have done to the lungs of the lead miners doesn't bear thinking about.

The fall-out did do something useful though. At the turn of the century it brought to light one of the few pieces of solid evidence for habitation of these parts by the Celtic tribes who are thought to have given the dale its name. A hoard of beautifully feathered flint arrowheads and hatchet tops was found lying just below the surface. The hoard also included chippings, indicating that the weapons were made on the spot. There are a number of things any amateur archaeologist could deduce from this. Firstly, that these Stone Age people must have either been well travelled or have established good trading links with peoples from other parts, for there are no flints hereabouts; secondly that there must have been game a-plenty to be on the receiving end of a sharp flint instrument; and thirdly that they must have been able to live, and

sight of early morning prayer sessions. Willy Parker remembers: 'Why naa, they wuz waalkin'on thon roadside, in thon bright orange robes, taalkin' tae thon nettles. Wid'ye b'lieve it?' Talk about culture shock . . . But in your own country . . . and in dear old Allendale.

Elia House is no longer a retreat, though the name Kailash Bawan remains and as it turns out was well chosen. Not only is Allendale, in all its spring or autumn beauty, a fit throne for the gods, but with its own resident underworld, a maze of tunnels and mine cavities going along the length of the dale, it is quite suitable for any self-respecting Sivaite of the netherly tendency, and has its own mountain glory too . . . Killhope.

Killhope Law stands at 2207 feet above sea level at the head of Swinhope valley: a small mountain, but an impressive one. On a clear day you can see across the Allen and Tyne valleys to maybe even settle, on the top of Killhope Law.

That final deduction is a sobering thought when you find yourself standing on Killhope in a force four gale, trying to remember which of your various numbered extremities goes in front of the other to get you quickly down the hill. But Killhope is not without its romantic qualities, as can be seen in this absolute gem of an extract from an 'Address to Killhope Law' by 'an Allenheads Love-Stricken Maiden', published in Robert Dixon's *Allendale Christmas Annual* from his printing house in Allenheads village, way back in 1871. Not content with falling head-over-heels for Dirt Pot's very own Casanova, she then presumes to engage the great hill in conversation:

> Grave old Killhope lend thine ear
> From thy throne above.
> Well I know you like the theme
> Which I treat of now,
> For oft I see the passing cloud
> Kiss thy wrinkled brow.

After a great deal of sighing and the sound of rending hearts, the maiden finds herself unable actually to come out with the story of her one true love, but asks instead whether life has been blighted by her own feelings, whether she'll sleep again and 'Never feel misfortune's thorn? Or be shaken on life's billow, Aching sick, from night till morn?' But we shouldn't jest: astoundingly, the hill answered, as she tells:

> Ha! a halo shrouds thy features,
> Something moves the craggy beard.
> And from out thy head so hoary
> Steal these words the vale across,
> 'If thou'dst have a mother's glory
> Thou must take a mother's cross.'

'Ha! indeed! You've probably heard it all by now, Buddhists talking to nettles, maidens to mountains, what next? Well, there's the story of the talking sill . . . But not now.

DOWN TO ELPHA GREEN BY SWINHOPE BURN

Down at the bottom of Swinhope Burn, on the road from Coalcleugh, approaching Spartylea from the south-west, there's a set of caves, a system of fairy holes called Elpha Green. Tradition has it that these holes were once inhabited by little people, by whole colonies of elves and bogies who used to come out at night and torment the people and the cattle in the neighbourhood. By moonlight they used to dance on Elpha Green, the ground of the elves.

In recent days the caves resounded not to the chatter of little folk but to the clang of metal from the equipment of pot holers, a new species of cave dweller, whose headlamps create light in the nether gloom, bringing to life a treasure of stalagmites and stalagtites. This had clearly been kept hidden by the elves for centuries, and it was thanks to modern mountain technology that we humans were at last able to get our own back on those dastardly sprites. Maybe, however, they had the last word: a rockfall blocked the cave entrance and the caves are no longer accessible.

The belief in local spirits, elves and the like, among our ancestors has to do with finding explanations for misfortune, and with shouldering the burden of blame on to forces unseen. The belief is not irrational, simply an intellectual response to a problem, cause and effect, with a touch of colour and romance thrown in. Many were the ways invented by our ancestors to control the uncontrollable, to reinforce the boundaries between the world of the known and the unknown, the ordered and the disorderly. And a legacy of this boundary confirmation can still be seen on the landscape around Elpha Green, and where else but in the shape and the state of its field boundaries, its 'dykes' or walls?

There are none finer, not anywhere in the whole of the North Pennines. Tall and solid, built from the best Allendale river stone, dragged from the riverbed to the farm and individually laid in place by craftsmen who inherited the art of 'dyke-laying' from their fathers and grandfathers before them. And not a touch of cement or mud holds these huge stones together. They're individually chosen to fit into one another, like a jigsaw puzzle. Chief of the Elpha craftsmen was George Phillipson, a man as solid as his walls, as gritty as the fells around. George had huge hands and a huge heart which somehow seemed to speak to the world through his walls.

Other farmers came for miles around to stand and gaze with admiration at George's walls; the way they seemed to go round corners without a bend in sight, or rise up and down hills and hollows in the ground without a sign of weakening. George's walls were impenetrable, 'mowdyproof' they said. Even the wind used to lie down before them, turning away from Elpha Green Farm to the hills around.

George died in 1983. He had lived the full life of a complete fellsman. Brought up on a farm, he first went down the mine, then worked on the roads, as a lengthsman responsible for keeping in order a 'length' or patch of road, roadside and ditch, before the days of council wagons and council teams. Then he worked the limestone for his father on the face of the escarpment below Elpha, where the elves had their holes. Then George took over the farm, a small one, but the neatest in the valley, with spart-free green grass pastures, and those wonderful walls. Any mowd, or mole, that dared rear his head near Elpha Green, George would be on top of it. The same must have gone for the elves. George saw none in his long life. When he died, you could not get near the chapel, it was so full. And the walls have never looked the same since.

George's friend from boyhood was Willy Parker. In the old days they used to go on drinking bouts to the inn at Allenheads, returning late at night across the fells. One night they stumbled blind drunk into the back garden of one of the Allenheads villagers. The lady of the house remembers finding them staring into the depths of her rain barrel, holding each other back from falling in and debating anxiously between them how they had managed to wander so far away from home that they'd ended up staring into the doomy depths of Byerhope Reservoir!

SPARTYLEA TO THE HAGG

There's a pretty church at Spartylea, St Peter's, built at the height of the lead boom. But it now attracts a different type of flock. For, like many Allendale places of worship, it has been given over not to the spiritual comforts of the people, but to the material comforts of local farm animals. It has become a hay shed, attached to the farm which runs from the old Cornmill. One of Willy Parker's strongest memories of the church

▼ Willy Parker, a man of the fell

▲ Ploughing at Sipton: earthworms beware!

in regular use was of the funerals. Apparently, when the funeral procession reached the top of the hill above the church, the church bell was tolled three times. When the procession reached half way down the bank, it would pause while the bell tolled twice, and then finally, when the procession reached the door of the church, the bell would toll once, one single, sad, final time, in honour of the deceased.

It tolls for us all eventually of course, and Willy, now in his late eighties and living at the top of the hill above St Peter's Church, has witnessed an entire generation of Allendonians

disappear for the last time down that path, while the bell tolls out their passing: his family and friends, war heroes and tramps, adults and little children. The graveyard is worth a visit, and Willy, if he's still active and about, will take you round. If you do, take a close look at the southern end of the graveyard near the wall, for behind a plantation of fairy thorns you'll find a series of little mounds. These are unmarked graves, the resting places of suicides and of the stillborn, or little children who died before baptism, before they became 'real' in the religious eyes of the world.

▲ May in Sinderhope

The locals are proud of keeping the graveyard in good condition, in paying proper dues to the dead. This custom is tied to the dalespeople's close affinity to their environment, an identity between people and place that makes the dead as much a part of the place as the living. Every year at harvest time, the graveyard committee, of which Willy Parker was the original chairman, meets to mow the high grass and mend the graveyard walls. Resting from their labours in the warm summer evening, there is talk of old times, and in this sacred place, the sacred heart of a dying community, wild nature and the fell is once more kept at bay.

The high road, the B6295, from Spartylea to Allendale Town takes you past two places where the landscape, in changing from the high brown fells to the lower grassy pastures, is particularly striking. The two places are called Sipton and Sinderhope.

A footpath takes you up Sipton Side, along the edge of dramatic Sipton Cleugh, a slit in the fellside through which tumbles Sipton Burn. An awful lot of Siptons, but your walk will take you on to the fellside to a point where it meets a gravel track called 'The Long Drag'. This was once used by the mulepacks of the old lead miners, but now only by the Allendale estate gamekeepers' jeeps on sorties to check the grouse numbers and to convey the visiting parties of shooters.

Walking on this track in high summer or in the autumn is an experience well worth the effort. It is also safer. If you go out in the spring you'll incur the wrath of the keepers concerned about disturbing the grouse, or suspecting you of poaching game. Even if you are within your rights to walk a public footpath, a brush with young keepers waving shotguns in the air, wearing bandoleers of shotgun cartridges round their shoulders, and that vague Rambo look in their eyes, is something we can all do without. And in the height of winter the Long Drag is indistinguishable from the South Pole . . . so watch out, you may be gone for some time . . .

This custom of burying those who died 'unnatural' deaths separately from the others is as old as the hills, a legacy of Celtic tradition and found among all the ancient and non-Christian cultures the world over. Often these burials take place outside the burial ground, a complete separation of the official and the unofficial dead, used as a way of emphasising separation, of trying to prevent the spirits of the unofficial, unhappy dead from afflicting the world of the living. At St Peter's though, these sad graves are actually in the graveyard, though slightly set apart, a sign of compassion on the part of the church.

But in high summer you'll see North Pennines fellscape at its best, with 'all around the bloomin' heather and the wild mountain thyme, so will ye go lad or lassie, go'. There are larks in the air, bees in the purple bell heather, bilberries underfoot, and if you're both quiet and lucky you may catch sight of a merlin hunting down an unwary moors mammal, swooping from the sky and into the heart of the heather below.

The Long Drag will take you past Sinderhope Carrs to the boundary stones which mark the edge of the ancient parish of Allendale and from there it is not far to Hangman Hill, a remote spot indeed to get strung up! After that you reach another smaller dale, the little valley of Rowley Burn in the heart of Hexhamshire Common. Pause and rest here, for there are breathtaking views across to Slaley Forest, the distant Roman Wall and Hexham itself. If you have the time at the end of your Allendale or even Pennine tour, it is worth making a special effort to visit historic Hexham. On the north edge of the Pennine Hills, it lies in the Tyne Gap overlooked by longer stretches of 'The Waall' as they say around here: the Roman Wall. For people living today in the valleys of the Allen and South Tyne, Hexham is the commercial centre of the area, the old seat of the shire, a bustling shopping and tourism centre with restaurants and a fine golf course and on Saturday, busy market stalls. It's a main Pennine town, but curiously left out of the Area of Outstanding Natural Beauty's scheduled area.

It's hard to imagine why. Set in rolling hills and parkland Hexham is a beautiful town, vying with Durham as the most attractive centre of commerce and administration in the north of England. Hexham Abbey at one time had the reputation of being the finest church north of the Alps. It's built from stones taken from the Roman fort of Corstopitum.

The Saxon crypt is the finest in England, and St Wilfred's Chair or Frith Stool, the Saxon throne of the Bishop, was, in mediaeval times, a place of sanctuary. Hexham didn't always prove to be a sanctuary though. In 1761 the Allendale lead miners were in Hexham to protest against new recruiting regulations for the militia. Eventually, the Riot Act was read out and the North Yorkshire militia turned on the assembly. Fifty were killed and 300 injured. For years afterwards the North Yorkshire militia went by the name of the Hexham Butchers.

Hexham is also the home of a strange story which you may not like to dwell on too long, out in the lonely moors. But here goes. In 1971 the eminent Celtic scholar and archaeologist Dr Ann Ross was asked to examine two carved stone heads of an unpleasant visage. She took them to her home and placed them in her study and that night she was woken by a strange sensation. On going to look she caught sight of a strange creature, half animal, half man. The creature continued to haunt the house until the heads were sent to the museum. Dr Ross had, it is thought, disturbed the ghost of a Celtic warrior or deity, who had lost his head, and was cursed with wandering the earth until he could put it back on to the rest of his stone body! Later, mysteriously, the Hexham heads disappeared without trace.

Back on the Long Drag, if you follow the path the other way, your OS map glued to your chin, you can in fact come down to Sinderhope by the back way via Hay Rake, an adventurous journey across gates and fences to the road below. Sinderhope is a tiny hamlet, a mere shadow of the populous community which lived here at the height of the mining era. But it has still got its post office, even if it is in the back of the postmistress's living room! And there is a thriving community centre where the villagers of Allenheads, Sinderhope, Spartylea and all the farms around come for get-togethers, to play darts and snooker, whist and dominoes and hold an annual Christmas party for the old folks.

The centre was once Sinderhope school, their school, where they were educated for life in the Allen valley. When it was closed in the 1960s it was turned into a field studies centre for children from outside the valley, an ironic arrangement which was not lost to the villagers. But when in the 1970s the Council decided to sell it off for a proposed ski centre development, complete with dry ski slopes down to the Allen and the prospect of après-skiers in gay abandon around their homes, all hell broke loose. An action committee was formed to fight for the building which was their community's birthright, paid for in the lead days out of public subscription. The press joined in and under pressure from all sides, the project was abandoned, and with a timely piece of community action, the centre was saved for local people to use and enjoy.

So if you are out in the snow and you pass Sinderhope Centre, hide away your skis, just in case you end up backside first on the slippery slope down to the Allen. And if you are there in the summer, go down the hill to the river ford below a farm called The Holmes. This is one of the prettiest walks in the whole of the North Pennines, through woods of oak and elm, past an old lead washing mill, to the riverside, rich with flowering water weeds, with mints and cresses, and where trout rise from the brimming Allen waters to catch fluttering butterflies and the ever-plentiful, ever-pestilent midge.

Between Sinderhope and Allendale Town there is a place called The Hagg, a collection of farm buildings past which runs the Hagg Burn, and there is another farm called Haggburn Gate. Hagg doesn't have anything to do with sorcery though; it's a Celtic word for an enclosed wood, similar to the old Norse 'hogg', meaning a copse or coppice. In lead mining times, wood was coppiced in this very place in order to provide a constant supply of fuel for lead smelting. The woods were managed so that new shoot growth from stands of the mature broadwood trees was cut down at certain stages in the growth cycle to produce firewood, but without killing the trees or harming the habitats. Some of Britain's best native woodland was once managed in this way, satisfying the needs of everyone, both commercial and amenity interests, and including the everyday needs of our wildlife.

ALLENDALE TOWN AND THE FESTIVAL OF FIRE

Allendale Town is not a large place. Its importance as the head of two dales, the East and West Allen, is more symbolic than real. Anciently known as Allenton, it has a current population of 600, which compares well with its population of 487 in 1881. And it is an attractive, sleepy sort of place, with a market square which seems to be fully taken up with hotels and banks. The church is notable for its carved lych-gate and a window mosaic of the Last Supper, and the tree-hung square backs on to a cricket ground and play area, where on many a long summer evening the sound of a crack on willow is matched only by the rattle and swish of emptying beer and whisky glasses.

The hotels are very busy in the summer months, for Allendale has for a long time been an embodiment for remote, tranquil, rural life, unspoilt natural beauty and clean air to folk from the great northern towns and cities. In the last century they came in their droves to improve their health and take away just a bit of Allendale's magic, a pilgrimage witnessed by Beaty in his original guide to the area, published in 1905:

Here comes the jaded business man to snatch a brief rest; the disease-worn invalid for renewed health; as well as those who, satiated with the gaities of town life, seek for change of air and scene. And many without doubt, have had cause to bless the pure bracing air of the Allendale hills, and acknowledged their indebtedness to it for restored vigour and health, giving them new courage and fitness to struggle with the cares and worries of life.

Many of the short walks around the town which Beaty describes are still there: some of them route-marked by the enterprising local Parish Council and available from the 'Toon's' busy post office. In particular the walk along the riverside around Wooley Burn is special. You can just imagine the scene in Victorian England, with long dresses and top hats, nannies and horse droppings, and many a tryst by the tinkling waters of the lower Allen.

Allendale was not, of course, always so tranquil and genteel a place. It was the location where for centuries the annual agricultural hirings were held, when labour was bought and sold, when 'serving' and skilled men and women formed relationships with employers and with local families which could last for as little as a few hours or as long as three generations. The hirings were major events in the Allendale calendar, taking place in May and November every year and coinciding with a fair for people and sometimes an animal sale, with stalls for corn, butter and cheese. The town was then a magnet for traders, tinkers and pedlars of all kinds.

The old fairs had their rowdy side, with drinking in the large number of public houses which dotted the 'Toon' and young couples courting and dancing to the tune of fiddles and clarinets stationed in each public house along the way. The combination of all this, together with the smell of the raw manure from the heaps of dung and household refuse dumped unceremoniously at the doorsteps of the Allendonians' proud town houses, must have proved highly intoxicating.

The old fairs have gone, but Allendale is still famous for an apocalyptic event of a different sort, one of the most spectacular folk festivals still found not just in England, but in the whole of Europe, an event fitting to Allendale's claim to be the centre of Britain. This is the famous Allendale Fire Festival or 'Tar Barling' ceremony, performed without fail every New Year's Eve. It is of unknown origin. But it is linked to a range of midwinter fire festivals performed throughout Europe since Celtic times and connected symbolically with the death of Balder, the Norse god of vegetation. It is a 'Bel', 'Bal' or 'Baal' fire, which elsewhere in Europe not only signals the turning of the sun upwards from its lowest seasonal point in the heavens, but celebrates the death and rebirth through fire of the spirit of

▲ The flames of the Allendale fire

spring, of vegetation and brings the promise of fertility and new life. Everywhere, the midwinter fire festival is a community rite of passage which re-forges ancient deep-rooted connexions between man and nature. The other best known midwinter fire festival in Britain is the 'Up Hell-iya' which takes place in Shetland in January and involves a tug of war, men dressing up as Vikings and the ritual burning of a Viking ship which is then put out to sea.

At thirty minutes to midnight every New Year's Eve, more properly termed 'Old Year's Night', a large crowd of dalespeople and visitors from all over the country assemble in the square in

▲ Snow lying deep on Slaghill

Allendale Town. The hotel bars are full to bursting and there is a tremendous air of excitement and expectancy. This grows alongside the throbbing of a huge bass drum, and as the minutes tick towards the magic hour when one year ends and a new one begins all eyes turn towards the lych-gate at the back of the square, where the Allendale Silver Band has struck up a medley of lively reels.

Without warning, the crowd is suddenly forced apart by a striding column of men in outrageous costumes, led by a man with a blazing torch, and several members of the Silver Band looking just a little the worse for an evening's solid tippling. And placed on the heads of each one of these 'guisers' is a blazing barrel of fire, the columns of flame reaching 6–8 feet into the now sparkling night sky. It is a truly remarkable sight.

The column of living fire then moves at rapid pace around the perimeters of the ancient square, re-marking the boundaries which mark out the living heart of the dale and the crossroads which connect it to the outside world. The barrels are dangerous, sawn-off tar barrels filled with sticks and paraffin, and the expression of the faces of these forty fire-bearing men, Allendale 'born and bred', bears witness to the

111

solemnity of the occasion and the danger to their persons which would follow from one false move of the foot.

This extraordinary procession quickly winds its way back towards the very centre of the square where a huge bonfire of wood is placed on top of a circle of old barrels foaming with petrol. Then one after another the 'guisers' tip their flaming load on the bonfire, taking care to retrieve their barrel and their singed skins as they make a hasty retreat from the scene. As the church bell tolls the final countdown to midnight, this great fire in the heart of the dale explodes like a bomb, sending sheets of flame and sparks soaring high into the sky, way above the heads of the crowd and the roofs of the houses, and on more than one historic occasion, above the church tower itself. There is a solemn silence as the crowd is hypnotised by the great column of fire, but it is quickly broken by a joyous rendering of 'Auld Lang Syne', as the onlookers join hands, encircling the sacrificial flames.

As the fire crackles and dances so do the people. Bacchanalia breaks out, and the square soon fills with people singing, dancing, hugging and exchanging 'happy new years'. The 'guisers' then first-foot it around the town, carrying embers of Allendale's ancient community fire to light the new year hearths of those fires which still burn in the houses of the town.

As the year turns, the home fires are kept burning. It is said locally that as long as there is a fire in Allendale, the community will not die. The fire which gives the dale of the shining water its heart and soul, and a lot of its character, shows all the signs of being kept alight.

Here we take our exit from the dale, on the B6295, following the signs for Alston and Whitfield at the famous crossroads at the centre of Allendale Town, and heading off west at Thornley Gate to Bearsbridge and into the valley of the West Allen. There is also another route, along the B603 to the village of Catton, a village of retired couples, named after its formerly large population of wild cats.

A WALK AROUND AND ABOVE ALLENHEADS
THE VILLAGE AT THE HEART OF THE DALE

This walk takes you back up into the high hills of the Pennines, this time part way up Killhope Law on the Carriers Way, lying at the head of the Allen valleys, with special views of the dales and of a little village at their heart: Allenheads. On this combined hill and village walk you will see where the lead miners carted their ore, follow the tracks of their horses, visit their old inn and see their heritage displayed in the old village houses and a new visitor centre. Allenheads is rich in the lore and romance of the past, yet to this day it has remained alive and thriving. The Allenheads to Dirt Pot village walk and back is about 2 miles, taking approximately 1–1½ hours. The walk to Carriers Way is about 4 miles and the combined one-way walk is about 6 miles, taking 3 hours.

Our story of the North Pennines began with a walk

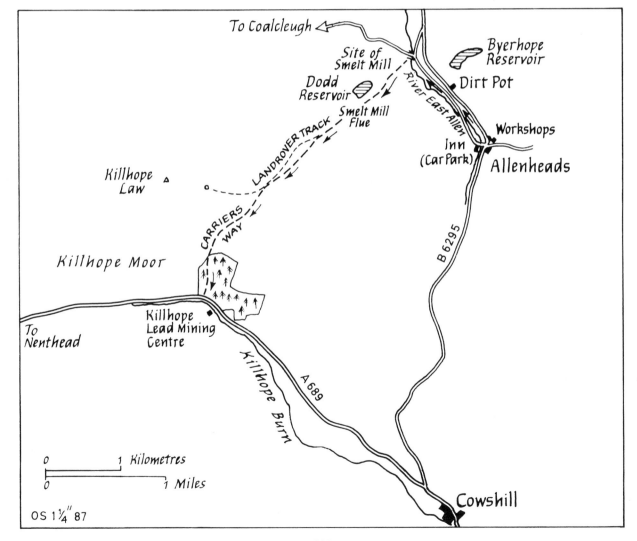

up Cross Fell with its expansive views of the region. Cross Fell is, however, an isolated place: the only inhabitants are those who, like us, go up and down it, and there are no settlements lying within its immediate shadow. Killhope Law, 2207 feet above sea level, is a less spectacular alternative for a hill climb, but it is an alternative none the less and it has the added attraction of a bit of Pennine heart – for our walk part way up Killhope begins and ends with the village of Allenheads, the highest inhabited village in the North Pennines.

If it is a 'rough' day for walking you may be inclined to park in the old village square beyond the crossroads, where the B6295 meets the lower village road. Here stands the old Allenheads Inn where many an old dale story has been told. At the back of the inn there's a gravel path leading up to the hillside which contains lots of waste from the local spoil heaps, including bits of bright purple fluorspar.

In the Allenheads Inn a fire blazes for a large part of the year, and you can sit for hours around the fire and chat with the locals. Allenheads is a friendly village and once you have broken the ice the conversation flows freely. The people are proud of their past, if a little apprehensive about their future in this remote corner of England.

Their pride in the past is being put on display at the new interpretative centre in the old mill opposite the inn. The two former main occupations of the village are very clearly shown by the number of photographs in the centre showing lead mining and agriculture. In the walk around and above Allenheads you're likely to meet examples of both, the latter very much a part of today, the former very much in the past.

The walk through the village starts down the lower road. If the workshops you pass by are open, walk in and ask to be shown the water-powered engine. If there is anything from the past of which Allenheads should justifiably be proud this is it, a unique example of a power source. These machines were originally produced in the area to replace the traditional but less efficient water wheels. They work not unlike steam engines, though instead of steam entering the cylinder and pushing the piston forwards, or backwards, water does the job.

You will see, either from the map or by entering the village from Rookhope or Cowshill, that there are reservoirs all round the village. These were part of the water power system, the powerhouses which supplied the water needed to drive these engines. The workshops included the drawing and planning offices where Allenheads' unique water power system was originally executed – on reams and reams of paper. These buildings, for many years in disuse, are now being reconverted into workshops; a potter is in one, and 'Crafty Heads of Allenheads', a craft workshop, is in another.

A look at these will have brought you out on to the top road, so you have to look out for the finger-post to direct you down the slope back on to the low road, running parallel to the B6295, through the village. Here you will come across Allenheads village's very own mini 'green belt'. Beyond the square, open-fronted farm building on the left there are fields and pine trees above the road on both sides.

On the hillside above you to the left are two cottages, an occupied one and a deserted one, typical former lead miners' homes. The fields in which they stand have been taken in from the rough moor for hay and grass for a horse, and a cow. More often than not there was a pig, but she had the run of the place, scavenging and eating and rutting all round and around the house. Higher up stands Viewly Hall, aptly named with its views of the hills on the other side of the narrow valley.

On your left you will see the Allenheads estate's former church, now converted into a home by one of Allenheads' leading lights, former ironworker Dave Flush. Then there is more open space round the bend, until after a few minutes' walk, you come to the stone terraced cottages and yet another converted chapel which tells you that you are in Dirt Pot, Allenheads' own suburb!

Up until now it's been all downhill through the village. But the settlement of Dirt Pot provides the taking off point for our final Pennine uphill trek. Dirt Pot is where the lead smelters lived in the 1800s when Allenheads was a busy industrial settlement enjoying the peak prosperity of the lead mining boom, and the hardships and heartache that went with it. At the back of Dirt Pot you will see a building known as Candle House where they made the candles that lit the village before the coming of electricity. On the steep hillside above the houses you can see the pines of Byerhope and on the verges run little water channels that turn into deluges when the winter rains fill Byerhope Reservoir and the wet fells above to their fullest.

On your left is the Methodist Chapel and Sunday School annexe where generations of Allenheads miners and farmers made peace with themselves and their maker. Beyond lies the terrace of Ropehaugh, a line of homes and holiday cottages as typical as you will find anywhere in the north-east. Inside many of them still have the original stone flag floors and iron hearths of the old days. Across the years many a happy couple and many a happy band of children will have come and gone within these little homes.

At the back of the stone terrace the River East Allen tinkles past, silvery with snow and ice as well as with silver crystals and moonlight, for large parts of the year. Between the river and the houses there are little grassy gardens, some with fluorspar-laden rockeries and with rose-decked arches where little wooden gates lead down to the stream. In the spring the grasses of some of these gardens are strewn with flowers, domestic and wild, including perhaps the saddest and most romantic of them all, the little blue forget-me-not. Once you've reached the bridge over the river at the end of the settlement, you have to make a choice: whether to undertake a walk up the Carriers Way towards the top of Killhope (and don't forget it's uphill all the way!) or to walk back through the village to Allenheads Inn.

If you decide to opt for the walk up Carriers Way, take the track leading south-west uphill past the Dodd Reservoir. This track is the old Carriers Way, used by the lead miners to bring lead ore from Killhope in Weardale to the smelter near the Coalcleugh bridge. The ruins over the fence which you pass on your left are all that remain of the mill buildings where the smelting of the ore took place.

Since galena, lead ore, is a sulphide, smelting gives off highly toxic fumes. So in the days of smelting, these were carried away by a long flue running for miles up to the top of Killhope. At the base of the Carriers Way you can walk on top of the flue, and peer down into the 'flume' or chamber – imagine having to clean that out regularly!

The Carriers Way was the pony track for the lead miners' pack ponies but now a track for Landrovers transporting shooting parties. Each pony carried about a quarter of a 'bing' of lead ore on its back, about 2 cwt of metal and rock from the bottom to the top of the hill. The breeding of these 'Galloways' or fell ponies was an important industry in the area. Stories have been told of men who would work double shifts in the mine, snatch a bite, and then walk over the felltops to Appleby Fair to buy a breeding mare, return and go into the mine after a catnap of a sleep and a bowl of broth. Their success in training horses and ponies for use in the mine or on the trail could mean a little extra food, or a little more comfort, for lead mining was not a well-paid living.

At least the miners and their ponies will have had some good views, and so too will you. If you look back down the dale from the point where the Carriers Way leaves the Landrover track, about 2000 feet high on the ridge, you will be able to see the whole length of Allendale unfurl itself behind you and you will begin to see some of County Durham's countryside, bits of Weardale and Teesdale, appearing over the far side to the south-east and south.

The Way diverges from the Landrover track you have been following and heads south across the moor, its route marked by an occasional 3-feet-high wooden marker post, and down into Weardale to the lead mining centre at Killhope about 1 mile below. If you have the time, it's well worth a visit, but it's also a climb back up to the Landrover track. Killhope is only 3 miles from Dirt Pot, and the return walk to Allenheads should take about four hours including time to stop and admire the views. Panning around, there are some tremendous Pennine visitas to be seen. To the south-west lies Cross Fell and the ridge over the Eden, to the west the hills of the South Tyne, and almost at your feet the valleys of the West and East Allen, the tip of the Derwent Reservoir, and Weardale and Teesdale. From up here there is another chance to take in the vistas which inspired this book, the seven dales and the hills of England's last wilderness, the great North Pennines.

5
THE WEST ALLEN
VALLEY OF THE FIVE BRIDGES

The Allen's sister river cuts a beautiful dash down a dale where Walter the Molecatcher caught his first mole, where Maddy Crow met a tawdry end, and where sunpower for years has warmed a swimming pool for the workers at Whitfield Hall. It is a dale of sharp contrasts, of peace and plenty fringed with wilderness, and centred upon a parkscape of great glory where every spring the lawns glimmer with thick crops of daffodils and crocuses.

Both the main westerly routes into the foot of the West Allen valley skirt the precipitous Allen Gorge and take you down over the fells, a true descent from heather moor and high wild and open Pennine views into an ordered landscape of lush estate lawns, pruned plantations and well-stocked pastures. We shall be touring the valley from north to south, but there is more lush splendour the other way too, north of where the waters of the two River Allens meet at Cupola and tear through the Allen Gorge past Plankey Mill and down to the River South Tyne. North and south, the West Allen is an Idyll, a setting of which Turner and Constable would have been proud, a hidden corner of old England where life is still lived under the shadow of a church, hall and farmstead.

But there's another side to the story of the West Allen, an older, sadder side which is something out of the ordinary, where those grand vistas are pierced by tragedy, just as the dale itself is pierced by the river which gives it its name. But this too is a part of Pennine life, past and present, a side which with all the awe-inspiring landscapes it is all too easy to forget, but which was once as real as the swish of sedge grasses in autumn wind, or the cry of the curlew when night falls over the fell.

To the unwary visitor, signs of the snake which has lain sleeping at the heart of this particular allotment of paradise can even be seen on the main road to the top of the dale: a series of 'S' bends slope down the fellside at an angle which defies even first-gear driving. When ice and snow abound they are a death trap without measure. And if you enter the valley further north from the Allendale side via the Thornley Gate and Burn Tongues road, you'll meet another such treacherous bend. At the bottom of this stands the Blue Back bridge. Look back up the valley from the Blue Back pub – it is one of the finest views in the whole of England's

Upper West Allendale: a picture of evening peace and plenty. What more could you ask of a dale? ▶

North Country. The thin spire of Whitfield church rises gracefully over the top of the trees and the curve of the river.

If you're on the Thornley Gate road, over Blue Back, then walk back across the bridge and look towards the other side. Here in the shade of the birches and hazels which overhang the road is carved a cross. Take some wet earth in your hand and rub over the writing on its face. The following inscription will appear, as if by magic from the stone:

> Lindsay Aulojo Jameson
> Born at Edinburgh 5th Oct 1870
> Killed by Accident
> Near This Spot
> 16th June 1895
> R.I.P.

It does not say how. One story tells of a cycle ride down the hill and round the bend which carried the rider over the bridgehead and into the river.

After making this sad discovery take the footpath which passes the cross and carries you into the woodland. It is clearly posted, 'Harlow Bank ½, Hindley Wrae ½'. As you pass the cross, look down to the right. There is a moss-covered stone on a little mound. Walter the Molecatcher used to walk this way as a child and according to him this was the original monument to the accident. He says that if you look closely, you can see a ghostly face in the rock. Look closely, for the face is indeed there. Shiver . . . and pass on . . .

The records show of other tragedies near these stone bridges. In 1868 a plumber from Newcastle who was working at nearby Whitfield Hall, a young man called Isaac Daniel Fisher, drowned while bathing opposite the hall. And in 1879, Jane Smith, a local lass and wife to a farm hand from up the dale at Ninebanks, lost her way after taking a short cut home near the bankside. Her wandering from the straight and narrow path proved fatal. She lost her footing and fell. The river was in flood, and she was drowned.

◄ Blue Back bridge

AROUND WHITFIELD HALL

The magnificent gardens of Whitfield Hall, home to the Blackett-Ord family, are clearly visible from the road, and open to the public at certain times of the year. They feature a collection of statues of Greek gods, gracefully presiding over a colourful display of rhododendron and roses. Alongside these silent watchers of another millennium there stands a monument to millenniums present and future: an array of solar panels. The panels collect the energy from the rays of the sun in photovoltaic cells. The heat generated is used to top up Whitfield Hall's electricity supply and to warm up a covered pool for brave winter swimmers.

On the other side of the river, budding naturalists can get a good view of the hall, from a standpoint within Monk Wood. This is a Site of Special Scientific Interest extending over 47 acres and containing oak woodland of a wide range of ages. It is ancient in parts and dramatic throughout, a natural drama made special by the presence of luxurious epiphytic flora featuring one speciality in abundance. Epiphytes may be ferns, lichens or mosses. Basically, they are plants which grow on other plants, not as parasites, but as plants which grow on organic debris which has built up on the surfaces of trees, on gaps in the bark, or clefts and hollows in branches.

They are a little bit like those tropical plants which you can purchase from supermarkets, plants which in their native surroundings live not on the ground but in the air, high in the forest canopy. You would think life in the air, just dangling there, was a bit uncomfortable, but epiphytes get the best of all worlds. There's no cow or sheep bred yet that can get up there to eat them (though no doubt our genetic engineers will have this one in hand!), and just think of all that fresh air.

In fact fresh air is what it's all about. The presence of the epiphytes in Monk Wood and in other parts of the North Pennines, like

Shipley Wood in Teesdale and the Woods along the Derwent Gorge, tell us a lot about the quality of the air in the North Pennines. It is the freshest you can get, and we know because epiphytic lichens only thrive in a pollution-free atmosphere. With the advent of the industrial revolution large parts of Britain's native woodlands lost their lichens. And even today, with the Clean Air Act having banished most of the nastier pollution, you still will not find lichens growing on the barks of trees near urban areas.

The lichens in Monk Wood do not just mean a blast of fresh air, they're also a bit of a blast from the past. Their presence is evidence to the botanist of the continuous survival of ancient woodland on a site for hundreds, if not thousands, of years. Monk Wood is part of Whitfield's ancient past and a testament to the presence of enlightened land management, ensuring its survival to the present. The current land agent at the estate is proud to have this woodland heritage in his charge, and pleased to welcome the parties of informed scientific visitors who come to Whitfield to stare at the strange looking ferns and mosses on the trees.

The name Monk Wood comes from a house of

▼ Cupola Bridge, in autumn peace

monastic correction based on the site of the tithe barn, a relic from the days when clerics lived partly off the land. They still do in some parts of Northumberland that King Henry's reformation could not reach, but not at Whitfield. Monk Cottage, further into the wood, was in an earlier guise first a retreat, then sanctuary from King Henry's men.

If your route through the West Allen valley keeps you to the far side of the river, stop by the side of the road past the Old Toll House and look across the valley at Monk Wood. There, in a clearing among the old grey oaks and the newer planted trees you can see the cottage and if you're lucky a wisp of wood smoke rising through the trees, to the sky. And if you look carefully and the light is kind, you can clearly see Whitfield's famous writing in the air: larches and pines planted in such a way that the differing canopy colours of these species spell out the message: GR VI. It is a commemoration by the estate of George VI's succession to the throne. In this small corner of England patriotic hearts beat hard, but as so often elsewhere now, those hearts when planted are not of oak but of larch. Larches grow faster, of course, and the wood is softer. But there is one consolation, they would never have done it for King Henry!

The village of Whitfield is actually located on the road to Plenmeller, and sits above the West Allen and the A686 to Alston which goes past the Hall and the new church. A short walk up the hill brings you to the village school, one of the few rural primary schools surviving in the Pennines. Its continued existence is only possible with the help of the estate. The old Whitfield church and graveyard is up here too, and there's a small green where an old maypole still lies, a relic of the old village celebration of maypole dancing on the first of May.

The new church, standing beside the main road, the well-supplied village shop, the pub and the estate offices are collectively known as Bearsbridge. In this little corner of England some of the old traditions are enjoying a revival. One

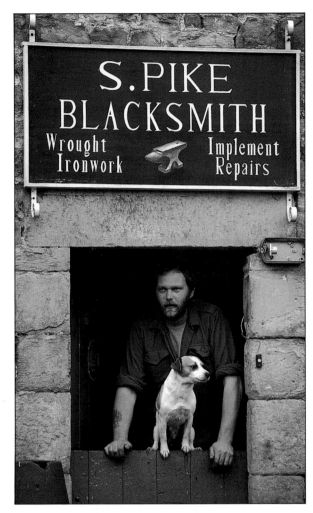

▲ Stan and dog: bringing life back to the smithy

very successful one is the blacksmithing business run by Stan Pike overlooking the village square at Bearsbridge. Stan moved into the former village smithy in 1980. It had not been used since the 1950s. He inherited a shell, but it was not long before he had installed a forge, and after a gap of forty years, had a fire burning again in the old smithy hearth. As Stan himself explains:

'Ah started as an agricultural engineer an' was made redundant. So ah set up me oon business,

121

repairin' cars an' tractors, an' practising smithing as a hobby in the night-time. Ah aalways wanted tae be a smith, and in time ah was able to turn the business to it full-time. Now the wrought-iron wark is a hundred per cent and the car repairs have disappeared. It's not as profitable mind, it's seventy-five per cent work an' twenty-five per cent a labour of love.'

Stan is that rare being in these days of instant creations – a true craftsman. Some of his jobs take years: the biggest being a 1756 Queen Anne gate and 60 foot of iron fencing he is lovingly restoring using the original methods for a private house in Warkworth in Northumberland. Months of labour, all done with fire-welding which is not common nowadays. He is kept constantly busy with new orders, particularly for his exquisite craft pieces, his ramshorn fireplace sets and his sculptured weathervanes. Everything is made to order, and sometimes the orders are strange, like weathervanes shaped like elephants or in one case, a violin, complete with strings!

At first in the West Allen valley, Stan found a lot of people were wary of his art. Whitfield is a traditional place and some old attitudes die hard. For in the old days, the village blacksmith was often regarded with awe and suspicion, as a figure connected with magic and witchcraft, with exorcism and the occult. But as Stan explains, 'T' old smith were also a philosopher, a bit of a pivot of the community, a man o' power who coul tak' somethin' unbendable an' unbreakable, an' yet create from it – ye had tae be in awe of that.'

But in time he and his remarkable art have found acceptance in the local community. After a certain point, all the old men in the village started to come in to warm themselves by the fire of the 'sorcerer's apprentice', and 'crack on'. Stan has come to accept the Victorian values of the community too. The doffing of the cap to the Squire is more than fairly compensated by the order that comes with living in a traditional community.

TALES OF THE MOLECATCHER

Before heading south up the valley and delving into Whitfield's ancient past, pause for a while in this neck of the woods. For back up the A686 road a bit there's a place called Staward, or rather an old manor, a farm and the remains of a peel which all bear that name. These places command one of the most breathtaking views in the whole of the North Pennines, a view across the depths of Allen Gorge to Crag Head. Below this pine-clad promontory a vertical cliff plunges down, down to the river far below. In the sunshine the Allen sparkles below, a deep blue trickle in the distance beneath. But up close, it's a tumult, overhung with thick, jungly vegetation, a haunt for heron and roe deer, for fishermen and for the explorer in all of us.

Staward is a justifiably celebrated place. The fourteenth-century peel tower was once the dale's first place of protection against attacking raiders from the north, a stone watch tower against all-comers. Below its hilltop base stands another piece of designated woodland, over 1100 acres of ancient gnarled oak, overhanging a variety of plants which are, as you might expect in view of the upland location, subalpine in class. But perhaps in local terms an even greater cause for celebration is Staward's historic role as the place where Walter the Molecatcher used to go fishing as a lad!

Walter, the local storyteller, as craggy and full of character as Staward Crag itself, remembers when 'th' river jes flowed with fish, there were so minny of them'. This was before the days of nitrates and phosphates, when the waters of the Allen, like so many of our upland rivers, were not so enriched. The river was its own oxygen tank, plenty of air for fish and plants, and everything could breathe more easily. The Allen's not as bad as many, and if you can get permission, you can have Allen trout for breakfast, dinner and tea. Of course Walter and his mates had the Squire's permission to test the Staward waters, but many a hook will have been slung in this

▲ From Allen Gorge, looking towards Crag's Head

idyllic spot that the Squire and his men will never have known about.

One of Walter's stories from Staward is the one about Maddy Crow. Maddy was the youngest son of one of the tenant farmers on the Whitfield estate, one of a large family of seven, two boys and five girls. According to Walter:

'Maddy was always kept doon, y'knaa. They reckoned that he tried tae droon 'is-self in Langley Dam [between Staward and Haydon Bridge], 'n' went three times roond it, swimmin' like, but couldn't do 'is-self in. One day he went missin' 'n' was never seen or heard of for two munth. Then these keepers were gannin' across Crag Heed, 'n' they spied somethin' hangin' off this hollow tree lyin' o'er the precipice. They climbed o'er some rocks across to thon hollow tree, 'n' saw it was a man – he'd hung 'is-self. But there was nuthin' left like, only bones and claethes. The only way it could be identified was the way it was dressed, like. They knew it was

123

Maddy because he'd always used tae roll 'is stockin's up o'er 'is troosers up to below 'is knee; 'n' this was the way he was when he was found hangin' there, dead.'

Looking up at the crag, a great lonely limestone buff with a single stocky Scots pine atop and a small derelict building at the back, it is not hard to imagine a swinging skeleton, an image from wild west country. And that, to a certain extent, is how Walter and his generation view these parts of their Pennine home, a wilderness of game and open landscape, filled with beauty and tragedy in equal proportions.

Walter Rutherford was born on the farm at Old Town near the meeting of the Allens, overlooked by High Staward Peel. But a tenant farmer he was not destined to be. Tiring of the routines and subordination to 'faidder', he left home for a life on the margins, for a career of casual work outdoors and on the fringes of fell and farm. He moved with wife and young children to Allendale, to the town's first council house, a former workhouse, and took work where he could, digging graves, catching rabbits, repairing walls and digging ditches. Like many an Allendale man he also worked down the local mines until they closed for good.

After that he took to casual working in the woods until an accident paralysed his left hand. He remembers being at a loose end, then, 'ah tried tae gan'oot on th' fell, pheasant shuttin' 'n' catchin' rabbits,'n' th' odd bit of fishin' like. Ah'd nivver bit on th' dole in me life afore, and ah wasn't goin't be put on it by this hear dead hand'. So he took up molecatching, and has never looked back since. Clearly neither have the moles. Walter's kill rate is legendary. On one stint in the West Allen valley he caught 10,000 moles. It is said that when Walter walked out, the ground shook with moles searching for their emigration papers!

Seventy-five years on, Walter is still clearing the Allen valleys of moles. He uses traps placed in the runs moles make between nests and the

▲ Keeping up the mowdy tradition: Walter and his son Peter, after a morning's work

mounds of earth they leave all over the place. He has used poison, but found it didn't keep the moles down, and also harmed the other animals and birds of the fell and field. Also there was nothing left to show that he'd been successful. The tradition has always been to hang the dead moles by the nose on a fence or line above a boundary wall. 'The fairmers wid'ne believe ye if yeh didn't hang 'em up, for them tae see.' So Walter's grisly lines can still be seen up and down the dale. His trademark is long lines: once he hung up 487 moles, all caught on a single farm: 'It was riddled, you could'ne see the grass for mounds of earth.'

Like many a hunter, Walter has nothing but respect for his prey. He talks of 'Mr Mowdy' with affection, and praises him for his wiliness and his ceaseless activity: 'Yeh wid'ne need th' dole if ivveryone warked like thon fella,' he confirms. He possesses a deep understanding of the ecology of the mole. He knows the mole has his place, as a creature which helps to drain the wet fields that lie below the fell. He knows its habits and rituals too: its aggressiveness and its territoriality; its six-week gestation period; its mating and chasing rituals; its extraordinary fertility, and one piece of behaviour you will not find in the text books: the female's practice when she's suckling of feeding her young off a larder of live worms she keeps trapped near her nest.

Walter needs no book of moles; he is the book. The mole is a creature of the margins, a denizen of the outlying fields which border the wet, marshy fell and moorland tracts of the country's uplands. He breeds well in pasturelands where the plough is never seen, where sheep and cattle have grazed and where nitrate fertilisers have not yet torn the heart out of the soil or driven off his livelihood – the common worm. Walter too is a creature of the margins, someone who has lived his life out on the felltops and the outbyefields, keeping down the moles and rebuilding tumbled stone walls; pursuing an ancient occupation which has itself become marginalised as farming has changed from a craft to a semi-industrial occupation dominated by machines and chemicals.

If you are lucky you will catch sight of Walter, out in the early morning fields of the lower East and West Allen valleys, alone with the larks and the curlews, 'settin' to' with his traps and walls. With his old deerstalker hat and his dark brown clothes he blends totally with his surroundings, with the grey brown moor, green fields and mottled stone walls. Hunched over his moletraps with his hat pointing down he looks, at a casual glance, not unlike Mr Mole.

One story he tells concerns a gift given to a local gamekeeper on the occasion of his retirement by the other men of the fell. The gift was a rocking chair, ''n' he only lived for a munth after it'. So as Walter tells, 'When th' nex' old 'un retired, a couple o' years later, one o' th' keepers, Heslop, had th' idea tae buy him a coffin! "But why th' hell should yae buy a man a coffin?" said another of the keepers. So Heslop turned roond 'n' says, "Well, yeh bought th' last yin a rocking chair 'n' he only sat on it once, so why not buy this yin a coffin – at least it'd be some use to him!"

'Y'see,' explains Walter, 'once you've finished with th' keepin' or once yeh retire up here, on this here fell, yer dead.'

The moral is clear. For hardened outdoor hillmen like Walter, the wild open fell and the outbyefields circumscribe their lives, giving them a definition, a purpose and a role lost to the rest of us, a communion with the wilderness. Their Pennine environment provides them with a majestic, all-powerful scenario within which men like himself, and like the wild animals they live with, act out lives and deaths as rich and as dramatic as the fell itself. Born with the fell to their backs, it's in their blood; once they come off the fell, their blood quickly runs cold.

GHOSTS OF THE WEST ALLEN

The magnificent Whitfield Hall was built in 1785 on the site of an older building, Whitfield Tower, one of a number of fortified buildings which could be found throughout the landscape of Northumbria since Norman times. Before then the place belonged to the Saxon Earls of Northumbria. After the Norman conquest, the tower and the lands around passed into the hands of the Scottish royal family. Indeed, one of the beneficiaries, the Countess Eada, was mother to two great Scots kings, Malcolm, and William the Lion. The remains of Eada Hall, possibly the ancient seat of the manor, can still be seen on the approach road to Old Town, birthplace of our friend Walter.

You can make out the foundations, now covered with grass and thistles, for the ground is too stony and hummocky to plough. The land is drained by the aptly named Kingswood Burn, and John Rutherford, the present farmer and now owner of the land, tells an interesting tale of how Mary, Queen of Scots is said to have sought refuge at Eada Hall in her attempt to evade the executioner's axe.

Long before Mary and the Scots line of kings came to a tragic end the estate passed out of the hands of royalty into the arms of the Church, to

▲ Whitfield Hall

the canons of Hexham in the twelfth century. Then, when the monasteries were dissolved by good King Henry in his pique against the Pope, the estate was bought up by its tenants, the Whitfields. Thereafter, it was sold to the Ords around the 1770s. A Newcastle family, they built the hall and renovated the estate completely, putting the land to rights for the first time in centuries. The estate has remained in the Ord line, to the present day owned and run by the Blackett-Ords in the manner to which the first Ords had become accustomed.

The Whitfield estate runs to some 20,000 acres and they are well run as you can see in the orderly fencing, the tended plantations, the healthy farms, the mannered estate gardens and the air of Old England in aspic which dominates the place. The Hall and its environs were described by the Northumberland historian Mackenzie, in 1825, in idyllic terms: 'The high bold rocks before the east front, the thick hanging woods, and the luxuriant plantations, form a fine contrast with the neatness of the lawn and the pleasure grounds. It is altogether a lovely spot, and appears like the Garden of Eden in the midst of a wilderness.' In view of the tragic ending of the Scots royal line, and the fate which befell a Blackett-Ord relative, another Eden, the famous Anthony, Prime Minister of England during the Suez crisis, Mackenzie's turn of phrase is an ironic one!

It is even more ironic when you uncover some of the more sombre details of the lower West Allen valley's more local history. For the estate has an unusually high legacy of suicides, high because its small population of tenant farmers and estate workers has never reached more than 200 at any time over the last sixty years. Yet within that period there have been at least twenty known tragedies. It's a circumstance not commonly advertised (who would wish it such?), but in the words of one local resident, who has now left the place: 'If you want to know what the area's really famous for – it's suicides.'

Older locals remember well the names of the unfortunates and their manner of death, but the dates and the events leading up to each death have blurred with the passing of seasons. One of the earliest is recalled by a local farmer from outside the estate. He remembers his grandfather telling about 'being foreman of the jury at a nearby farm . . . a man committed suicide there. He was in his twenties, and he was found hanging from a tree in a wood, and they held the inquest in the barn, 'n' the jury had to view the body . . . up in the loft, in the granary. Yes, they'd just left it there. It was a crime then and they weren't supposed to be buried in consecrated ground. Well I think the rectors that wus here, they just waived that rule – they were just buried.'

Another story concerns an entire family from another outlying farm: 'The mother committed suicide, she poured paraffin over herself and put a match to herself . . . there wus two of the family buried the same day through the flu, this bad flu around 1919; and there wus one o' the sons attended the funeral . . . and he, when he went back to work, he was found in the reservoir drowned. Me father was at that funeral. He said that when they wanted to carry the coffins down the stairs, they couldn't get them because they'd taken them up with their lids off . . . at the finish they had tae slide them owt the window on a ladder. When they put on the lid . . . it makes them go that much wider on each side . . . and they couldn't get them owt the doors. They had to go and get the joiner to take the windows owt, 'n' they were late, an hour late . . . terrible.'

The gravestone of this unfortunate family can still be seen in the old churchyard at Whitfield. And unfortunately they are not alone . . . and neither will you be – if the stories are to be believed about ghosts being sighted in the area of the graveyard.

The earliest tragedies have become absorbed within the local mythology of the place. There is a story told by a farmworker about a tree in his neighbour's garden where a woman killed herself: 'Thon tree, they reckon, there's red apples on one side and green on the other . . . why there was a family and they were all a bit touched y'knaa, and I don't know how she did it, but they reckoned that she banged her head against the tree and all the blood ran down, and that's why them apples are all red on thon side.' The pattern of the past is even reflected in the massive broadleaved trees which drape the roadside of Whitfield. There's a local saying, 'When the leaves are falling, the suicides start; when the leaves are falling, as they turn red and brown.' As the year turns, so do local lives.

Suicide has always been a part of rural life everywhere, an untimely falling of leaves to be sure, but a part of the great seasonal cycle of life and death that is a part of every country-dweller's daily round. Country villages have always been intense places, where gossip and feuding rule the roost, and where a bit of in-breeding is part of the package. Those people in Whitfield who are aware of the suicides see them as natural to a small place.

Whitfield, the place, almost certainly plays its part in this eerie puzzle. The village, with its hanging woods, its cross-marked bridge, its deep pools and high crags, silently and without fuss absorbs its timely dead. No local has ever tried to count the tragedies and the matter is not dwelt on. But they are a part of the place, as much a part as the wild fell, the woods and the rough waters. One old story tells of how the body of a local man who had drowned himself well upstream of the estate perimeter was discovered only when it had come eventually to rest by Bearsbridge . . . in the very heart of the old Whitfield estate.

A WOLF IN ARCADIA

Observant map readers will notice the appearance of the word 'wolf' in the place names of the Allen valleys, in Wolfcleugh Common and Wolfhills and Wolf Cleugh Farm. There's a reason for this, and a good story too, a story which somehow blends in well with the Whitfield saga – you can just imagine the howls of a lone wolf in the graveyards of a winter's night where the ghosts walk and sorrows hang in the silent air like willows over the moonlit waters of the West Allen river. And it's a tale which fits in well with the ancient history of the wild, wild fell, but we're not dealing here with an ancient natural past, it's a story of not so long ago . . .

One wild dark night in the winter of 1904 a strange apparition was observed on the fellside between the Allen passes. A huge grey wolf could be clearly seen stalking the hills for unwary prey. The local man who'd seen it rushed to tell his fellows in the village, but was met with incredulity: his vision consigned to the realms of a whisky-sodden haze, or 'too lang spent oot on th' fell'. But in the days following, his sighting was backed up by a large number of reports of sheep-worrying.

At first these were thought to have been the responsibility of a dog, but then when all the local dogs had been shut in, the people began to think otherwise. The worryings turned to killings, not just of a few sheep, but of many, with the carcasses just left lying about. These became a temptation to local dogs. After tasting the blood of the dead sheep, even faithful sheepdogs turned to worrying, and the numbers escalated. There was an evil abroad within the canine community and something had to be done – but what? And the wolf was still only a rumour, based upon the flimsiest of evidence, and one sole witness.

Then a Captain Bain of Shotley Bridge in the nearby Derwent village let it be known that he had recently purchased a wolf cub from a zoological garden, but it had escaped, and was at liberty on the fell. He put a price on its head of £5, for the capture of his cub, dead or alive. Up and down the shires of Hexham, Allendale, Cumberland and Westmorland rusting guns were hauled from cupboards and from out under bedsteads in preparation for the hunt of the century, the hunt for the now notorious Allendale Wolf.

The wolf's activities led to the wildest stories, of ghost wolves and wolf packs, of werewolves and hauntings, of eerie howling in the night and fantastic tracks in the snow. While out on the cold bleak fell a solitary half-starved animal roamed in blind obedience to deeper, ancient instincts, the hunters gathered in their scores, planning their routes and oiling their weapons. Fortunately few ever got the chance to use their weapons, as according to one old dialect storyteller of the area, ''Twes lucky sum on 'm didn't hetta fire 'm 'cose they wad mebbies hev deeun mair dammish ti' thirsels than ti' the wolf.'

The rag-bag of hunters and adventurers that crawled out of the woodwork included an old game hunter who showed everyone a picture of himself with a dead tiger that he'd shot from the back of an elephant out in India. The Haydon Hunt even had a go, but the hounds were either too terrified to trail a wolf or were naturally inclined to stick to more familiar paths. According to Old Joe, the storyteller, 'The hunds nivver fa'n'd ony cents 'cep o' foxes.' The farmers of both dales organised great gun parties and they roamed the fells in search of the wolf. But without avail, and without even another sighting. Meanwhile the sheep losses continued unabated, the carcasses (thirty-five at one point) mounting up. Shepherds watched, ever more anxiously; there's been nothing like it since the last snows melted on the hilltops at the end of the great Ice Age.

But the end of the Allendale Wolf was sudden, and ignominious to the great white wolf hunters. After a very bad night of sheep-worrying near Alston, news came in that a large grey wolf had been killed by a train at Cumhinton near Carlisle. The body of the dead animal had been put together by the railway workers and photographed and measured. It turned out to be over 5 feet in length and 5 stone in weight – a monster, and a match for any dalesman or dog. The poor creature was eventually stuffed and taken to the headquarters at Derby, where it was displayed in splendour until a flood destroyed it just before the Second World War. A celebrity for years, it even inspired a song of which the ending still exists: 'If thoo dissent beleev mi, or think Ah's tellin' a lee; just ax for the wolf at Derby – it's theer for o' ti see.'

At one time of course, the Pennines would have been home to thousands of wolves, for the grey or timber wolf had the elevated position of being top of the food chain for thousands of years before man muddied the scene. Around 5000 BC its numbers must have peaked. The ice had all melted away and a forest of hazel and birch would have covered the upper fells, while the passes below were dominated by a thick cover of oak and elm. These were ideal conditions for game and for cover, and troops of wolves lived well on a diet of wild pig, deer, small mammals and birds.

The wolves moved easily across the wetter patches which opened up the forest cover, and hunting in troops, were able to bring down large and swiftly moving prey with ease. A lone wolf is capable of bringing down a full-grown deer, and when hunting as a pack there is nothing too large for them to tackle. So in those days even large mammals like wisent, bison and auroch would have been fair game. The wolf does not out-run his prey, rather he runs it out. Moving in bursts as part of a carefully laid-out pack strategy, with wolf after wolf coming in from the side to wear the prey down, the prey eventually tires and the wolf moves in for the kill. No wonder these animals put the fear of God in the animals of hill and forest, and ultimately in man himself.

The wolf in England, though hunted down in the end, was a victim less of the hunt than of the undermining of the afforested environment to which he was suited. He was a victim of deforestation, of the coming of agriculture and the opening up of the area for commerce and mining. As with so many wilderness species and wilderness areas, it is the knock-on effect of the presence of people, rather than our direct activities that have sounded the death knell of change and even extinction.

FROM NINEBANKS TO
THE CRAGS OF CARR

The upper West Allen valley is more familiar outbye Pennine terrain as the arcadian slopes of Whitfield give way to open fell, gutted by deep burns. These watercourses, locally known as sikes, tear down the hillside giving cover for alder, oak, birch and willow, and in the spring, banks of bluebells and golden primroses. The waters of the West Allen form out of a group of three main tributaries which meet at Black Bridge below Conyhill. But the main road up the valley divides before this, and you have a choice between travelling up the west side towards Alston on the A686 or right up to the valley head on the minor road to Carr Shield and the wilderness beyond.

For the moment we'll take the Carr Shield road, turning off at the Trap Gate and crossing the Allen at Blackett Bridge to the pretty hamlet of Ninebanks, named it is thought, from the lie of the land around it. This is the heart of the old

▲ Ninebanks village

parish of Ninebanks, and the site of a church built in 1764, with the gravestones around supplying the names of the local families who have lived and worked here generation after generation – the Martins, Reeds, Lees, Keenleysides and Taylors. The church is well kept and well attended, particularly at harvest time, when the gifts from the land are placed in a glorious display around the altar.

In earlier harvest times the last sheaf of corn to be cut from the fields in the river bottom was safely stored with an apple in it until Christmas morning. Then the apple was given to the youngest daughter of the household and the sheaf to the best dairy cow, to procure good luck and magically transfer the benefits of fertility from a successful harvest of the past to the harvests of future years. After the harvest thanksgiving in the church, there would be a 'kern' ('harvest' or 'corn') supper in the household at the end of the day, with drinking and dancing through the night.

the back of the farmsteads. During the height of winter their seals are broken and the preserved sweet hay, high in mineral traces and nutrient content, is fed to the sheep and cattle until spring returns with a promise of fresh pasture on the ground.

You can get a feeling of what village life was like in this country corner from the writings of the Reverend Joseph Ritson whose *Reminiscences of Allendale* was published in 1930. Ritson was born in Ninebanks, and it is to his childhood there that he traces his inclination for the religious life, inspired like many before him to emulate God's great pattern on earth through a churchly vocation. But as a child he wasn't beyond the odd bit of 'help-herself', like 'surreptitious raids on the bowls of cream in the dairy'. In this passage he records a far more serious form of 'devilry', the beginnings of that historic change in the English countryside, when human labour began to give way to the machine:

The hay harvest had special charms. I remember seeing the mowers bending their backs to the scythe, making the long swathes. The disastrous exposure of the field-mice had special and peculiar interest for me and I made various fruitless attempts to rear their blind and hairless families. Then there was the 'leading day' when the pikes were made into a great stack, a day of unwonted stir and activity. A little later the advent of 'the devil' in the form of a hayrake, startled the village; and later still came the mowing machine which ended the activities of the mowers and their scythes, so that the musical sound of the scythe sharpening was heard no more.

The parish of Ninebanks and Carr Shield was originally an established Saxon property. It was part of the dowry of Ethelreda, wife of Egfrith, King of Northumbria. Ethelreda, like the Reverend Ritson and the Throstle Hole Buddhists who followed, was a religious soul and perhaps inspired by the spiritual tranquillity of the place, she gave it up to the Church. The recipients, in

▲ Harvest festival in Ninebanks church

The late summer and early autumn is the time to see Ninebanks in its glory. The fields are brown and yellow where the crops have been culled, and there is a rich smell in the air of newly mown grass from where the late season hay crop has been taken up for silage. If you are lucky you will see the men out with their haymakers and their silage balers, a piece of new technology which has found a warm welcome in these parts. Great rolls of compressed hay are packed into black bags which are laid in piles at the year 674 AD, under some complicated medi-aeval transaction, were the Bishops of York, Hexham and Lindisfarne. But just over a couple of centuries later these bishoprics were dissolved, not by any order of Rome, but by the axes of the invading Vikings. By 881 AD, the warriors of Thor and Balder, without setting foot in the upper West Allen valley, had changed its destiny for ever.

Thereafter, the parish changed hands between the Bishop of Durham, William the Conqueror and, with his blessing, a long list of archbishops from York. When Henry VIII dissolved the monasteries, he took direct control over this part of the world, taking revenues out of the hands of the Church, and giving them control only over matters spiritual. The Church, for the people of West Allendale in those times, was no longer the landlord, but an affair of the spirit only.

The lie of the land in the upper dale has changed a lot since those early days. Much of the mediaeval tree cover of oak, elm and ash has gone from the valley floor, but alder, willow, pine and sycamore still grace the river banks and the banks of the deep burn valleys which eat into the side of the fell. But if you take the road beyond Ninebanks village, through Carr Shield and up towards the former settlement of Coalcleugh, the country opens right out. You enter a kind of no-man's-land, where the land is neither fell nor dale but something inbetween. It is empty here – only the odd car, a couple of farms and the flight of the curlew. As you climb up towards the pass which takes you over the top and into the Nent valley, you will notice all around you signs of abandonment, of a once busy landscape and inhabited houses where there is now no longer life.

Indeed, life at this height must always have been difficult. It is marked in indelible ink, even on the 2½ inch map, in place names like Hardstruggle, Shivery Hill and Scum Hill, Sting End, Old Shafts and Black Hill. By the riverside you can even see the remains of old mine workings, old miners' sheds, iron trucks and rails and even mine openings carved into the bankside and surmounted by wooden posts. Some of them were re-opened in recent years, for the extraction of minerals like zinc and barytes. Now and again, men come back to look for traces of the old metals.

In the heyday of lead mining the big mine in these parts was Coalcleugh. There is nothing there now but a scattering of old spoil heaps on

▲ Coalcleugh, the village at the end of the world

Peat bog above Coalcleugh ▶

which plants still refuse to grow, some broken dykes and a couple of houses. For some time one of these houses was occupied in the 1960s by one of northern England's leading poets. And despite the desolation, it's not hard to see many sources for poetic inspiration within the landscape around. On the fell above Carr Shield there lies a great wallscape of crags, Whitleyshield Carrs, home only for swooping birds of prey and the odd sheep requiring shelter, but a marvellous viewpoint – a harsh and haunting place.

On the road above Coalcleugh, which takes you back under Killhope Law, over to Allenheads in the East Allen valley, there is another inspiring spot, a sudden bend in the road at a place known as Whetstonemea Burn. If you stop here and look north down Carrshield Moor to Blackway Head there is a long line of abandoned smallholdings which dips down into the valley. This is a Pennine view which is both uniquely Pennine and different from any other upland view in the country: a wonderful mixture of desolation and tranquillity, for the line of house ruins takes your eye right across the top of the Allen valleys to Hadrian's Wall and the Cheviots beyond. The brown and grey of the moortop merges in the distance with the green estates of Northumbria and only Scotland and the sky lie beyond.

The village of Carr Shield contains a field centre for adventurous school parties, in what was originally the village school. On the side of the building you can still see the stone signs which marked the different entrances, one for the boys and one for the girls. Sadly, there are very few local children left in Carr Shield now. And the post office, like the school, has gone the way of all flesh . . . or should that be stone. When Katie Forster, the postmistress, retired after forty years' service to the local communication industry in 1978, the post office was retired too. The sign remains though.

People still live in Carr Shield; there is even a village computer operator and an active parish council, and where the sign invites you to buy fresh milk there's a farm selling the real thing. It is unpasteurised, thick creamy stuff, just like it used to be in the old days, and it pours down the throat like velvet.

Coalcleugh is no longer even a village and there is no longer any coal to be found, just some houses and a large 'cleugh' (gully). When the mining industry collapsed, Coalcleugh became hoary and ghost-haunted. In its heyday this was the highest village in England, at 1760 feet above sea level, higher even than Tomintoul, which claims to be the highest village in Scotland. Coalcleugh has been a long time in going downhill. There's a wonderful description of it in the *Allendale Christmas Annual* printed in 1871. This is part of a tale told by Old Feg the Storyteller, alive at that time. According to him:

There are no young plantations there, nor nice hall, and one half of the houses are empty and tumbling down, and the other half looks as if there were no girls in them who cared much for scrubbing. The reason for this is that the mines, which used to be so prosperous here, are now very poor, so that many miners have had to remove with their families, and others go and work all the week in other mines, and only come home from Saturday till Monday. It is no wonder the girls will not scrub and keep smart houses when all the young men are away.

And Feg adds:

People say funny things about Coal Cleugh. They say that the folk who live there burn cats for fuel; but then the cats are only balls made of clay and powdered coal, so that there is nothing so wonderful in it after all. People also say that Coal Cleugh is the end of the world! Just as if the world has an end like a cow's tail! The world, you know is round, like an orange, and so has not got an end; besides when you go up the road above Coal Cleugh, you see Nenthead on the other side of the hills, so that this story of Coal Cleugh being the end of the world is nonsense.

Feg's story takes us out of the Allen valleys and

into Nentdale, the beginning of our next journey, down into the valley of the South Tyne. But before we leave the West Allen valley it is worth pausing for reflection, not just on the dramatic, desolate views with which we leave the place, but on the words of 'Vagabond', the pseudonymous author of one of the original guide books to the area. For this part of the world, these two Allen valleys, contain places where there is mystery which 'is as eternal as the stars, and it is that which fascinates, holds, refreshes the soul and mind and gives to you and I, the sources of meditation. As there is that valuable social contact with the countryside folk, so are there comparisons to make between their lives and ours: we enjoy it more, perhaps, and while revelling in the novelty, subconsciously absorb the spiritual.'

And it is not often you can say to anyone you've been to the end of the world – and back.

A RAVINE AND RIVER WALK
THE ALLEN AT PLANKEY MILL

One of the most favoured walks for people living in the north of England, this is a busier route than any of the others we've suggested, but it is relatively short, about 3–4 miles in length and very beautiful – ideal for a family with small children. You will want to take your time on this pleasant effortless stroll along wooded riverbanks and rocky gorge, so allow 2–3 hours.

From the A69 Hexham–Carlisle road take the A686 Hexham–Alston road south-west past Langley Castle, Langley Dam complete with anglers and romantic boatshed, and Langley itself, with its woodyard and derelict lead smelting mill. Watch out for a turning north at Carts Bog where there's an inn, Carts Bog Inn, and a campsite. Take a sharp turn opposite the inn to the north-west following the sign for Plankey Mill. Turn left at the first T-junction and keep following the Plankey Mill sign. After another mile or so, the road goes down a steep hill into the Allen Gorge, with spectacular views looking down on the tree-hung Briarwood Bank on the far side.

There is a car park at the bottom of the hill, and awaiting your arrival is the farmer from Plankey who will tell you all about the walk and relieve you of a very small amount of change from your pocket for the privilege of messing up his grassy sward with your car.

The walk begins by crossing the first of two suspension bridges over the river. It is made from cable and planks, and while not as hair-raising as a rope suspension bridge across the Kosi river in the high Himalayas, it can be fairly shaky – particularly if there are children on it making it sway from side to side. So hold on! Over the bridge turn right, facing due north.

The riverside here is very rocky and cuts deep into the bank on the side of the car park, showing clearly different layers in the rock. The river at this point is a powerful force, its currents driven by the waters of both the West and East Allen rivers. They have already met below Staward further up the river and in joyous unison are pummelling their way towards the Tyne, meeting that great river at Morralee.

The path takes you at first deep inside a dense woodland of hazel, alder and sycamore, with here and there the first of many encounters with some mature beeches. These, together with some great Scots pines and Douglas firs, grace a great clearing where the National Trust has kindly provided some seating, which is well used by children and more elderly Plankey enthusiasts. The path divides here. The upper one goes towards Briarwood to a place

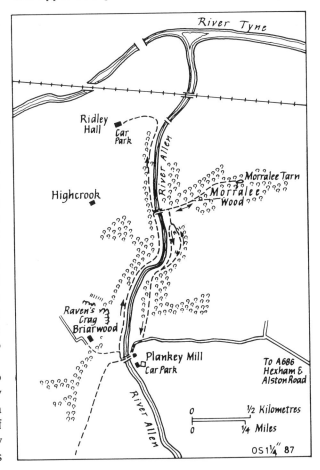

where the floor of the path is made from sheep bones, an uncanny sight on the forest floor. Returning to the lower one you are a short way from the side of the river, with ramsons and crossworts strewing the distance between path and water.

The lower path then begins an ascent past some large horse chestnuts until it reaches a great crevasse on the left, Raven's Crag. Here there are signs warning you to beware of falling rock. And if you look up you can see why – a tangle of stones and twisted tree roots on the top of an exposed rock face seem to wait for an unwary passer-by.

Past Raven's Crag the rock face slopes away from the river. There is a small cave at the base and a series of stone steps which do not appear to go anywhere. Below this the land flattens out in a great open sweep, a level, which goes right down to the river. Here there are good river views and a shingle bed, where you can swim on a warm day.

The path goes up again towards Highcrook and the grounds of Ridley College which was once a castle and now known also as Ridley Hall. But before going too far watch out for a diversion down towards the river which leads on to the second of the suspension bridges. This hangs and shakes over the water and leads you into Morralee Wood, where there are some more seats and an interpretation board erected by the National Trust who own 193½ acres of this lovely mature riverside woodland – all except that strategically placed little earner, Plankey Mill car park. And this is your objective, for once on the other side you're on the home stretch.

For the more adventurous there's a second and even third walk that can be attempted from the second suspension bridge. One walk before you cross the bridge will take you down the Allen to picnic grounds in National Trust territory beside Ridley College. The other, on the far side of the bridge, will take you deep into the woods to a hidden surprise: Morralee Tarn, a wonderful stretch of woodland water where in summer white water lilies bloom.

On the return path to Plankey, the river can be clearly seen from above, pouring its silver coils deeper and deeper into the gorge which guides it eventually towards the Tyne. The views here are second to none, and you can get an even better perspective by going up the stone steps provided at intervals to take you higher and higher into the woods to give you more and more spectacular views. There are a number of these steep little 'nowhere' paths'. On some, logs overhang and fences drape. Sheer rock faces filled with little caves, fox holes and the odd hole in the ground abound, giving plenty of room for mystery and imagination.

After a while the path runs between a herb-rich haymeadow and the riverside. The fields here look like good arable land, but perhaps because the farmer spends his time overseeing the cars of the visitors to Plankey Mill he has not got the time or the inclination to plough this waterside field. The result is a joy to the eye, a field on the river bend high with flowers and grasses from spring into summer, and decked with wonderful smoke-coloured hay pikes in the autumn between all the rusted beeches.

Watch out for nesting kestrels in the trees above the haymeadow and barn owls in the evening. Where the ground flora is rich and natural, there will be insects and small animal life for these birds to feed on. And there are the remains of the original Plankey Mill on the river bend to provide a bit of extra cover for the owls. Beyond this, you are soon on the side which took you into Plankey Mill originally and you are on a tarmacadam descent down to the newer Plankey Mill farmbuildings. Here there are refreshments and a pretty garden where you can reflect upon the beauty and tranquillity of a stroll by the silver River Allen.

6
THE OLD STONE DALE
VALLEY OF THE SOUTH TYNE

South Tynedale, lying between the fells of the West Allen and the Vale of Eden, is the centrepoint of the North Pennines, with Alston as its capital. But it is one of two Tyne dales – its sister valley, the North Tyne, lies far to the north, from where the River North Tyne rises at a place called Deadwater on the Scottish border, to meander through the Cheviots and the great dark green coniferous forests of Kielder and Wark. Fortunately, there are few acid forests draping the banks of the South Tyne. The valley consists of heather-topped open fell, populated by sheep and wild birds, worked by shepherds and gamekeepers, and graced by a series of pretty hamlets and its very own fairy castle.

The little town of Alston, formerly 'Auld Stane', lying at the head of the valley, over 1000 feet above sea level, is the highest market town in England. With its cobbled main road and Dickensian back streets set on a hill overlooking the early meanderings of that great northern river, the Tyne, it is also one of the finest of market towns. And the rest of the valley, from little Garrigill lost in the downdraft at the back of Cross Fell near the head of the Tyne, right down to Coanwood where the land levels out, features some of the very best of Pennine scenery.

The dale itself is narrow, with river, two roads, farm fields and even fell appearing to compete for a little bit of level space. There was once a major train link too. It's a wonder there was room for it at all. There are few detours though, on the main road up the dale, so we'll keep close to the riverside and, with a picnic hamper filled up at Alston's excellent shops, hope that you do too.

Our approach from West Allendale brings us from Coalcleugh on to the A689 and down a steep gradient from Killhope Law's tumbling back. Looking south-west there are some wonderful views of the back of Cross Fell and Great Dun Fell before they make their mighty swoop into the Eden below. If it's winter or spring they will be snow-covered. If it's late spring, summer or autumn the land that lies around, a mixture of moorland swamp, cotton grass and heather moor, will roll green, brown or purple before you. Curlew and snipe rise in the crisp fell air, and the ground moves with grouse, feeding, chattering, breaking cover or warning you away: 'Go-Bak, Go-Bak'. They're busy talking aversion

Tynedale from Hartside Cottage ▶

tactics, making plans against the annual August offensive, and do not respond too well to being disturbed.

THE ROAD TO NENTHEAD

In the middle distance you will see a lone chimney, a solitary reminder that you are still in the country of the lead men. On closer examination you will see its pronounced lean, and at its base the remains of a tunnel, the flue which connects it to the lower fell. 'Lean' is, in fact, a piece of descriptive kindness. Pisa has nothing on this one. It does not lean, it *bends*, to the point where you wonder how it stays up at all. It is an old smelt mill chimney, a flue for the heavy metal toxics and gases which lead burning created. The idea was to draw the fire, and the residues, away from the smelter. The fell got them instead. You can see the effects upon the vegetation behind the chimney: after a century of no smoke there's still no sign of recovery. Of grass, heather, sphagnum moss or rush there is no trace, just bare grey-tinged peat. Suction will have drawn this detritus up the chimney, but its own weight will have brought it quickly down.

The underground flue which runs down the fell beneath this leaden smokestack goes past a reservoir from the lead days and a complex of abandoned mine buildings. This is Shaw Side. But Shaw and all the other gold diggers are long gone. Instead you might see on the waters of the reservoir the luminous red and day-glo yellow anoraks and lifejackets of the kayak brigade, practising their turns, twists and ice-water spills in this remote but beautiful location. Even at the height of midwinter, if the waters are ice-free, they are there, hardier than the grouse themselves.

On your way round the bend of the road to Nenthead and on the right-hand side you can clearly see a most unusual looking cluster of trees, a small forest of dwarf Scots pines – unusual · because there's no such thing as a

▲ Victims of lead: dead, dying and dwarfed Scots pines above Nenthead

dwarf Scots pine. For these are amongst our tallest pines, the stately stalwarts of our ancient Caledonian indigenous woodland. So what is the explanation? The answer lies in the soil beneath the trees. It is not what it appears. It is not really soil but spoil; spoil from the lead and fluorspar mines, piled in heaps on the hillside.

The trees were planted in the 1950s to stabilise the heaps, to give them some cover and colour, and no doubt to create a commercial forest crop. There is not much chance of that. These trees were doomed to a short life before they even had a chance to set root. The lead in the spoil has poisoned them from the bottom up, stunting the growth of some, but having a delayed effect on others, allowing them to grow to a reasonable height, and then killing them suddenly from below – a truly leaden punch. The result is partly an eye-catching landscape curiosity, a piece of Pennine wonder, and partly an eye-sore, like a Scandinavian advert against acid rain, with tree tops dead and withered, broken branches.

The River Nent, a tributary of the South Tyne, rises in the fells behind Killhope and Knoutberry Hill, and tears down the valley of the Nent through more old lead mining country, sloping woodlands and valley sides and into Alston. Here's how Nentdale is described in Hodgson's *History of Northumberland* (first published in 1840):

The little valley of the Nent was once a fairy land, and had its flowery meadows, and wild shaws, and bosky breays, and Nentsbury for its capital, till the wealth of mining speculations began to improve and enlarge the narrow stripe of enclosed land that fringed the margins of its chrystal stream; and blotch its gemmed and emerald fields with the rubbish of its mines and levels, and gutter its head and sides, and poison its sweet waters.

▼ Nenthead: a model village cast in lead-soldier days

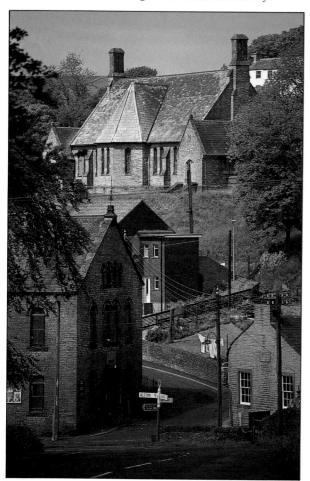

That's quite an introduction to the sweet and sour landscape of this area. But the area still has a ring of the fairy tale about it, as we shall see.

The village of Nenthead at the valley head was at one time the very centre of the lead mining industry, with most of the mine leases under the control of the London Lead Company, a firm of Quakers. It may not look quite that way now, but Nenthead was designed and built by the Quakers as a model village. The smelt mine and buildings were first erected in 1750, and later extended with a 'mine shop' to house the miners working away from home. They lived where they could, in great poverty, in old farmhouses and outhouses on the Alston Moor, so the mine shops with their comforts compensated for the hard life down the lead mines.

By 1820, the company realised that it had to make more permanent arrangements. So it called in the architects and builders and a new village was planned with thirty-five cottages, a clock tower, market hall, school and chapel. Later a post office was added, a public water supply was fitted in 1850, and baths and a public house were provided. They say that cleanliness is next to godliness. Well, the lead miners of Nenthead were certainly amongst the cleanest of their time, and according to one report the godliest too. As the new village developed, trade in the established pub fell off, the people, it was said, preferring 'books to drink'.

There is one feature of the industrial development of Nenthead which must be mentioned, the Nent Force Level. This was a mine drainage channel nearly 5 miles long which was driven into the ground between Alston and Nenthead. It was a remarkable feat of engineering for its time. It had many purposes: to drain the water from the fell and make mining operations safer, to expose new, predicted mineral veins, and to transport waste products down the valley. It was the last of these functions that was the most interesting, for this made the level in effect an underground canal. It took sixty-six years to complete from its starting date of 1776, and when it was finished it ended up being put to an unlikely extra use – as a tourist attraction.

This is how one section of the force was described by Sopwith, the mining engineer based at Allenheads in the next valley:

It is navigated in boats 30 ft in length, which are propelled in four feet water by means of sticks . . . and thus may be enjoyed the singular novelty of sailing a few miles underground . . . The hanging rocks suspended over the entrance with the romantic scenery adjoining, and the neighbouring waterfall, render a visit, even to the exterior, highly interesting; but this is much increased by a subterranean excursion, which is frequently undertaken by strangers, and not unfrequently by parties of young persons resident in the neighbourhood. The old and often grotesque dresses worn on such occasions add to the mirth and cheerfulness which prevail – while the fine effect of vocal and instrument music, and the exercise of propelling the boat, add to the singular feeling which is excited by the idea of so bold an adventure.

The irony of the enterprise is remarkable: sailing underground at 1500 feet above sea level, under one of the highest inhabited places in England. But the visitors to the Nent Force Level did not just stop at sailing. On one section of the canal there was a dancefloor too, known as Jennie's Dancing Loft! Sadly the dance is over and the sailboats gone. The portal of the level is now gone, and the buildings which served it have also gone. But it is said that noise and laughter from those gay days can still be heard coming from the ground below, from the ghosts of the Nent Force Level.

Nenthead village itself prospered and grew under the London Lead Company. Its population reached its peak of 2039 in 1861, greater than that of Alston. As the lead industry collapsed Nenthead did not go so quickly into decline as Allenheads and the other lead villages. For in 1896, a Belgian company, Vielle Montagne, took over the lead leases and started to increase the extraction of ore for its zinc content, before pulling out in the 1920s.

The shape of the countryside in and around Nenthead was largely determined by the actions of the London Lead Company. For the Quaker firm's improvement policy extended beyond the village to the fell itself. They limed and drained the higher pastures so that the miners could work them as smallholdings. They supported horticultural activities and planted Scots pines on the knolls of land around the village. Some of these evergreen landforms are still visible today, a rich contrast to the brown moors and the pale stone of the dykes and farm buildings which line and dot the area.

Now, over a hundred years after the demise of the lead mines, much of the improved pasture has been reclaimed by the fell, 'improved' in true wilderness fashion with an invasion of rushes and mosses. Drainage is again unrestrained, and the River Nent fills once more with minerals and organisms from the fellside rather than from pastureland. The result is good for the wildlife, but a poor prospect for the people. So too, many of the fellside smallholdings, and even the houses within the village, lie forlorn and abandoned. Today Nenthead shows little sign of its former bustle.

If you chance to walk through the village today, and take the public footpath up to the church for the excellent views over the valley, you will find your path takes you through some of the gardens of the old mining cottages. If you are in luck you may even strike up a conversation with Nenthead's last Quaker, a humble man who will tell you about the hardships and the glories of the past, the pride and hospitality of the local people, and Nenthead's great tradition of producing scholars and scientists who, from humble beginnings, have had important roles in the great world beyond the Nent.

And if you are not in too much of a hurry, he will tell you of the changes that have come to Nenthead, the closure of the school and the decline in the population, and the changing attitudes too, the loss of intimacy among local folks and the coming of the 'hippie types' to the village. They arrived with the 'back to nature' movement in the late 1960s, and taking advantage of the low property prices in the area, the availability of attractive farm buildings and the tranquillity of the countryside, have stayed. In fact they have now been there so long that they're almost as institutionalised as the grouse on the local moor. Coloured caravans and buses, anti-nuclear stickers and the signs of the zodiac inlaid on house and car windows tell of a gypsy mentality which has blown into Nenthead with the wind.

FROM THE HEAD OF THE TYNE TO ALSTON

From Nenthead there is a choice of routes, one down through the Nent valley, stopping off for refreshments at either of two first-class establish-ments: Nenthall with its swimming pool and (brrr) outdoor jacuzzi, or the enticingly named Lovelady Shield. Or alternatively you can come with us on a small trip back to the very beginning of Pennine time and place, to the source of the Tyne itself.

Take a left turn at Nenthead along the route of the Dowgang Hush, where the lead miners exposed the silver, lead and iron ores that lay like hidden treasure beneath the surface of the fell, until you reach the little village of Garrigill. From here there is a road up to West Ashgill which goes past the great Ashgill Waterfall and eventually peters out into a private road and then a fell track. This is definitely a boot job, though if you ask the farmer's permission he may allow you to cheat and drive up the track. The track is, in fact, a road maintained for many years by the Nature Conservancy Council to provide access to Moor House at the back of Knock Fell.

Moor House was used for some time as a

▼ Garrigill: the finest air around

research station by the NCC, Durham University and other research institutions, to facilitate botanical and zoological studies on Moorhouse National Nature Reserve. Many a black wellington and fell boot, armed with microscope, plastic bag and ten inches of weatherproofing, have emerged midwinter from the back door of Moor House in search of the magic species that make up a PhD. However many a Darwinian resolve has been shaken after several accidental slips into the blanket bog or moorland mire which make up this wonderful, squidgy site. But it was all good fun in the name of science; and the studies which resulted led eventually to this piece of terrain being designated as a World Biosphere Reserve (the biosphere is the living surface of the earth), an area so rich in diverse plant communities that it forms part of a chain of crucial sites which straddle the surface of the globe.

You can see some of that terrain quite clearly from the roadside, acres and acres of blanket bog, hosting just about every shade of green known to art, and riddled with little waterways where the water is so pure that it's almost invisible.

Eventually after you have passed the site of the deserted village of Tynehead, west of Dorthgill, the valley narrows between Round Hill and Tynehead Fell, until it meets the little valley at the head of the Tees. In fact the watershed of these two rivers is so close that the rivers almost touch at their source. In midwinter storms it must be impossible for the water to know whether it is coming or going; it is touch and go whether it turns east and joins the Tees or starts the long journey north and slips into the Tyne. Either way, the chances are that it's going to end up a good deal dirtier than when it started out, at this watershed of the rivers.

It is not all water, plants and bog. The valley of the Upper Tyne is dotted with old mine workings and amalgamated smallholdings where the old lead miners used to grow their oats, vegetables and turnips to feed their sheep, their single horse and their milch cow. Under Noonestones Hill can be seen a single disused lime kiln where they burned lime to spread on the fields and neutralise its acid overcoat. This made a more balanced soil, essential, especially at this height, for many self-respecting vegetables. There are mine remains at Noonstones, where they used to work a 300 foot sulphur vein known as 'The Backbone of the Earth', and also at Calvertfold (just under two miles from Dorthgill) and Metalband Hill and Tynehead itself. This is prime adventure country for geologists. The old mine workings are littered with pieces of quartz and fluorspar crystal, iron ore and even pyrites – fool's gold. The old miners were not fools though. Gold itself was once found, a thin seam of treasure hidden where it had been deposited thousands of years before, at the head of the Tyne.

Back down the road-track at Garrigill the George and Dragon will be opening its doors to welcome evening visitors. Formerly a seventeenth-century coaching inn, the George and Dragon does a roaring trade for Pennine Way walkers, lost botanists, tourists and local people. On the flag floors of the bar the real ale flows into the night and in the hearth a log burns, spits and crackles throughout the year, casting a red light on the rugged faces seated before it. And when the bar shutters finally go down there's a treat in store for the sober: a complete illustrated rendering, hand-drawn in the old style, of a poetic version of George's mythical slaying of the dragon has been laid across the shutters. If the dragon in the drawing moves or if the lines do not seem to rhyme, then you're clearly over the top!

Garrigill is well known for the quality of its air. It is said that no purer air can be breathed anywhere. Even in the height of the lead mining epoch, when the miners were subject to poison dust from the mining and the smelting of heavy metal ores, the air lent itself to longevity. It is on record that at a great tea in Garrigill to celebrate the passing of the Reform Bill of 1832, John

Martin and his wife, both 102 years of age, sat at the head of a great table placed on the village green. And if you do not believe us, check it out in the local graveyards!

The Pennine Way connects Garrigill to Kirkland in the Eden valley, a route which traverses the side of Cross Fell, stopping off at the infamous Greg's Hut. This is where the walkers rest for the night or longer after traversing Cross Fell from below or from the south. Its infamy lies in the stories about the 'goings-on' associated with the place . . .

This route also gets a mention in the history books as the 'Old Corpse Way'. The people of Garrigill used to bury their dead at Kirkland on the gentler side of Demon's Fell, as it was then still known, and there's a story from the seventeenth century about a corpse once being taken along this route in the middle of winter. By the time the party had reached the summit of Cross Fell, a snow storm had blown up. Fearing for their own lives, the party fled, abandoning the corpse on the top of the fell. There it stayed for a whole two weeks, perfectly preserved by the snow and ice, a corpsicle. When the weather cleared they set out again and retrieved it, but were forced by the snow on the passes to bring it back to Garrigill. It was buried in the glebe land, and the Bishop of Durham informed of the circumstances. He then ordered the glebe land to be walled in and some time after, he came to consecrate the ground. This was the beginning of the burials at Garrigill, and some say, the last time the Corpse Way was used. The existence of the Way, and the connection with Kirkland in Cumbria, has been given as the explanation for why this part of the Pennines is in Cumbria rather than Northumberland, its more 'natural' neighbour.

The road from Garrigill to Alston sits on high land overlooking Leadgate and the valley of the South Tyne river, as it gathers momentum for its eventual meeting with the main body of the Tyne. You're soon on the B6277 Alston to Langdon Beck road and the views from here are quite

▲ Annat Walls Farm between Garrigill and Alston

special. The road runs above a farm known as Annat Walls, which according to a local author, William Wallace, who was writing in the 1880s, was a place where the Border reivers used to pass. He relates how watches had to be kept as a precaution against them, and tells of how as a boy, 'my grandmother used to tell me stories of the olden times. Most of these I have forgotten. One, however, I well remember was that during her grandfather's time, the family was careful to arrange axes and other weapons at the head of their beds, in order to be in readiness to defend their property against the Scotch.' Tough times indeed.

Alston itself is a bustling centre for traders and tourists, with antique shops, a wine shop with very fine wine selections, a cheesery behind the Market Place where fine Alston cheese is moulded before your eyes from local cow and goat milk, a gallery for arts and crafts and King Arthur's bottle shop. Here a modern-day version of the mythological king – more Merlin than Arthur, but no less colourful for that – sells his wares, a fantastic variety of glass bottles of all shapes and sizes, and the odd antique. And after you've worn yourself out buying your wares, you can refresh yourself at one of a number of hostelries and cafés, the most traditional being the Blue Bell Inn, and the Alston Country Kitchen where afternoon tea is served in style, in heavy hammered bronze teapots.

Alston, like Nenthead, was originally a mining town. The land on which it grew was once in the ownership of the Earl of Derwentwater. But after his execution for his part in the Jacobite Rebellion of 1715, the estates were confiscated and put in the hands of Greenwich Hospital. As the lead industry grew, Alston's population expanded to some 6858 souls in 1831 and the town became the main service centre for the area, providing food and raw materials for the local households, with supplies drawn from Brampton, Hexham and the towns of the Eden valley. Later, supplies came by rail, and a branch line from the main Newcastle–Carlisle line ran for 124 years from Haltwhistle to Alston, terminating at a junction near the confluence of the Rivers South Tyne and Nent. It was a sad day when in 1976 the railway to Alston finally closed, to be followed not long after by the iron foundry which had been the iron-cast centre of the town's economy for most of this century.

The population of Alston is now just a little over 2000. The old railway station is a tourist information centre and cafeteria, and a train of sorts still runs for a short way down the track to Gilderdale Burn. The track is now narrow gauge

and the engine a small one. The South Tynedale Railway Preservation Society (who have revived it for tourists) have done a wonderful job, and it is a major attraction for a family on a day out. There are now plans to extend the line back into Northumberland. When the sun shines, the line is busy and the town's main cobbled streets are a major thoroughfare for tourists, adding new colour to the Pennine grey of the Auld Stane from which Alston takes its name.

Once upon a time the locals made their own colour, particularly on pay days, or 'Pays', when Alston was open for business with a vengeance.

▼ Caleb Reed, with bike and broom, on Alston's cobbles

Here is an account by a reporter for the *Cumberland and Westmorland Advertiser* who was inspired by the events of the Alston Cattle Show in October 1888 to reminisce about the festivities he had known fifty years previously. Remember, this was a time when the mines were in full swing and lines of mules with ore carts were a common sight on the open fell and in the heart of the town. As he relates:

The pays in those days were events to be remembered. Their leading characteristics were a plethora of cash, a cheap-Jack bawling in front of every house,

▼ The Butts, Alston

a free fight at every corner, and a glorious spree generally. Life was worth living in those days. There were no myrmidons in blue to hoist the toper from the gutter to lock up. There was no lock-up to confine him in and no town hall to try him in. The parish constable was selected from the deafest, blindest and lamest of the inhabitants, and gave himself no concern whether the locals were closed at ten or twelve, or two or four; and equally little concern whether the inmates were drunk or sober. If by any chance he manifested a curious interest in the conduct of the inns he was quietly ducked in the millpond.

How things change. On a more orderly note, the excellent East Fellside and Alston Moor Countryside Project, originally based in Alston but now moved downdale to Carlisle, has produced some detailed walks which take you around and beyond the town of Alston. One of our favourites takes you past Gossipgate and above the former foundry site, to a waterfall above the town, named the 'Seven Sisters' after the seven tongues of water which pour across a rock face set high in the river. The spring flowers here are a treat. There is everything from early purple orchids, globe flowers, wild pansies to water avens, primroses, cowslips and marsh marigolds.

Another walk takes you round The Butts, the oldest part of Alston where there are houses so old that at least one of them has to be held by stilts. They date from the early 1700s, and a few still have the outside staircase leading to the ground floor of the house – on the first floor! The ground floor proper was used to keep the animals in during the winter. At the time this was an excellent source of alternative energy. The heat from the animals' bodies rose through the floor to warm the people above. It's an old principle, hot air rises, but so too did the smell!

BARHAUGH AND THE SHEPHERD'S YEAR

Travelling down the South Tyne valley from Alston there is a choice of roads. There is the main A689 which runs parallel in parts to the Pennine Way on the left bank of the river as you go down. There is also a small gated road on the right bank, off the A686 as you leave Alston, towards the hamlet of Randalholme. This is our chosen route down the valley. The nuisance of opening and closing the gates is more than made up for by the delightful scenery and the narrowness of the dale at this point. Also you never know who or what you might meet!

As you climb down towards the river at Randalholme there is a recently cleared plantation to your right, but some stands of trees remain, a thick black forest of dark timber below and evergreen above. On the roadside there are elms and birches which provide a graceful backdrop to the singing river below, as it tumbles and chortles down the valley. The riverside here is special, with flatland beside the water ideal for passing herons. it is an idyllic spot in the summer when the haymeadows are high, and in the spring when filled with cowslip and spotted orchid.

When you look around it is hard to believe that this was once prime coal mining country. Right up into the early part of this century the landscape was dotted with small open-cast and tunnel openings, with coal hoppers and pit refuse. On your way down to Randalholme you may have noticed one such mine on the hill to the north, Ayle Colliery, with its pit head, slag heaps, coal hoppers and pit props. This is a working anthracite mine, delivering regular supplies to British Coal. But it is the only one left. You may still be able to see the scars where others have been, the loading platforms where the coal and anthracite were piled high and put on to the trains for transport out of the valley, and even concrete structures which held the posts of bucket lifts used to take the coal across the river.

It is a fact of life that the old dual economy of the Pennines, of mining and farming, has been replaced with a new dual economy of farming and tourism. These too depend upon one another to survive, and in the new economy the incomers have as important a role as the locals. Where true progress for these hills and dales lies is where there is a meeting of minds, of new ideas with old talents and skills, the mixing of the spirit of new enterprise and new knowledge from the outside with the resources and knowledge that exist locally. There are signs that this is already happening over much of the dales. Good local examples in South Tynedale are the cheese making at The Butts in Alston and the manufacture of Cumberland Mustard, an old local recipe given a modern garnish and marketing push, by a couple based in Slaggyford.

Another good example of the meeting of new minds with old matter is the development at Barhaugh House, an old stately building with towers and outhouses, located just above a beautiful tree-hung river bend where the Barhaugh Burn meets the South Tyne. The manor at Barhaugh dates from the seventeenth century when the estate covered over 500 acres of the surrounding land. The name comes from the Saxon 'bere' for barley and 'haugh', a piece of flat river-formed land. For about a hundred years it was in the hands of the Dryden family who built the folly tower and spiral staircase and planted the limes and beeches which you can see to this day. In the 1970s the building became uninhabited, and started to fall into disrepair. Most of the estate grounds had already been lost to sheep farming, and a question mark lay over the future of this once beautiful building.

A cooperative has now turned it into a focal point for North Pennines recreational development, a study and conference centre. Courses planned cover just about every aspect of the North Pennines human and natural environment, with training on rock climbing and cross-country skiing, natural history studies and introductions to the mining and railway heritage of the area.

The road peters out at Barhaugh. To get back into the main valley by car you have to return the

On the road to Randalholme ▶

way you came, through Alston, and join the A689 road going north down the valley. However you can cross the river by foot from Barhough to the hamlet of Slaggyford by following the track under the Williamston Common, over the Barhaugh Burn bridge, coming eventually to the Williamston bridge. Here there is a nature reserve, complete with mountain pansies, spring sandwort and grass of parnassus growing on old lead wastes and river shingle.

The old culture of these and the other Pennine hills and dales lives on in the hearts, minds and working ways of the dalespeople who remain, particularly the outbye men, the hill shepherds and their families. Men like Willy Parker and Denis Short, Ray Dent and Frank Collingwood, despite accepting all the trappings and comforts of modern-day, high-tech, four-track living, have changed little in outlook from their fathers and grandfathers, from those of their ancestors who tended flocks out on the fell before them.

The hill shepherd's year is set by the seasons. The working year beings with tupping, or mating, which at these heights begins in November–December. Selected tups or rams are put on the hills to mate with their ewes for the new year's crop of spring lambs. The most popular breed are Swaledales, selected for their good wool, their hardiness in all weathers and their ability to feed on coarse herbage, which in the North Pennines is plentiful. They replaced the more indigenous Scottish Blackface, a smaller and therefore less economically attractive beast. But the Swales' longer legs mean that the old stone dykes built for the Blackfaces have had to be extended in height with wire netting to stop them jumping over!

After tupping there is the long wait until lambing starts. Often this coincides in late March–April with the worst of the snow.

So for shepherd and dog it's an icy job, up at dawn, hauling lambs and sheep out of the snow

◄ Barhaugh House: a new centre for some of the twentieth-century's outdoor pursuits

drifts. But these days they try to bring the ewes off the fell at the first sign of snow. In this period the sheep require constant supervision and the quick response of the shepherd, as one older man explains:

'At big lambin' time, ah used t'gan when it turned dark an' had a look an' see if there's anything, an' if there wasn't, went t'bed for a couple of hours. 'N' waken. Th' same fer eighteen days. Y'check them three times a day, forst thing in th' morning to see that she'd got plenty o' milk. At dinner time t'see that the third lamb has had milk again. And then at night, just before dark y'walk an' see them again.'

All living proof that there's one area of work, hill shepherding, where counting sheep does not send you to sleep – the exact opposite is the case! When lambing is over, the ewes are returned to the fell, where they have been 'hefted', become attached, of their own instinctive accord, to a piece of terrain from which they will then not tend to wander.

By early summer it is time to gather in the old ewes and the new lambs. This is a great sight on the fells. The air is filled with burbling larks and curlews, the grass is high and herb-strewn, and if the sun is up shepherd and dog enjoy a Pennine day at its very best. But the work is hard, dosing sheep for worms, marking lambs and castrating new tups. For this the new lambs are separated from their mothers for the first time. But before long, they're all back together again and out on the fell to enjoy the summer. By mid summer they are gathered again for shearing and dipping. Then comes the autumn and the final gathering of those lambs which are to go to market and those rams which are to go to the breeder sales run by the Swaledale Association.

The sales held in Weardale and the Eden valley are great meets for sheep farmers from all over the Pennines. Sheep change hands, but so do information and ideas. Old friendships are maintained and old relationships cemented. After the sales there's a great deal of socialising.

▲ Sheep in the snow: the Pennine seasons are often far from kind

There used to be one type of get-together of the sheep farmers which was, however, more famous for its socialising than for business.

This was the gathering of strays, when the shepherds of the valleys would assemble in a chosen spot with any stray sheep that had got into their patch in order to pass them back to their rightful owners. It never quite worked out. The trouble started with the nature of the chosen spot: always a public house. As drink flowed and the long Pennine evening wore on there was considerable confusion about which sheep belonged to which farmer. In the end the shepherds always went home with the wrong ones: a perfect excuse for another gathering.

The Pennine hill shepherd has a romantic image for many of us, and no doubt there is romance in their lives spent on the lonely fell, with only a dog and wild nature at their side. But they have a hard life, a life which breeds independence and a self-esteem firmly based upon experience and graft. And among the shepherds themselves, the most prized ability is that of 'ettling'. Our old shepherd explains:

'A good shepherd's a good "ettler". "Ettle" means

he can judge wats gannin' te happen befor' it happens. He thinks that this is going te happen, an' if he happens to be right he's a good "ettler". And a good "ettler" is a good shepherd.'

ALONG THE MAIDEN WAY TO FEATHERSTONE CASTLE

On the main A689 down the valley, brown moors rise up on all sides, steep fells where even sheep find it hard to manage, where not too much 'ettling' is carried on. The population levels in this part of the Pennines are low. There are no villages, only tiny farming hamlets like Eals, Lambley and Coanwood and the odd scattered farmhouse.

This road shares in parts the line of the old Maiden Way, the Roman road through the Pennines to the great Roman Wall. The Maiden Way was the name given by the Celts to the road the Romans built between Catterick and the Scottish border, well beyond the Roman Wall itself. In its Pennine section the Maiden Way skirts Cross Fell itself before entering the South Tyne valley and reaching the former Roman station at Whitley Castle near Kirkhaugh church and on the north side of Gilderdale Burn. There is nothing to see of the road now, though the remains of Whitley Castle are still visible, in the form of eleven well-preserved ditches. Archaeologists working in the early 1800s discovered the remains of a perfectly preserved middenstead, a good old-fashioned Roman dungheap! Shortly after its discovery it quickly disappeared: the explanation comes from the journal of mining engineer, Thomas Sopwith. According to him, the heap 'furnished many loads of excellent manure to the neighbouring fields, and been hitherto the productive mine of several interesting curiosities'. Unfortunately, the good taste of the times prevented Mr Sopwith from telling us what they were!

The station was known by the Romans as Alione, headquarters of the third cohort of the Nervii. In the late 1700s an altar was found dedicated to the god Hercules and on which was once stood a colossal statue and carvings of mini-deities attacking serpents. Also found were Roman sandals, copper breast pins, carved earthen tiles, fragments of lead and glass and a huge battle axe. These finds inspired a moment of reflection from Sopwith:

The ruined station and heathen altars remind us of a warlike, superstitious and powerful race of people, regarded without any congenial feelings of sympathy. But on examining such articles as shoes, combs, spoons and breast pins, their familiar and everyday nature induces that social feeling which is always inspired by similar usages or wants; and it is singularly interesting to contemplate them remaining in so perfect a state after those who constructed and wore or used them have slept the sleep of death for sixteen hundred years.

The old Maiden Way becomes a small stretch of the A689 as that road enters the hamlet of Slaggyford. As you approach the village, watch out for a piece of roadside curiosity kitsch made for visiting parties of campers. It's a Lilliputian caravan park where all the caravans are the colour of the trees around, and where a little train takes the children around a mini lake complete with island, gnomes and Disney-style deer. Slaggyford is small too, typical of the other settlements of South Tynedale.

The bird life on the wet heath and patches of blanket mire which straddle the fells is extraordinarily varied. These lonely places provide excellent, undisturbed nesting grounds, and where there is water there are invertebrates to feed on. So the fells are home to a large number of birds that you would normally expect to find not on mountaintops but on seashores, for they are migrating waders: lapwing and golden plover, dunlin and snipe. Some are internationally protected species with the North Pennine attracting a significant percentage of their total European population.

153

Apart from the eponymous curlew, the golden plover is perhaps the most attractive of these salt and heather dipping birds. The plover nests in peat and moss on the exposed high plateaux, its presence indicated by a solitary, plaintive note that rings out across the fell even on days when mist and rain encircle the hills. In August the plover with its new chicks heads for the lowlands, and for the big seaside feed before departing for foreign shores. On lowland pastures it keeps company with lapwings, and in the twilight hours can be seen flying rapidly in circles in the formation of a crescent moon.

The dunlin is a bird of sandpiper stock. It is a little bird which flutters across the fell at the slightest disturbance, anxious to keep intruders away from its nest of eggs or chicks. Another hill wader for which it can easily be mistaken is the snipe, which when disturbed flies upwards for a short distance before falling again, out of sight in the rushes and fell grasses. Its sudden zig-zags in flight and its larger size distinguish it from the other waders. If you do not see one, you will certainly be able to hear them, particularly in the early evening. For above their nesting sites the male snipe wheels and dives through the warm spring night air, giving out a distinctive bleat and fanning the air with its tail feathers. It creates a remarkable drumming sound, which added to the whirr of wings, fills the night with unusual sound.

Perhaps in general the one bird of South Tynedale and of the North Pennines that arouses the strongest passions of all is our old friend the bonny moor hen, the red grouse. The vast tracts of heather moor which are the skyline pride of these great northern hills are an ideal habitat for this unique British bird. It is our only true endemic bird, found in no other country. The grouse nests openly on the moor, producing a clutch of five to ten eggs each year. The maturing chicks quickly become as tough as their parents, able to survive well on the high land in all manner of conditions. In the latter part of the year the grouse migrate in large packs across the

▲ The curlew, whose lonely cry haunts the Pennine moors

moors, moving from place to place and along routes well established by their ancestors. Their Pennine pilgrimage is one of the great sights to be seen, but sadly only some make it to the other end, back to the ancestral breeding ground.

For the grouse is much prized as a game bird. Every August the hills are alive to the sounds of gunfire, as shooting parties converge on the fells, and under the cover of stone and turf butts they fill the sky with lead and flurrying grouse feathers. The North Pennines offer some of the best grouse shooting in the country, and therefore the world, and a whole industry of beaters, keepers, gun-makers and cooks rely on an annual slaughter to keep themselves in livelihoods.

No matter what your view of grouse shooting, whether you find the slaughter and the eating of this game bird to your taste or not, the fact is, without it we would have no heather moor. For heather moor is a managed habitat, encouraged by burning in winter small patches of heather in a gentle enough manner to allow its regeneration. The result is a fresh crop of young heather shoots for the grouse to eat and tall leggy heather nearby for the female grouse and her chicks to shelter from the wind. And then, of course, there is the restraint of the predators and the management of trackways, drains, bridges, walls and butts in readiness for the Glorious Twelfth. On all the great Pennine estates, Stainmore, Raby, Whitfield and Allendale and on the fells of the shooting consortiums, moor and grouse management is a full-time activity for dedicated teams of gamekeepers.

Perhaps the most dedicated of all is Eddie Fairless, now a resident at Plenmeller at the bottom of South Tynedale. In his seventies, Eddie was a keeper on both the Whitfield and Allendale estates, which he joined in 1936, returning after the war to become, in time, head keeper. Now he does a bit of part-time keeping on Plenmellor Common to keep his hand in. He has been a dedicated bird man all his life, developing a keen ornithological interest not just in grouse but also all the other birds of fell and dale. Because of all the time in his early life spent watching creatures that flew, it's no surprise that when he joined the war effort he went in as a pilot!

The keeper's year starts with heather burning on any fine days between January and March. The local beaters control the blaze, to ensure that the whole shooting match does not go up in flames, and the grouse count along with it. In April and May the keepers are busy keeping down foxes, crows and stoats. In June and July the butts and moor tracks are prepared for the new batch of shooters. August is taken up with shooter management, controlling drives, organising beaters and flankers and collecting the catch. The keepers are busy throughout, and it's much, much more than a nine-to-five job.

Eddie Fairless never takes a walk on the moors without a purpose. He is always watching for signs of nesting, the marks of a grouse, the progress of a family, signs of sickness in the stock or the tracks of a predator. At a glance he can tell the progress of breeding within his patch or 'beat'. There are other similarities with the 'boys in blue', for a keeper is very much the policeman of the fell, who keeps out intruders whether poachers or predators, and admits only the authorised. If you're unfortunate enough to be a predator caught in the act, a crow, stoat or weasel, you'll end up like many a North Country criminal of old, strung up on a piece of wire known among keepers as a 'gibbet'.

Grouse shooting is a serious business, but there's humour in it too, in the poems and stories that go with it, in the friendship and camaraderie among the keepers and beaters of the hills. Every year in a secret location in the valley of the South Tyne, the keepers of the North Pennines assemble in their own 'keep', a piece of grouse or pheasant shooting country where they have a free shoot of the cock birds left in that area, this time for the benefit of their own larders. Afterwards they assemble for a whisky-drinking session in an old blacksmith's shop, the scene for many an annual gathering. The shop has one use, and it shows – the imbibing of the drink of the heather moor. From top to bottom the cupboards are full of one thing and one thing only: empty whisky bottles, in their hundreds. No prizes for guessing the blend: Famous Grouse!

If you have not been diverted on to the grouse moor, or done a quick diversion out of South Tynedale to the North Country grouse bars of the Tyne Gap, we suggest one last port of call in this pretty dale – the drive to Featherstone Castle at the foot of the dale. You'll need to turn off the A689 at Lambley, taking the northern road to Rowfoot. The castle itself can be seen from the small road on the left at the Rowfoot T-junction. Set in rich meadowland and tree-laden lawns

▲ Featherstone Castle: destination of a ghostly bridal

this small castle was founded on the site of a peel tower built to keep out the 'sporran-wearing brigade'. The estate has been in the possession of the Featherstonehaughs since Saxon times, one of the most noted of this long family line being none other than Sir Albany Featherstonehaugh himself, High Sheriff in 1503, and killed in a border feud, no one knows why. The event of his departure from life and from the castle of his ancestors has been celebrated in song by Robert Surtees, Durham historian and nineteenth-century ballad writer, in typical apocryphal manner:

> Hoot awa', lads, hoot awa'
> Ha'ye heard how the Ridleys and Thirlwalls and a'
> Ha' set upon Albany Featherstonehaugh
> And taken his life at Deadmanshaugh?
>> There was Willimoteswick,
>> And Hardriding Dick
> And Hughie of Hawden, and Will o' the Wa'
>> I canna tell a', I canna tell a'
> And mony a mair that the de'il may knaw.

Surtees does not tell us much about the man, sadly, or his fighting prowess.

In the 1780s the castle passed for ever from the Featherstonehaughs into the hands of the much more pronounceable Wallaces, and now a hundred years later it is in the hands of a local estate agent, with an even more pronounceable name, Clark. Sadly, the castle now looks a bit run down and is not generally open to the public.

But we're not quite done with the Featherstonehaughs, nor, if the old stories are to be believed, are the people of South Tynedale. For the woods near the castle are believed to be haunted by the ghostly Bride of Featherstonehaugh. According to legend, Abigail, daughter of one of the mediaeval Featherstonehaughs, was in love with a local gallant, but her father forbade him to marry her, and arranged instead for a union with a nobleman of comparable birth, and as they say in these stories, noble lineage and character. Abigail, having no choice, acquie-

156

sced, and the day of the big wedding was set. Her scorned lover went into hiding.

Then on the big day after the ceremonials had been performed, but before the nuptials were complete, the bridal pair set off to ride the ancient bounds of the barony, along Ash Holme, past the Slaggy Ford, through Coney Wood, over Wolf Hills and Tods Wood, past Pinkyn Cleugh and so back home. While they rode forth preparations were completed for the wedding feast, and all waited for the party's return.

Return they did not. The afternoon waned, then dusk fell, then night set in and midnight approached. The baron, Abigail's father, traversed the hall in a great fury, and giving up on the whole affair, packed the guests, minstrels and servants off to their homes. He alone waited in the great hall of the Featherstonehaugh castle for the return of the bridal party. In time he fell asleep. Then as midnight struck, he was awakened by the sound of thunderous hooves approaching the castle from a distance, entering the yard and turning to footsteps by the door. As the taciturn wedding train entered, he sat bolt upright seething with rage. Within seconds of the party entering and seating themselves at the banqueting table, the baron's rage turned to horror. For he saw that each of his guests, his daughter and son-in-law included, had the unmistakable ashy pallor of death on his or her visage, only relieved in the case of many of them by long streaks of blood and ghastly gaping wounds, while the features of some of the party were painfully distorted, as if they had died in great agony; and all their eyes were wide open, with a cold glassy stare, horrible to behold. A shudder ran through the baron's frame, and his limbs trembled beneath him. He rose to his feet and crossed himself mechanically. That instant a sound, as if of a mighty rushing wind, hissed through the hall, and deadened, while it lasted, the sense of everything else. When it ceased, as in little more than the twinkling of an eye it did, the unearthly bridal throng had disappeared.

The baron went into a coma and never recovered, except to tell the tale. It transpired later that the party had been surprised by Abigail's spurned lover and his troop of robbers. They had engaged in mortal combat at Pinkyn Wood. In the struggle the bride was accidentally killed by a sword, and the bandit and her husband had locked together in an embrace from which neither of them emerged. Their blood apparently ran together and mingled in a hollow stone where, it is said, the ravens drank, in joyous carousal, their very own bridal banquet. From that time on, on the anniversary of this foul massacre, the ghosts of the bridal party ride through Pinkyn Wood, gliding through walls and hedges, following an original route long lost . . . a route which many an unfortunate traveller has wished had remained forgotten.

If that does not speed you on your way west on the wide comfortable, modern trunk road leading you to Brampton, and around the northern edge of the Pennine foothills, to the treasures that await you in the garden of Eden, then nothing else will.

A WALK OF RAILWAYS AND ROMANS
FROM SLAGGYFORD TO ALIONE AND BACK

Slaggyford is on the A689 road between Alston and Brampton. It was once one of those lucky villages which had a railway running through it, the station a part of the village. It was on a branch line from Alston to Haltwhistle where trains could be caught to either Carlisle or Newcastle. Businessmen could travel to board meetings in either town, or on to London, Glasgow or Edinburgh. Excited children, summerclad and winter-white, would wait expectantly with their buckets and spades for a trip to the seaside sun of Whitley Bay. The line at Slaggyford is now closed and the track lifted but the station remains, shuttered and forlorn. In its guard there stands a remarkable Pennine ghost, an old steam engine, looking perkier than in recent years, for there is good news at hand. The railway is coming back: the South Tynedale Railway Preservation Society intends to extend its narrow gauge system from its present terminus at Gilderdale Bridge to Slaggyford.

Among the first passengers who alight at the old station there will be those who wish to walk in this wonderful area. Until that day dawns we have to content ourselves with getting there by car and parking on the village green. In the past the villagers of Slaggyford could get out to see the world, or little bits of it, come past their doors, for their village lies on the Pennine Way. We are going to make use of this route for our walk. The distance is about 8 miles and takes 3–4 hours.

You begin by walking back from Slaggyford along the A689 in the Alston direction for a few hundred yards to Thompson's Well Bridge. Through the trees beside the river are tantalising glimpses of Slaggyford's only current working railway, the one that goes around the Island campsite. Cross the river via the bridge, beside Williamston Nature Reserve. The narrow road follows the gurgling river upstream and the grass verges, which are never hacked by flailing machines, are rich in wild flowers. At a sharp bend in

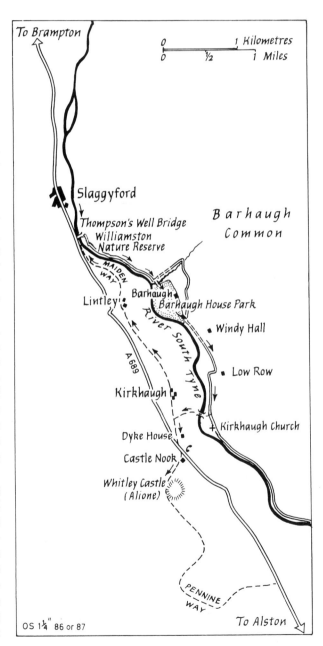

158

the road as it turns away from the river there is a gap in the stone wall with an open space beyond.

This turns out to be a wooden platform and the most extraordinary bridge you'll ever meet. It leaps out from the high bank of the Barhaugh Burn to the haugh, or low ground, on the other side, and so it has to be supported on very tall pillars. Then you descend a steep staircase to the lower bank. This is the parkland of Barhaugh House. The path climbs alongside the burn through the beech trees, up some steps to help you up to the top of the first rise. The second electric pole up the hill from the bridge is a useful guidepost! There is no definite path up through the park, but like all good parkland there are trees and a sizeable copse which should be kept on your right-hand side. Soon the house comes into view, a sturdy building. Continue to climb and look for the exit gate out on to the road.

The views across the valley to Geltsdale Forest fells are fascinating. Above is the brown high moorland of Barhaugh Common; beneath is the green of the river valley. High up on the left is a farm with a magnificent view, Windy Hall. All the way along to Low Row it is the views both up and down the valley which hold your attention. Across the valley on a mound below the ridge sits the Roman fort, one of our objectives.

At Low Row follow the road down into the valley, but pause and look at the farm. There is a modern farmhouse there today, but there is evidence of older farmhouses. Look out for the byre, a one-time long-house with the humans living at one end and the cattle at the other, and an Elizabethan building with glazing bars still firmly fixed in the stone windows.

At the graceful Kirkhaugh church (still on our side of the river, not like Kirkhaugh village, on the other bank) the door is always open. The vicar has written an extremely informative, and witty, account of the church and parish and answers your question of why the church has a Black Forest look about it!

Retrace your route to the path leading to the footbridge across the river. Did you notice the farm opposite the church, high up on the other side? This is Dyke House. Head diagonally up the slope towards

it. There are ladder stiles over fences beside the dismantled railway, but they only have one operative side – you can climb out of the railway site but not into it. Fortunately the new fence has a much simpler stile across it.

The path in front of Dyke House is the Pennine Way, approaching a telephone kiosk. It makes you wonder how many footweary travellers have phoned home from here! Once across the road and through the farmyard of Castle Nook, on the horizon can be seen the humps and hollows of Whitley Castle Roman fort, known to the Romans as 'Alione'.

Stand on the ramparts overlooking the river and you'll understand why it was built just here. There are views in all directions except one, the view behind, where the defences are at their most complex. For the Romans, danger could always be lurking in the hills at their backs. The three or four moats and walls concentrically arranged were intended to protect occupants from a sudden surprise attack.

Going back to Dyke House, cross the road to the finger-post beside the telephone kiosk. The first gate gives the instructions DON'T GO DOWN THE FIELD, THE RIGHT OF WAY IS BETWEEN THE TREES and also suggests that you visit the Kirkstyle Inn, 1 mile north of Slaggyford, where you can enjoy good food, good beer and even a room for the night. The Pennine Way is well marked all the way back to Thompson's Well Bridge. There is a kink in it at the next farm, Kirkhaugh. You arrive below the farm and leave via the gate marked PENNINE WAY behind the farmhouse, which is dated 1692 on the back wall.

The next tricky change of route is at Lintley where another finger-post directs you under the railway viaduct over the Thornhope Burn on to a footbridge. The Maiden Way, the Roman road from the fort to Hadrian's Wall, runs straight ahead here, but you can't see it. So just follow the stream down to the river and walk alongside. It is tempting to use the swimming pool where the lifebelt is tethered . . . and if the sun is out and the day warm, why not? If you've got this far you will have earned a cool, refreshing swim, and Slaggyford is only half a mile away.

THE VALE OF EDEN

The western edge of the North Pennines is taken up with a valley so beautiful, so rich and subtle in its aspect, that it has been rightly called the Vale of Eden.

The Eden at its widest spread separates the North Pennines from the dramatic hills of the Lake District to the west. Its North Pennine section covers the valley's eastern edge, the landscapes on the east bank of the River Eden, where it rises and where its tributaries drain the slopes of the Pennine escarpments, an area also known as East Fellside. This landscape, its villages, hills, fields and rivers are the vale's truly Pennine section, the slopes of Eden.

It is a fitting place for us to end our Pennine journey: a vision of North Country paradise, the beginning of beginnings. If you approach the Pennines from the east, over the ferocious pass of Hartside, through the darklands of Stainmore or around the tip of the Tyne valley, then a tour of Eden will give you a journey's end which will stay with you for ever. If you approach from the west, and it is your first Pennine port of call, then its character is all the more memorable for its contrast with the other Pennine dales.

The Eden valley as a whole is a place which has inspired tomes of local poetry, crafted by many an aspiring child of nature, but topping the list are none other than Poet Laureates Alfred, Lord Tennyson and William Wordsworth. For it is a place which inspires romance and thoughts of valiant times, when King Arthur and his knights strode the land, and when the forest which once covered most of England was still in its prime, virgin if not verdant. Wordsworth was quite old when he discovered the virtues of the Eden, giving an old twist to a new song, for this paean to the River Eden was composed when he was sixty-four:

> Eden! till now thy beauty had I viewed
> By glimpses only and confess with shame
> That verse of mine, whate'er its varying mood
> Repeats but once the sound of thy sweet name:
> Yet fetched from Paradise that honour came,
> Rightfully borne; for Nature gives thee flowers
> That have no rival among British bowers;
> And thy bold rocks are worthy of their fame,
> Measuring thy course, fair stream.

Mallerstang, in the Vale of Eden ▶

Not Wordsworth at his best, we will concede. But he was right about the Eden's flowers.

From the north you can follow the line of the Eden river which gives the valley its name, to its source in the richly mythological dale of Maller-stang where the Pennines meet up with the Yorkshire Dales and where Cumbrians turn into Yorkshiremen.

FROM BRAMPTON TO THE WRITTEN ROCK OF GELT

Our Eden tour starts with our backs against the wall – Hadrian's Wall, a landscape shape unique in the western world which outcrops and mean-ders along the banks of the Irthing and the Tyne. The roads from deep Northumberland and from South Tynedale converge at the pleasant market town of Brampton. From here we must follow the B6413 which takes us south along the bottom of the Pennine hills with the River Eden on our right.

Brampton itself gets its name from the bram-bles which once used to grow in profusion and, no doubt, played their thorny part in obstructing the various armies which chose this area across the ages to dispute the rival claims of English and Scots kings and queens. For it was here that the Jacobites met to plan their rebellion, here that Bonnie Prince Charlie planned the siege of Carlisle, and near here in the battle of Hellbeck that an army of 3000 men and women rose in support of Mary, Queen of Scots but were slaughtered by Elizabeth's royal cavalry. It is said that a tributary of the Gelt known as the Hell Beck took its name from the blood of the dead rebels which flowed down its course for three days after the battle was concluded.

Hell Beck itself flows under the B6413 between Brampton and Castle Carrock, out of a lake called Talkin Tarn situated at the bottom of Talkin Fell which rises gently away to the east. Looking up at the hills at this point, you can completely lose all sense of upland landscape, the slopes seem so gentle and the countryside so verdant. But it is but an illusion: the gates of Eden are made of the flimsiest and prettiest of veils.

The tarn, or lake, at Talkin has an underworld connection: it is fed by a spring which rises so far underground beneath Talkin and the aptly named Cold Fell that its waters are permanently icy. It is not a place to swim, and how those windsurfers manage to keep their limbs and their wits about them after the odd accidental icy dip is astonishing. Perhaps it is what they see and hear underwater which recharges their batteries, as well as those of pike, perch and roach which bring anglers like mayflies to the tarn's shore. For there's a legend that at the bottom of the lake stands a ruined city, the ghostly inhabitants and church bells of which are said to talk to those who will listen.

An old story tells of how once upon a time a prophet was sent by God to punish the inhab-itants of the town for their wickedness. The prophet was not well received – except by one aged and inevitably quiet widow who offered hospitality to God's chosen messenger. On tak-ing leave of her, the grateful prophet, fortified with porridge and compassion for the widow, told her to throw her shovel at a spot beneath her house to save her house and life. She did so and when the flood came and drowned the unwary sinners of Talkin and all their houses, her cot-tage and life alone were spared. Her former kith and kin were forced by their thoughtlessness to converse instead with the fishes. A tall, even 'tall kin' story, you might say, but if you do not believe us, ask the tarn, then we'll see who's really 'talkin'"!

After the tarn you can do a small backtrack, going north back over the railway line then left before Brampton on to a minor road to Low Geltbridge, where the Gelt runs out from within a bank of rich deciduous woods and across more even ground to its meeting place with the by now voluminous River Eden near Warwick Bridge.

162

From Low Geltbridge back up to the source of the Gelt is a mini paradise for naturalists, one of the most important sections of the Pennine wilderness and a must for bird enthusiasts of all types. But before taking a bird's eye view there are a couple more features of the landscape which are worth noting.

Most prominent of these is the red colour of the earth, the rock and the buildings. This is St Bees sandstone, a rich, light deposition from Permian and Triassic times, which perhaps more than anything else gives the Eden valley its unique and warm landscape flavour. It was laid down when this area was another type of

▼ The red earth of Eden

wilderness, a desert, boiling and blooming with desert shrubbery and animals under a burning Permian sun nearly 200 million years ago.

It is hard to think of Eden as a desert, though it is worth remembering that at other geological times it was also a shelf on an ocean floor and at other times again the edge of two vast rivers of moving ice, one with its glaciers centred in the Lake District, the other centred on Cross Fell itself. But the Eden and the far coast of Cumbria alone display this red rock and red earth, a welcome and youthful landform relief between the ancient surface grits and limestones of the North Pennine escarpment to the east and the older exposed Lower Palaeozoic lavas, shales, slates and sandstones of the Lake District to the west.

On the southern bank of the river below a farm named Unity you can see a cave cut into the new red sandstone, known as Abraham's Cave. Not another biblical reference point apparently; but according to tradition a watching place for poachers carved out of the rock by Abraham Bird in 1814, acting on the orders of the Lord of the Manor. There is a tradition of cave building in these parts and perhaps there were other, more spiritual motives, as the cave has also been occupied in its time by hermits and refugees seeking sanctuary in Eden's garden from the troubled world outside.

On the northern bank of the Gelt can be seen another unusual landscape feature: the Written Rock of Gelt. This apparently was the product of a bit of graffiti remaining from the time of the Romans. It records the quarrying activities of the second legion and was done while they were repairing gaps in Hadrian's Wall. Clearly the section where legionary Ustus Uphisjumperus carved sweet nothings for his love, left pining back on the banks of the Tiber, was erased by an over-zealous centurion. But there's enough romance left in the writing for it to give rise to a brief elegy by Tennyson in his 'Idylls of the King', where he mentions the 'crag-carven o'er the streaming Gelt'.

UNDER EAGLES' WINGS

Across the years the lower Eden valley has become accustomed to occasional visits by one of Britain's rarest and most dramatic birds, the golden eagle. The eagle has been known to drop in briefly during the winter months en route to the Lake District and further north. You have to be exceedingly lucky to catch sight of those majestic wings soaring across the crags above the high fells of Tarnmonath and Cumrew, but once seen, the sight is unforgettable. Swift as the wind he flies, a god of the air watching with sharp eyes over the garden of Eden.

One reason why the eagle graces Eden with his presence is because the River Gelt from Greenwell to the Old Water is managed by the Royal Society for the Protection of Birds as a bird reserve. This managed reserve is part of an important SSSI which includes Glendue Fell and Hartleyburn Common on the South Tynedale side, Bruthwaite Forest and Tindale Tarn with its rich feeding edge for waterbirds to the north, and the upper Gelt valley itself, known as the King's Forest of Geltsdale, and despite its name, remarkable for the total absence of trees.

There are plenty of trees in the middle stretch of the river – blocks of ash, wych elm and sessile oak. They are found on the drier soils, with clumps of birch, hazel and alder flourishing on the wetter ground nearer the river's edge. Again this is ancient woodland, ancient in the sense that it is all self-regenerated from species native to the Pennines and has been there for as long as anyone can remember. This stretch of old, rich, valley woodland supports lots of mini habitats for flora and fauna, making it ideal for woodland birds, while up the dale there are large stretches of blanket bog, managed for sheep and grouse and heather but featuring some of the more unusual species like cowberry, cranberry and cloudberry.

The observant and the lucky could fill their bird books in the space of an afternoon with the variety of birds to be spotted. But you do not have to take our word for it; there is an expert on site to watch over you as well as the birds. He is the King's man, the King's Forest's reserve warden, John Miles, who is based at the site headquarters, also his family home, at Jockey Shield. In John's own words:

'The site was given over on a lease basis to the RSPB by an enlightened local family who had the shooting rights but, aware of its ornithological richness, were keener on its conservation. But the grouse management regime adopted by the old keepers, including the practice of strip burning the heather which creates open areas on the moor, has encouraged the presence of breeding birds, in particular wading birds like dunlin, golden plovers, curlew and redshank. Careful control of mammal predators like stoat and weasel has contributed to a bird abundance: ninety breeding birds recorded in some years. And that's why we're here, because of the diversity that has resulted from the diverse habitats.'

John will tell you that the old alder and birch in Geltsdale are great for the holes they produce, a magnet for woodland birds like short- and long-eared owls, nuthatch, redstart and great spotted woodpecker. In fact in the higher woods the older mature trees are so full of inviting holes that John has had no need to put up nestboxes to encourage species. But he has done this in the lower woods, where the beech and elm do not come 'holey' enough, and has been able to push up the numbers of pied flycatchers from ten to one hundred breeding pairs in Geltsdale.

He'll also tell you that the Gelt is rich botanically, because of the old woodlands and the controlled grazing which encourage the presence of a rich ground flora on the limestone edges and the wet acid peat margins of the Pennines. Over 450 plant species have been noted, including some of the Teesdale rarities that have escaped from across the hills, plants like three species of gentian as well as herb Paris, early purple orchid and sword-leaved

▲ Strip-burning last year's heather bloom

helleborine. At the lower altitudes there are herb-rich haymeadows, and in patches of standing water, where the drainage is poor or the river has been careless, there are water-loving plants, including the lesser butterfly orchid.

Another reason why the bird life of Geltsdale is so interesting is because of the proximity of the Tyne Gap to the north. Migrating birds take advantage of the shortest gap between the east and west sides of Britain, and the lower altitude, to fly a bit lower in massed flocks from coast to coast, stopping off on the few bits of waterway that they chance on in between, places like Tindale Tarn at the back of Cold Fell. Migrating seabirds spotted resting inland by John Miles and other local birders include avocet, smew, fulmar, kittiwake, shelduck, little bittern and red-backed shrike, as well as species of geese including barnacled, pink-footed, greylag and Canada.

'Living on the Gelt,' says John, 'you never know what you're going to bump into. One year was marvellous for raptors, red kite and hobby, rough-legged buzzard and merlin in profusion. There's lots of prey, meadow pipit and small woodland birds and a fair bit of carrion still.' Because the Pennines are not under the same pressure from the public as the Lake District, there's more chance for these shy birds to breed in quiet and safety, and there's many a predator has made its escape from the Lakes to the Pennines, to get away from the predations of surplus *Homo sapiens* – so plentiful in parts of Cumbria now, that they outnumber the sheep!

THE CROGLIN BAT AND NUNNERY WALKS

Leaving John Miles enraptured with his raptors, we move further back up Eden vale to lift another veil of magic off this dramatic western edge of the North Pennines: a veil of dark superstition terminating in a sacred walk, the beauty of which will take your breath away. The place is the Croglin Water, a fine stretch of wild water which plunges from 2179 feet at the top of Black Fell down to a spectacular junction with the calm Eden at Fieldgarth near the pretty village of Kirkoswald.

The year is 1875, twenty years before the appearance on the world literary scene of Bram Stoker's book *Dracula*. Suddenly, the quiet little village of Croglin had a strange visitation. A family of young Australians, Amelia, Michael and Edward Cranswell, had been staying, like many a holiday cottager today, in a country retreat: the farm at Croglin Low Hall beside a road bridge over Croglin Water. Late one summer night after the company had gone to bed, Amelia lay awake gazing out over moonlit lawns and fields, watching the trees swaying in the gentle breeze of the warm night.

Suddenly she saw two small pinpoints of light moving across the garden. In a flash they were outside her window, the eyes of a demon whose claws were scratching at the window. She ran to the door but before she got there, the beast had broken through the window, dragging her to the bed and savagely biting at her face and neck. The creature smelt of death and decay, its withered skin and bones only partially hidden by a huge black cloak, a shroud from a long-forgotten tomb. She screamed with terror and pain.

Hearing the commotion, the brothers Edward and Michael smashed down the door and saw the cloak-winged creature escaping out of the window and across the countryside up to the fells above the house. Amelia was alive but badly bitten, bites diagnosed by a doctor as being those not of any human, but of an animal of some sort. The Cranswells went on holiday to Switzerland to forget that terrible night at Croglin. But they returned in September, Amelia taking up her old room and the brothers the rooms next door, armed with axes and shotguns should the beast return.

Return it did to Low Hall, but not until many months had passed, with reports of other 'bat' attacks in the neighbourhood. This time however, before it had got fully into the room one of the brothers was after it, chasing it across the countryside and up to the village cemetery where it appeared to vanish into a vault.

The next day a posse of men went to the churchyard and opening a tomb found that all the coffins had been smashed, their grisly contents lying around the floor. All that is but one, where the lid was removed to reveal the semi-decomposed body of a tall man in a cloak, with fresh blood dripping from the fangs on either side of its mouth. Not a moment was wasted. Edward Cranswell took a stave of rowan wood and drove it deep into the creature's heart. The coffin and its terrible contents were then lifted out of the crypt, placed on a pyre in the churchyard and set alight. As the flames leapt up into the sky above Croglin church and village, the coffin opened one last time, and to the horror and astonishment of all, the Croglin 'Bat' sat up. Its horrible head and socket eyes gazed for one last time at its chosen prey, the children of Eden.

The Cranswells, their vision of paradise impaired, returned to Australia and that lucky continent's undiminishing sun. The room where Amelia had been attacked was closed and the window remains bricked up to this day. The north of England's most celebrated vampire bat never returned and Croglin remained at peace . . . well, until now. You may of course want to raise a few ghosts yourselves. In which case you can retrace the steps of the beast and walk from the Hall up by the river to the old churchyard, to the Robin Hood Inn where the locals will fill you in on other escapades of the Croglin Bat, as it came to be known. And they'll point you up to the river walk which leads past Scarrowmanwick Fell to Watch Hill and Black Fell.

After you leave the little village of Croglin behind, the landscape quickly empties, and you'll fairly quickly discover that you are in one of the most desolate, uninhabited areas in the whole of the North Pennines. For as the locals attest, 'There's nuthin' up thear, nuthin' upon

▼ The lonely road through Scarrowmanwick Fell

nuthin'.' Even the ever-present upland curlew seems quiet, no place even for her haunting call.

There are a few isolated ruins to the north of the tumbling Croglin Water, and to the south the remains of an old quarry working and track where hardened quarrymen and miners must have at one time struggled away, determined to ignore the stories of the 'Scarrow-Man', the beastly Bat of Croglin. And high above one stretch of Croglin Water there is an eerie series of broken and cut stumps, all that remains of a thorn forest which once grew in profusion on the side of the fell.

After a while you come across a small vision of peace and tranquillity, an unnamed waterfall, tumbling down from limestone pavement over a section of darker harder rocks below. There are trees and ferns here, birches and alders hanging high over the small gorge which runs from the waterfall, and no doubt bats too, possibly even populations of whiskered and Brandt's bat, present in the North Pennines at unusual altitudes and at the northern limit of their habitats.

If you trace the rest of Croglin Water's tortuous path down to where it meets the Eden there is another surprise in store, more pleasant than a vampire story but no less dramatic. A small diversion off the B6413 to Kirkoswald brings you to a large rectilinear sandstone building, formerly a Benedictine nunnery built on the site of a twelfth-century nunnery and part of a monastic and contemplative tradition which grew up across the centuries in the area of Kirkoswald, the home also of a unique split-site church and church college. The Nunnery is now a holiday cottage, but remains a perfect place to stay to take in the famous Nunnery Walks, which have by no means lost their spiritual character.

They start just behind the Nunnery. You simply go through a gate round a corner and look down, for the ground opens up before you, and a waterfall plunges over 100 feet down into the depths of the earth. Great vertical cliffs of red sandstone, strewn with ivy, mosses, ferns and

lichens and overhung by great Scots pine, oak, beech and planted exotic species, form the walls of a vast and narrow chasm which takes your breath away. And at the base the foaming Croglin Water tears across a pavement of limestone, complete with pot holes, hollows and clints where stones have eaten away at the rock surface.

You have a choice of walks, long and short, along the paths that the nuns once followed, and you can see signs of their contemplation in this womb of the earth, in the remains of a summer house complete with mediaeval carvings, in stone benches and in solitary prayer caves carved into the rock face at the bottom of the gorge. One wonders how they got down there originally: rope-climbing nuns? monks with ice picks? Paths were cut down the rock face, but most of them have long been worn away. The whole chasm, with its magnificent views and its religious relics, inspires a sense of awe and fright in equal amounts, so much so that Wordsworth was forced to observe that he had seen nothing like it in his life, not even in the most awesome corner of his wild and beloved Lake District.

The vista ends however in a scene of pure tranquillity and light, as the wild Croglin Water is tamed by the superior force of the Eden into which it pours. The woods open out on to banksides carpeted in the spring with primroses, celandines, wood anemones and willow fronds. On the far side of the river runs the railway line from Settle to Carlisle, and on a clear day the passengers have staggering views across more measured cliff faces above the Eden toward Croglin Water and the High Pennines in the distance. The views from the train are indeed awesome, but few who look out realise the beauty and the fearsome stories which lie behind a peaceful vista of trees and fields . . . along the wild waters of Croglin.

◀Croglin's Chasm makes a watery veil at the head of Nunnery Walks

KIRKOSWALD AND THE RAVENS

The village of Kirkoswald back on the B6413 beneath the fellside is one of the prettiest in Cumbria with an equally charming church devoted to Oswald, King of Northumbria. In the seventh century the people of Kirkoswald used to worship a local god at a spring beneath the present bell-tower hill. King Oswald, converted to Christianity by the monks of Iona and a great missionary in the north, came across their practice and 'persuaded' them of the error of their ways. Their new calling came from a bell tower placed on the hill above the spring, no doubt sited there for optimum cosmic effect, as well as sonic resonance. The church was built on a different site beneath the hill, perhaps on the very site of the spring itself, and there is a well dedicated to Oswald on the west side of the church into which fresh springwater flows. The various Norman and Saxon carvings and headstones which lie around the church walls attest its antiquity, and there is a magnificent carved wooden porch which dates from 1523.

Below the bridge in Kirkoswald there is an old stone mill and a beautiful little cottage – Raven Cottage. This is named after the Raven Beck, another riverine veil of Eden which rises from Haresceugh Fell beside the Hartside Pass where the A686 joins the Eden and South Tynedale valleys. Raven Beck does indeed provide sanctuary and a hunting ground for our friend the raven. Time was when these interesting birds were regular breeding birds in the North Pennines, but for a large part of this century they have been absent from their haunts in the hills. Then suddenly in the early 1980s they were noticed by the RSPB warden, breeding again on the Geltsdale site: three pairs had returned, émigrés from pressurised parts of the Lake District, and perhaps encouraged by the new moor management systems, and by the abandonment of poison as a way of controlling unwelcome predators.

In local and national folklore the presence of

ravens is always a good thing, a sign of luck and prosperity. Indeed from an ecological point of view, breeding ravens point toward a healthy ecosystem. The trouble here before was that with the intense sheep breeding programmes, which came to the hills with the introduction of the EEC hill sheep subsidies, local farmers were keen to banish the ravens because of their habit of attacking young lambs and sheep over-heavy with wool. Ravens are persistent and pugnacious creatures: not only will they harry larger birds like the buzzard and attack foxes for the sheer fun of it, but they will watch over a flock of sheep for days on end after spying an ailing specimen in the hope of being first in on the poor animal's deathbed.

So the return of the ravens, nesting in the high crags overlooking the Eden valley, in the same sites as their ancestors hundreds of years before, was greeted with joy by the birdmen. But perhaps their return was not welcomed so cheerfully by the local farmers, and at least there must have been loud boos, or baas from the sheep. John Miles remembers how pleased *he* was anyway: 'When I first came to the fells, it was the thing I really wanted to see back, because it's a lovely sound when you're walking the fells to hear the raven honking up above and that beautiful display. It was great when they returned.'

In 1986 however this black bird of good omen for the hills suddenly disappeared again. Only one breeding pair remained, and even they were seen by one farmer moving out across Tynedale for pastures far and new. But neither sheep nor farmer cheered, for this sudden emigration coincided with the cloud of radioactive particles from Chernobyl which drenched the Pennines and the lakes in a light wash of radioactive caesium. The caesium is now thought to have largely dissipated, but sadly the ravens have yet to come back again to the little Pennine fellside valley to which they have given their name. Meanwhile all eyes, except those of the local sheep, are on the fell for their return.

LONG MEG, CROSS FELL AND THE LITTLE RED VILLAGES

Travelling south from Kirkoswald we must take our leave of the B6413 and start a slow meander across a complex of small country lanes. Slow, because this is Eden's rural heartland, where small villages and hamlets (children and animals too) pop up at almost every other bend in the road. This is a corner of Old England where the village pub and post office still make a living, and where you still find farms and farm buildings overlooking the village square. Geese and goslings routinely cross the 'highway' between pond and field, cows take their own pace en route to the milk parlour, and stray sheep and tractors still rule the highway. It is a vision of great charm and peace. Out here they are the ones with the true right of way.

Watching over the buzz and bluster of these little red sandstone villages from another time, a time of peace and plenty, of Brooke poems and Palmer paintings, there are two ancient sentinels, themselves the product of another aeon. Their origin lies lost in the mists of time, but their visual power remains constant today. The first is Long Meg and her Daughters, a circle of standing stones, overlooking the Eden and the countryside around from a hilltop near the village of Little Salkeld. The second is great Cross Fell itself, highest point in the Pennines and a standing stone of considerable drama and stature. Viewed from below, Cross Fell is a magnificent spectacle, rising above the little red villages like a Goliath among men, and touching horizons only with the mountains of the Lake District which lie on the farther side of the Eden valley.

According to legend Cross Fell is so named because of a visit to the summit by St Paulinus during the seventh century. At that time it was known as the place of devils, as 'Fiends Fell'. As part of their campaign to convert the local Celts to the Christian cause, a mass was held on the

Cross Fell ▶

170

top of that wild hill to drive out the demons. A cross was erected, which no longer stands, but the name has stuck, Cross Fell. One demon remains, the famous Helm Wind, a mighty draught which tears at man and beast and everything that stands or moves beneath the fell when it blows.

The demon Helm shows its face when all about is quiet. According to Cumbrian historian Bulmer, 'Sometimes when the atmosphere is quite settled, hardly a cloud to be seen, and not a breath of wind stirring, a small cloud appears on the summit, and extends itself to the north and south; the Helm is then said to be on, and in a few minutes the wind is blowing so violently as to break down trees, overthrow stacks, occasionally blow a person from his horse, or overturn a horse and cart . . . The sudden and violent rushing of the wind down the ravines and crevices of the mountains occasions the loud noise that is heard. Its effect on the spirits is exhilarating, and it gives a buoyancy to the body. The country subject to it is very healthy, but it does great injury to vegetation by beating grain, grass and leaves of trees, till quite black.'

We'll spare you the various meteorological explanations; suffice to say that it has to do with the gradient of the mountain, with hot air rising, suddenly cooling at the top, and rushing back down the hill to meet the warm air below and a contradictory west wind. Needless to say, all hell breaks loose as the winds wage war on one another and the inhabitants of the villages around Cross Fell, Milburn, Kirkland, Ousby, Melmerby and Gamblesby. If it were not for the fact of it being an occasional, rather than a regular occurrence, and not a summer phenomenon, it's the kind of thing which could make you all heated up, even quite cross!

Cross Fell is famous for something else too: its natural history. It is listed in the prestigious catalogue of internationally important biological sites known as 'The Nature Conservation Review', put together by the government's agency for such things, the Nature Conservancy Council. It is a National Nature Reserve, part of the World Biosphere Reserve, an SSSI, and has just about every other classification you can think of. So what has poor old Cross Fell got to deserve the attentions of the world's leading ecologists, apart from a biting wind and a pleasant aspect from the valley below?

The answer is an exceptional range of plants including some heath and grassland species more typical of Scotland, and a wide variety of grasslands, flushes, bogs and rock outcrop habitats. The latter provide food, shelter and companionship for a wide range of upland birds, including merlin and buzzard, dunlin and other winged lovers of wet boggy ground, but more significantly for a large number of lonely botanical rarities. The catalogue of these includes the shy flowering cloudberry, the crowberry, with its pink flowers and purple to black fruit, and on wetter ground, amidst all the sphagnum mosses, the slender, star-like bog asphodel, a tiny yellow upland lily, and the innocent-looking but highly insectivorous common sundew. These are all plants well suited to the thin acid soils, the wet ground and the semi-arctic conditions experienced up here. If you venture up these parts and you see a pretty flower, by all means look it up in your guide to flora, but leave well alone. At the same time watch you do not put your foot in a hidden bog or flush. Apart from the obvious risk to leg and life, there's a risk of damaging a flower habitat many thousands of years old.

Teesdale communities are relics from the Ice Age, enjoying the cold and the isolation from man. Over 13,000 years ago, a minor corrie glaciation centred on Cross Fell itself created on these hills the drainage system that we know and rely upon today, but it also left a few other things as well, including a series of ice-worked patterns known as stone strips. They lie along the summit and are a nationally significant and rare landform. Subsequent action by cold water within the hills has also led to the formation of the most perfect maze passage cave in Britain, visible at Knock Fell cave.

▲ Long Meg; older than the Pyramids, an ancient marker for the winter's turn

Long Meg herself, well below the hill escarpment, but with wide views of the countryside around, is the most prominent stone in one of the largest Neolithic or Stone Age circles in Britain, facing an opening circle at least 300 feet across and made up of between sixty-six and eighty individual stones known as Meg's Daughters. Various legends are attached to the stones, including one which explains their origin as a company of witches who chose this sacred spot to perform an 'infernal' dance and were, at the prayers of a saint, turned to stone. It is unlikely that this impressive alignment resulted from either a piece of common or garden hocuspocus or from the intervention of a holier-than-thou spoilsport.

For the real story of Long Meg we have to go much further back into time, further back than the Egyptian pyramids, back to a people whose environment was mostly oak and elm forest, who began to cut down and ring-bark the hardwoods which grew in profusion on the ground which had been scoured clean by the melting glaciers of the Ice era. These were a people whose main tools were axes of flint and stone, who hunted and grew crops, and who lived close to the rhythms of the earth and the animals around them. But they were not primitive. They had the technical ability and organisation to build these and the many other circles, megaliths and Stone Age fortifications which litter the Eden valley, but are rare in the hilltops of the Pennines. They also had a knowledge of the movements of the planets and the stars, the earth and the sun, and an understanding both of mathematics and of geophysical forces. Nothing airy-fairy at all, though the systems of symbols used to interpret the world around them may have had mythological colouring: the attributes of gods and spirits, magic and mystery; but no less scientific for that, as any good anthropologist these days will tell you.

But why stone circles and why this one here, and in this configuration? The answer is a combination of factors and of beliefs, for these ancient circles served a variety of purposes. Amongst other things the stones were clocks, their alignment calibrated to the movements of the sun and the moon, providing the basic parameters of calendars by which they could help time the planting of crops and plan the division by festival of the social year. As with Stonehenge on Salisbury Plain and Newgrange in Ireland, the solstices throw light on the matter, and if the sky is clear, on the stones too. With Long Meg it is the midwinter sun, which at its turning point in the heavens casts a beam of light past Long Meg and between the gap in the stones into the heart of the circle. Then, as now, this was the signal for the turning of the year, the beginning of the end of winter and the coming of new growth and a new life or rebirth, a reincarnation for men, women, animals and the land.

Three symbols of rebirth can be seen clearly on the south-eastern flank of Long Meg, spiralring marks incised on the Penrith sandstone of this impressive angular block, a feature shared with megaliths across Britain, Ireland and Europe. The remainder of the stones are of a flinty limestone, indicating possibly that they replaced an earlier sandstone circle, or that the two types of rock had different qualities. Long Meg is aligned in such a way that her four angles point to the four points of the compass. But it's not all mathematics and stone-masonry, there is some magic too. If you stand facing Meg from the south-west you can clearly see the face of a witch, her mouth and nose and eye . . . and what's that strange bloodcurdling noise behind you!

There are new theories about the relationship between the siting of these ancient megaliths and patterns of unusual geophysical activity, rock faulting and earth tremors. The circular alignment of large stones is supposed to reduce levels of radioactivity and electromagnetism within their walls: to create order and peace within hidden unseen space. The Eden valley is of course the product of great faulting on the earth's surface between the Pennines and the Lakes, so the frequency of megalithic sites within the area could be related to this. Even in Stone Age times, humans endeavoured to control wild nature and forces well beyond their command. A measure of their success is our presence here today, as their descendants upon the earth, but whether humanity will be successful enough in understanding our world to last as long as these great stones is another question altogether.

If you haven't turned to stone by now, there's just a little more we should tell you about the Long Meg site. Some stones are gone from the site, and it is possible that there was once an outer circle of stones which has been pillaged. In any case an accurate assessment of the number of stones present is no easy feat. And if you count them twice you'll get a different number. In the last century there were clearly more, but you'll not be too far out if you get a number in the high sixties, though we bet your companion will get a different figure. It is also said that if anyone ever does count the same number twice, Long Meg will come to life, or the devil will drop by for a bit of fire practice. But no calculators please – and watch your back!

In 1725 one Colonel Lacey of Salkeld attempted to blow up the stones for milestones. But a storm blew up and the workmen fled for their lives, terrified that the stones were going to punish them for the desecration of their circle. He must have learned a lesson about the earth sculptures from this incident, for he himself tried to make a national monument by carving a complex of caves into sandstone cliffs near an ancient cairn on the bank of the River Eden near the weir at Eden Lacey. The caves are there for all to see, in their bright red glory, above the river and in view also of an impressive weir, mill complex and railway viaduct. There's a local walk you can do from Little Salkeld which takes in both the stones and these red carved caves. The caves are good,

▼ Lacey's caves, above the Eden

but on a warm summer night as the sun sets, casting red light on the land around, the stones win hands down.

Let's then leave Long Meg to her magic and the words of a local poet who wrote:

> Mark yon altar. This wide circus
> Skirted with unhewn stones: they awe my
> soul
> As if the very genius of the place
> Himself appeared, and with terrific tread
> Stalked through this drear domain.
> Know that thou stand'st on consecrated
> ground;
> The mighty pile of magic planted rock
> Thus ranged in mystic order, marks the
> place
> Where, but at times of holiest festival
> The Druid leads his train.

Between the ancient stone structures of Cross Fell and Long Meg, with their respectively natural and human sculptured shapes, lie the villages of East Fellside, refreshingly rectilinear but cosy in their design and colour. The warm red sandstone of local quarries has been shaped by craftsmen masons across the centuries into blocks which provide the raw materials of barns and farmhouses, cottages and stone walls, homes ancient and modern for people and animals.

One group of villages well worth a visit includes Skirwith and Kirkland, Blencarn and Milburn, after which a minor road takes you over, past Acorn Bank, to the main A66 road to Appleby and beyond. Or else you can stick to the sides of the Pennine ridge to see Knock and Dufton en route to the walk up to High Cup Nick, where the great volcanic Whin Sill outcrops above the limestones of the Pennine escarpment, and the views of the Eden valley and the Lakes are unsurpassable.

Either way, your route from Long Meg should try to include the working organic watermill in Little Salkeld, to pick up fresh supplies of stone-ground flour and muesli. Here the millers will show you their working wheel, one of the last of the traditional cornmills in the country, still using the clean, self-renewing power of water to grind their flour. Weather and miller permitting you can see the wheelrace that runs off the Melmerby Fell from its source high up on Melmerby High Scar, and powers the wheel, without charge, without pollution – and without VAT! And if you want to sample the final product, hot wholesome bread from Melmerby Fell powdered flour, then there's the village bakery at Melmerby where the bread is simply delicious.

The villages of Skirwith and Kirkland, through which run the tributaries that feed the little Briggle Beck, are connected by history too. Until 1980 they were part of a single ancient parish which also included Blencarn and the chapelry of Culgaith. The old halls at Kirkland and Skirwith which pre-date the present farmhouse settlements at the furthest end of the two villages once had the same owner, MP for Westmorland between 1774 and 1806, Michael le Fleming. This character was one of a common breed, an absentee landlord. So the estate was managed by an impressive agent, John Moore, who with his successor, Thomas Harrison, took upon himself the task of restoring the halls to their original splendour. An interesting document survives from that period which prompted action on Kirkland, a report to Harrison about this once fine building's poor state of repair, and its effect upon the tenant farmer for whom Kirkland was a working home.

Thomas Atkinson of Kirkland came here last night with a lamentable tale of the great distress he and his family are in from the late snow (which almost filled their house) and the water they had to carry out in consequence thereof. He says . . . that if he has not a new House built immediately he will leave the farm this Spring and expects . . . an answer very shortly. He brought with him a Plan and Estimate upon a rather smaller scale, and says that he will undertake to have a House, and Cowhouses as he wants it, built and finished for Eighty Guineas, having the materials of the old House and the old slate which came off the old Mill at Skirwith, and also having Liberty to cut the necessary Oak Timber upon Skirwith Demense and having the Oak Bark, but not the top.

The farmer got his new home. To re-cement the sandstone and to plaster the walls and ceilings, the estate even built a lime kiln near Kirkland to prepare the lime, and that kiln can be seen today, one of the most impressive of the strange monuments that dot the Pennine Hills in various states of disrepair. Around this time too, work commenced on the rebuilding of Skirwith Hall to the fashion still evident today, a large farmhouse in deep red well-pointed sandstone with a large courtyard and outbuildings on three sides. Today it's a mini fort, with superb views over mature woods which grace the Briggle Beck. However, a tragic story is attached to this reconstruction of the ancient Hall. It seems the Hall did not take too kindly to renovation, for in a newspaper report from 1775:

on Thursday last, as Mr Thomas Addinson and his men were pulling down Skirwith Hall . . . they undermined a gabal end to let it down together. Mr Addinson standing at a little distance called to the men when it began to shrink, who all got from it, but . . . in stepping backwards [he] stumbled over a log . . . and a great part of the building falling on him, he was crushed to death, and his body for some time buried in the ruins.

Perhaps in commemoration of this event, the date 1775 is carved crudely on the milkhouse window sill. And even more strangely, on the gable end of the barn facing, possibly the very place where the accident happened, there is a mason's carving, just above the iron gate where the courtyard opens to the land and water below. The carving is eerie, resembling a Celtic head, with hollow eyes and mouth. Ghostly by moonlight and even by sunlight, it may even have been the product of an exorcism to rid the new Skirwith of the ghost of Thomas Addinson. Such carvings were common at one time, placed at gateways and door openings to frighten away the old Celtic beliefs about spirits occupying boundary posts and openings, the betwixt and between places of the physical and spiritual worlds.

It must have worked, for there is no ghost at Skirwith. There are however lots of rooms in this big farmhouse, as also at modern-day Kirkland Hall. The enterprising farming families of both old halls let these out as short-stay holiday cottages to the many visitors to the Eden valley who also like to bask in the Eden sunshine and sleep in peace in comfortable and tasteful red sandstone surroundings. With the trout fishing at nearby Blencarn under the shadow of Cross Fell, with historic landscapes all around, walks and pony treks a-plenty, and deep local history for the connoisseur, it's a perfect place to be.

If you do get the chance to visit this part of the valley, and the other East Fellside village greens – places like Knock and Long Marton, Kirkby Thore and Temple Sowerby, Newbiggin and Milburn – you'll discover that, like Kirkland and Skirwith, each place has its own story, a long history and no doubt the odd ghost or two. And before leaving the area, take the walk up Cross Fell, along the route signposted from Kirkland. Watch out for buzzards and flowers, and we'll leave you to interpret for yourself some of the other mysteries which you'll find on its slopes, mysteries like the discovery of coal on its steep sides, and mysteries like the true origin and function of the cultivation terraces near Kirkland which enjoy a dramatic title: 'The Hanging Walls of Mark Anthony'. But do not broadcast your theories too much: some things are better left as mysteries.

ACORN BANK AND APPLEBY

By the banks of the Milburn Beck which rises from the heights of Knock Fell there lies a

▲ Acorn Bank: herb garden of the Eden valley

modern-day miniature Garden of Eden. There may be no 'truths' inside this particular Edenic garden, as in the popular 1960s song, but there are plenty of flowers and a magical display of aromatic herbs. The garden is called Acorn Bank and you'll find it near Temple Sowerby, off the A66, the main road between Appleby and Penrith. Originally a home for the historic Knights Templar in the eleventh and twelfth centuries, by the twentieth century the house and garden at Acorn Bank came into the ownership of a far-sighted lady, Mrs McGrigor Phillips, who after restoring the garden and creating a wild flower and bird reserve, gave it in 1950 to the National Trust. The house is now a home for elderly people, run by the Sue Ryder Foundation, while the garden and riverside parklands are managed for nature and for an extensive collection of herbs.

There are newts in the well garden and a carpet of spring flowers in the orchard, including the double wood anemone, the yellow wild tulip and the pheasant's eye narcissus. Over 20,000 specimens of the little daffodil or Lent lily have been propagated on the oak bank beside the water, just one of an incredible 60 varieties of daffodil and narcissus which nod and dance in the spring sunshine every year. But prepare your nose for an aromatic treat: a grand tour of some 250 species of herbs for just about every pot and ailment under the sun. There's everything here, from good old familiar thyme and basil to stranger, more exotic varieties, like asarabacca which makes you sneeze, the poisonous bane-berry used as a black dye, black snakeroot, an antidote to rattlesnake bites, burning bush which gives off a vapour which can burst into flame, to the narcotic poke weed and the beautiful water flag, with its lowly uses as a purgative and a cure for syphilis.

And if after sniffing that lot you do not end up as high as a kite, or as sick as a parrot, we recommend another short detour, along the A66 to Appleby in Westmorland. Appleby is a pleasant small market town, clearly the good apple in Eve's fallen garden. Every year it is host to a large horse fair which attracts Romanies, or travelling people. They come in their hundreds from all over the country, in old gypsy caravans and the odd brand new Mercedes Benz, to trade their stock and to tell the fortunes of the passer-by. They have races and they wash their horses in the river, customs as old as the hills under which these ancient traditions are practised year after year.

Appleby is notable for something else too: its castle. A Norman edifice of the motte and bailey type, it managed to survive not just the to-ings and fro-ings of successive generations of these new Englanders, but also the wars with Scotland in the thirteenth century and the odd ad hoc assault by gangs of reivers. It also survived the plague and all the other calamities which beset the ordinary poor people of Appleby across the ages, and after a bit of restoration by the celebrated Lady Anne Clifford, it even survived that other plague on the fortunes of English royalty – the revolution by Cromwell, and its aftermath. It's a monument, in short, to the principle of conservation: good and sensitive management of ancient resources, with just a little bit of occasional meddling, thereby creating a heritage for future generations.

Today conservation at Appleby is alive and kicking, in the shape of a remarkable assembly of rare animal breeds which are maintained in the castle grounds, and rare birds which are kept there too by the current owners, Ferguson Holdings. Animals to see include white park cattle brought here by the Romans, longhorn cows, the Pennine-bred whitefaced woodland sheep and bagot goats. The latter are beautifully horned animals which are now sadly listed as one of the most endangered breeds of British domestic animals. A remarkable array of birds includes rare ducks like the blue Cumberland runner, eagle and snowy owls, the beautiful Lady Amherst pheasant, ravens and red-faced parrot finches, spoonbills, ibis and exotic Chilean flamingoes. There are whistlers: whistling swans and wildfowl like the Cuban whistling and fulvous whistling duck.

All that and the pretty town of Appleby too, proud of its ancient associations to the point where the citizens even attached the name of the old county, Westmorland, to that of the town's name, to keep at bay yet another unwelcome extinction. Appleby has three churches too – what else would you expect from the biggest settlement in a valley which not only has its own little biblical Eden in Acorn Bank, but an Ark as well, Appleby Castle!

If further proof is required that the age of innocence is not lost in the Eden valley then a visit to two little churches further south up the dale towards Kirkby Stephen is in order. These are the churches at Warcop and Great Musgrave on the B6259, places where an ancient ceremony of rushbearing takes place every spring, involving young maidens, pretty posies of spring flowers and a plant, the common rush, for which few other uses have yet to be discovered. Warcop farmer, Neil Richardson, chairman of the rushbearing committee at St Columbus's Church, takes up the story:

'They reckin' it all started from when they used t' put rushes 'n the church flaars, fer warmth. 'N what happens now is on th' 29th June iv-very year, on St Peter's Day, th' girls carry very light wooden crowns, bound with moss 'n' flowers, 'n' th' boys carry crosses 'n' rushes. There's two bands, one supplied by th' local military, 'n' a procession starts from the Chamley Arms, up to th' Lord O' th' Manor 'n' round here, tae th' church. It's queer really, why it's on St Peter's Day, when it's St Columbus's Church.'

Only history could explain that one. And of course like all old customs, the rushbearing at Warcop is not what it was, as Neil relates:

'When ah' wuz at school there wuz any amount of girls tae carry crowns and the boys didn't carry anything. But as the years heve gone by, there got tae be less girls, an' after ten or eleven they're young women and won't carry it.'

Mr Richardson's observation is a fitting reflection of the mores of our times: all that's young and pretty is no longer pure of heart and mind, growing old before their time. There's another rushbearing down the road, at St Theobold's Church at the little village of Great Musgrave where the River Belah, rising on distant Bowes Moor, meets the Eden in the shadow of Musgrave Fell.

Here, the rushbearing takes place on the first day of May, when St Theobold's becomes the only church in England where there is dancing every year. According to a church scroll, on this day:

. . . twelve young maidens from Brough, approved by the vicar, assemble on the first of May at ten in the morning at the foot of Brough Bridge, their white dresses decorated with flowers and garlands on their heads, in the shape of crowns formed of rushes with flowers entwined on the outside and blue ribbons on the top. Accompanied by the band, the maidens proceed through the fields to Musgrave but a mile

distant, the band playing and the rushbearers dancing. The rushbearers are led up to the north aisle of the church, and they hang up their garlands on the side of the church there to remain until the next year.

Then, after a bit of gospel and a few psalms, a lot of local hair is let down. Fiddles are produced and a space is cleared near the altar where the dancers assemble and let rip until late in the day.

The dancing and the date of the Musgrave rushbearing give us a clue towards the real origins and meaning of the ceremony. It's clearly a festival of the spring, a hangover from the

▼ Flower maidens at the Warcop rushbearing

Celtic feast of Beltane, named after the Celtic deity 'Bel' or 'Baal', marking the beginning of the light part of the year, a time of growth and fertility, of promise and fulfilment.

It is the spring equivalent of the Allendale Fire Festival, though here no fires are lit, for the sun is blazing in the heavens, and there is fire and passion in the breasts of the dancers, the singing and the fiddling, and in the colours of spring displayed in the garlands and head-dresses of the dancers. All is well upon the earth, for the spirit of a Celtic Persephone, the power of the corn goddess that lies dormant within the earth during the long winter months, has returned to confer blessings upon the world of men. Its incorporation within the church calendar at Musgrave, as with equivalent festivals in the nearby Lake District, shows the power of the traditional, of the folk memory, within modern English rural life. Long may they bear the rushes in the spring at Great Musgrave and Warcop!

THE GATES OF EDEN: RETURN TO AVALON

Our passage through the garden of Eden is now almost at an end, the head of the valley and the source of the river is in sight.

Kirkby Stephen is particularly well appointed for the traveller, with a good bookshop, antique shops, a well-fitted outdoor equipment and clothing shop, public houses, tea shops and arguably the best vendor of fish and chips in the country. It is a focal point for Pennine visitors, for people crossing the hills or heading for the Yorkshire Dales and the Lakes. At this crossroads of the dales, there is also a beautiful church dating from the twelfth century and known as 'The Church of the Dales' because of the length of its nave. The Settle–Carlisle railway line also enters the Pennines for the first time at Easegill Head near by. And this is a celebrated way of seeing the hills and the dales at their

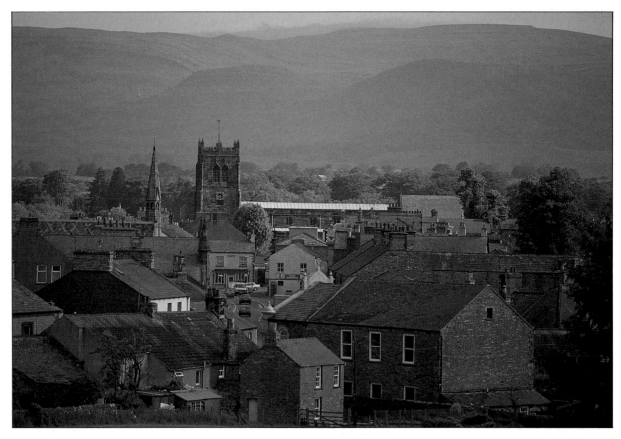

▲ Kirkby Stephen, crossroads of the dales

grandest. For many years a threat of closure has hung over this line, and a local campaign group has been fighting all the way down the tracks. So far it's still running, but only time and the great Station Master in the sky will be able to say for how long.

The product of another local campaign, this time by enlightened local individuals, government officers and rural community councillors from the Eden valley, is the East Cumbria Countryside Project. A team of local enthusiasts, volunteers and government trainees have been embarked since the early 1980s on a series of projects designed to revitalise the dwindling economy of East Fellside, to put life back into a rural community which had begun to lose confidence in itself. The results have been impres-

sive, new small businesses geared towards the new economy, more tourism and broken-down bits of countryside rehabilitated. The Eden valley has been put on the national map, thanks to their imaginative and award-winning series of interpretative leaflets, covering just about every walkway and footpath in the dale.

And there's some good walks to do around Kirkby Stephen, to Steukrith Bridge, Hartley and Winton, if you want to stretch your legs in those gentler bits of countryside at the crossroads of the Pennines. One walk takes in nearby Brough. This is, in fact, not one settlement but two, Church Brough and Market Brough, divided by the great A66 trunk road descending from out of the Pass of Stainmore, where Eric Bloodaxe met his end, through the Eden valley to the Lakes and beyond. And from Brough there is a walk to Helbeck Quarry which takes you past ancient 'cultivation terraces' or lynchets. In spring the verges of the roads are a feast of colour, a rich blue with forget-me-nots and speedwell, white with sweet cicely and dog or moon daisies, and red with foxgloves, wild rose flowers and hips and the ever-present rosebay willowherb.

The final flower-strewn road on our journey up the Eden is the B6259 which goes up through the Pass of Mallerstang, across the Cumbrian border into Yorkshire and the Yorkshire Dales National Park. These are our gates of Eden, a place to find a high point, to pause and look back on the beautiful green grass and red stone valley lying below, from where the mighty North Pennines rise, vying for a place in the sky with the neighbouring hills of the Lakes and Yorkshire.

> At times I think there are no words
> But these to tell what's true
> And there are no truths outside the Gates of
> Eden.

So wrote Bob Dylan. But there is one area of outstanding interest within the gates of Eden where truths are hard to come by, where myth, magic and history intertwine: the castle (so legend has it) of Uther Pendragon, father to the noble king, in the Mallerstang Pass. It can be clearly seen above the road with full views of the Eden valley and Pennine escarpment in the distance. Approached through a wooden gate, you see a moat on three sides, with the Eden on the fourth – though how they got that water up there to fill the moat is a complete mystery. Maybe Merlin the magician had a hand in that one. The castle is a ruin, but a magical one for that, a fitting location for the conception of the once and future king, with delightful window arches overlooking the trees and waters of the Eden, and brilliant blue clumps of common violets and ivy-leaved toadflax growing high up on the castle walls.

Pendragon is privately owned. The owner, Raven Frankland, lives near to the little village of Ravenstonedale, just off the A685, in the no-man's-land between the North Pennines and the Yorkshire Dales. For many years, Raven, a local politician and leader of the Pennine community, has kept a visitors' book where you can join Spike Milligan and others rich and famous, poor and humble, who've come to pay their respects to this symbol of a lost kingdom. Raven owes his name to the appearance over his father's Ravenstonedale house of three ravens at the time of his birth. As the future restorer of Pendragon Castle breathed his first draft of fresh clean Pennine air, the ravens gathered above and flew away over high Harter Fell.

Looking at the castle close up, signs of Raven's restoration are evident, but the castle has remained a ruin, a place lost in the mists of time where one can still be free to dream of another Eden, of Avalon, where Arthur sleeps on, but ever ready to reclaim his land from the invading hordes. Standing on the castle walls, your eyes almost cast about of their own accord to look for the stone out of which Excalibur was

▲ Pendragon Castle

pulled. While at the castle's feet below, the River Eden runs its immortal course, wholly silent on the subject of Pendragon and his line, giving no clues to Excalibur's origin.

The link between this ruin and the tale of Arthur possibly owes much to the activities of Robert de Clifford, Warden of the Scottish Marches during the fourteenth century, in the reign of Edward I. He crenellated the castle and changed its name from Mallerstang to Pendragon during a time when the cult of Arthur was fashionable in royal and aristocratic circles. There is a theory that the renaming was a re-creation and not a new piece of romantic fiction. For there are many associations between Arthur and his knights, a range of local ancient monuments and the towns and countryside of Cumbria and the north of England.

Indeed historians agree that in the vacuum created by the collapse of the Roman Empire at the beginning of the fifth century, Arthur was a Celtic leader who led his cavalry of knights and soldiers up and down the country in campaigns against the Saxon invaders, keeping them at bay and delaying Britain's descent into the chaos which has since come to be known as the Dark Ages.

Various parts of Britain lay claim to the legend of Arthur – Cornwall, Somerset, Wales and the North Country – but as a folk myth with some historical basis, all competing claims are fair. No one is likely to prove one place above all others as the rightful home for Arthur and his court. The one thing these places do have in common, apart from a number of Arthurian place names and associations, is that they were Celtic strongholds, to the last. The Welsh Cymri, for example, are also the Cumbrians of the western Pennines and the Lakes. Arthur was a defender for them all, a Robin Hood figure who roamed the Albion of the Celts, giving rise to local legends wherever he fought his campaigns against the forces from without. But perhaps Cumbria's greatest claim to the legend of Arthur, history apart, is its role in inspiring the poet Tennyson, who as a young

man frequented these parts, to produce his immortal epic, the 'Morte D'Arthur' and the 'Idylls of the King'.

Arthur's very last battle, against his own treacherous nephew Mordred, is thought to have taken place at Camlann, a site identified as lying between Carlisle and the Roman fort of Camboglanna near the Roman Wall. Both Penrith and Carlisle are attributed as being the location of the Round Table itself. Ravenglass on the Cumbrian coast, ironically now the home of one of the world's oldest, biggest and potentially most dangerous nuclear installations, the Sellafield plant, has even been identified as one of the sites where Avalon was placed. According to legend, the mortally wounded Arthur was taken from there to the Isle of Avalon – probably Ireland – by the witch-fairy, Morgan le Fay. The faithful knight Bedivere watched his going, from the great deep to the great deep, in the stillness of the dead world's winter dawn:

> Then from the dawn it seem'd there came
>   but faint
> As from beyond the limit of the world,
> Like the last echo born of a great cry,
> Sounds as if some fair city were one voice
> Around a king returning from his wars.

The ravens that accompanied Arthur on his mythological journey no longer roost on the estuary that bears their name, preferring instead to inhabit the safer heights of the Cumbrian and Pennine mountains. There they wait and watch, for the passing of Sellafield, and the return of the king.

From Pendragon Castle, the road through Mallerstang Pass, the B6259, winds up to Aisgill, the last place in the North Pennines. The names are Norse in origin, a testament to the Viking presence in these parts, though what they actually stand for is a matter of some scholarly dispute. These days this is where Cumbrians

Blencarn, with Cross Fell in the background ▶

182

▲ Wild Boar Cairns: stone sentinels on the backbone of England

become Yorkshiremen, and where you can see a vista of great hills impressive enough to rival the claims of Cross Fell and High Cup Nick to represent the Pennines at their craggiest. On one side of the road above the cottages of Aisgill Moor is the path to the source of the Eden, a short and sweet walk past another dramatic waterfall, Hell Gill, back to the very beginning. The Eden rises as Red Gill beneath High Seat on the great Black Fell, and within yards of its marshy beginnings it has carved a dramatic but narrow ravine. Hell Gill Gorge, into the soft limestone below. The gorge is an impressive landform, complete with ghylls, clints and grikes at its base, birch and alder climbing out of its sides. Stare into its cavernous depths and you will feel that you are looking into an ancient womb, the beginning of time itself.

From a hell below ground, we cross the pass, to a heaven above it. For that last perfect view of this section of the Pennines, of the Eden valley, the dales and hills beyond, there is no place better than atop Wild Boar Fell. This can be approached from Mallerstang with permission from the farmer at Aisgill Farm by a route up Aisgill Beck to the top, but the correct route is really from the village of Ravenstonedale on the far side of the fell. The Aisgill route also takes you across dangerous sink holes into which the unwary can easily step, to a cavernous and lonely end, and across deep blanket mire. Fall into that and you may become a well-preserved curiosity for palaeoecologists in the year 4000 AD trying to understand the meaning of your credit cards and puzzling over the uses of your Swiss Army knife!

Wild Boar Fell got its name from the local Lord of the Manor, Sir Richard Musgrave, who died in 1409. Legend has it that the noble Sir Richard killed the last boar to roam on the felltop, a conquest of which he was inordinately proud. So proud was he in fact that he even insisted on being buried at Musgrave chapel along with a tusk from his prize pig.

But Wild Boar Fell is a remarkable summit, and a fitting place for a journey's end. Its peak is a desolate escarpment plateau, at a height beyond the point where flowers grow and the curlews sing, where it seems there is only you and the soaring buzzards. It is a hill to climb when your heart is heavy with life. Or it's a place to go when your thoughts are with the years gone by or are dwelling on a love lost in time . . . It's a place to go to be on your own. But having struggled an epic struggle to the top you will discover that you are not completely alone. Behind you there stands a line of high cairns. The line ends on the site of an ancient Celtic mountain burial place. The location is fitting, for from the bottom of the hill these sculptures of wind-driven stone resemble an assembly of standing stones, even a group of petrified people. But neither casual interpretation of the eye is too far wrong. For they have a presence all their own.

From where you and they stand together, take a last long glimpse of the hills and dales before making the long descent along White Scar to the sheltered ground below. But leave a stone for the cairns to show that you have been there. And as you go, count the cairns. There are nineteen or more, rock statues made out of stone put there one by one by many people over many years. And there they stand in the teeth of the wild wind, silhouetted against the open skyline and the hills beyond, stone sentinels guarding the gates of Eden, atop the North Pennines, the backbone of England.

A WALK ON THE EDGE OF EDEN
DUFTON TO HIGH CUP NICK

If you have not the energy for the full-blown Cauldron Snout to High Cup walk in Teesdale, bringing together the devil (Old Nick) and his cooking pot (Cauldron Snout), there is another way, from the Eden valley side. This is a walk where the views of the Eden as you ascend the western-facing escarpment of the Pennines are nothing short of spectacular. High Cup Nick itself, more properly termed just High Cup, is one of Britain's greatest geomorphologic landmarks – featured in just about every secondary school geographical textbook in the land. Allow a good 3–4 hours, for the distance you will cover is about 9 miles, wear good boots and take something warm. There is a local saying in Weardale: instead of the catchphrase 'take a jump', they say 'tak a waalk off High Cup Nick'. So as you can gather, this is serious walking country, with a narrow footpath on the edge of a precipice and it is worth taking good care, particularly with children.

You can get there from Appleby which is on the A66 main Eden valley road. From Appleby follow the signs north-west for Dufton. Once past the railway bridge, turn north-east.

The walk starts from Dufton. Leave your car in Dufton and walk back to Billysbeck bridge. There is a turning right over Billysbeck bridge just before the village, on the Appleby road, which signposts the Nick and the Pennine Way which we will be following throughout this walk. You can drive some of the way if you prefer, as long as you do not block the road or leave the gates open, and if it's a morning walk you are doing you might even snatch a bit of breakfast at Bow Hall Farm en route, leaving your car there. The tractor-track-cum-footpath passes between a quarry and a rounded hill up towards the first of the limestone outcrops at the bottom of Peeping Hill.

The views here are good, but they get even better as you round the bend leading up to High Cup. The land rises steeply below and above you. You are on the edge of the cup directly opposite Middle Tongue Crag. This is aptly named, a great tongue of hard volcanic rock, the Whin Sill, 1495 feet high, protrud-

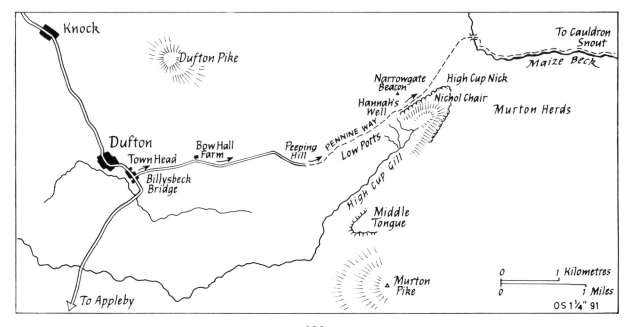

ing out over the Eden valley and dividing the High Cup Gillbeck from the waters of Trundle Gill to the south. In shape it is like one of those flat-topped mesas which featured in old cowboy movies. It is a fitting analogy, for this is wild country, where there is only the wind and the odd peregrine or plover around to accompany you.

Round the corner from Peeping Hill, the path leads through a metal gate and sheepfold into Low Potts. There is often a puddle before the gate, and beyond this lies a mini gorge, with huge clumps of white limestone rock lying all around in various stages of topsy-turvyness. Above, on the left, can be clearly seen a small cave-like opening into the limestone hill, with an arch of chiselled limestone marking the entrance and inviting a closer look. Careful inspection will reveal a simple hollow, frequented by the odd late-night Pennine trekker, and providing essential shelter in any sudden rainstorm. It is the remains of a lime kiln where the farmers burned the local limestone to put on their acid upland pastures to make the grass sweeter and allow them to farm at higher altitudes.

The presence of the kiln in this spot explains why there's a cart track this far up the Pennine escarpment. The combined activities of man and nature in this spot have left a surreal landscape, complete with limestone grotto – ideal monster country for younger trekkers.

From here the track continues up in a steady climb until you are on the open top of the escarpment directly overlooking the High Cup valley at 2000 feet. Where the escarpment above is closest to the escarpment below, the path itself narrows and skirts along the edge of the precipice. Here in winter some feeder streams, including Strands Beck, cascade down towards High Cup Gill way down below you. If the sun is shining you have a full view of the immense glaciated valley of High Cup, from top to bottom. You will hear the gill tinkling way beneath you, looping many ox-bow loops on its way down through a barren lime-clad landscape to the softer greener landscape of the Eden below. On the far hillside you will see little white dots moving across screes and sparse pastures. These are High Cup's own version of the Pennine Swaledale sheep, who have developed an uncanny ability actually to graze on slopes as near to

vertical as you'll get anywhere in the North Pennines.

The rim of High Cup is formed from the hard rock of the Whin Sill which outcrops as High Cup Scar around the head of the valley. Below it, screes of limestone, shale and even weathered whin hang like tresses of hair from a Scandinavian troll. Around and about, updale, downdale, whips a Pennine wind.

The footpath runs above the scar under Narrowgate Beacon, past shallow pot holes and Hannah's Well, a little lonely spring which issues from beneath a boulder. Who Hannah was is anyone's guess. It is a romantic spot: water, wilderness, heath and stone, and on every available patch of thin soil a covering of wild mountain thyme . . .

In view from the path is a slender pillar of basalt known as the Nichol Chair, named, it is said, after a shoemaker from Dufton who not only climbed it but even heeled and soled a pair of boots while on the top.

Beyond Nichol Chair you will come to the nick after which the whole valley has come to be named. This is a narrow cleft in the escarpment, a chip in the old block. That, and indeed the whole valley, looks as though some giant in ages past has taken a fancy to a bit of Pennine Pie and has bitten off a whole chunk in one go leaving behind his crumbs – the screes – for others to pick up.

Before long you're at High Cup Gill head and looking down the length of the valley to the Eden below. For the adventurous the path actually goes on past Watch Hill and Murton Herds to run alongside Maize Beck and into Upper Teesdale, connecting with the Cauldron Snout walk described on the Teesdale walk. In fact a short detour along Maize Beck will lead to some interesting features including a ford, a footbridge, a limestone gorge, complete with rich limestone flora, and eventually a mine shop and mine.

Unless you're going the whole hog, over to Teesdale, complete with the promise of a lift on the other side, the return journey is back along the route you came. The views do not change, but the perspective does, particularly if the light has shifted, picking out the different features in the dramatic landscape lying below and above. But one stunning view you might not have noticed on the way up is the north view as you round the corner past Peeping Hill. This includes

Dufton and Knock Pike, laid in a descending line which continues behind you south, to include Murton and Roman Pikes.

A pike in these parts is a conical hill, and these Pennine pikes are the product of the great Pennine fault, a series of fractures which led to these hills being separated from the main body of the Pennine chain. Collectively they are known as the 'Cross Fell Inlier', an inlier being an older rock surrounded by up-and-coming younger ones. And 'in-lying' is probably what you'll most feel like doing the day after you have finished this walk. But if you fortify yourself with the refreshments provided at the excellent Stag Inn in Dufton village you'll soon be more than ready to walk another day, through the unique landscapes of the North Pennines.

INDEX

Page numbers in *italic* refer to the illustrations

Abraham's Cave, 163
Acorn Bank, 175, 176–7, *177*
Addinson, Thomas, 176
Aisgill, 182, 184–5
Allen, River, 8, *95*
Allen Gorge, 116, 112, *123*, 136
Allendale, 18, 88, 94–115, 155, 179
Allendale Town, 109–12, *110*
Allendale Wolf, 128–9
Allenheads, 54, 94, 96–8, *96*, 99, 108, 113, 114–15, 134, 142
Allensford, 79, 80
Alston, 129, 138, 141, 146–7, *146, 147,* 148
Annat Walls, 145, *145*
Appleby, 18, 175, 177–8, 186
Appleby Fell, 11, 17
Arnold, Ralph, 74
Arthur, King, 16, 18, 82–4, *85*, 160, 181–2
Ashgill Head, 48
Ashgill Waterfall, 143
Atkinson, Thomas, 175–6
Attwood, Charles, 64
Aukside, 32
Ayle Colliery, 148

Baal Hill, 65
Backhouse, James, 36, 41
Backstone Bank, 65
Badger Men, 79–80
Bain, Captain, 128
Balder, River, 28, 30
Baldersdale, 32
Barhaugh Burn, 159
Barhaugh Common, 159
Barhaugh House, 148, *150*
Baring Brothers, 64
Barnard Castle, 24, *25*, 26, 35
Basire, Dr Isaac, 59
Baybridge, 88, 90, 92
Baynbrigg, Roger, 39
Bearsbridge, 121, 128
Beaty, 109
Beaumont family, 97
Bedburn, 65, 67
Bedburn Beck, 65
Belah, River, 178
Bewick, Thomas, 78
Bird, Abraham, 163
Bishop Auckland, 56
Bishop Auckland and Weardale Railway, 62–3
Bishop Oak, 65
Bishops' Park, 55

Black Bridge, 129
Black Fell, 166, 167, 184
Blackett Bridge, 129
Blackett-Ord family, 119, 126
Blackhall Mill, 76
Blackway Head, 134
Blanchland, 87, 88, 89, *89,* 90, 91–3
Blencarn, 175, 176, *183*
Blue Back bridge, 116–19, *118*
Blue Circle Industries, 50
Bolbec, Walter de, 89
Bollihope Burn, 62, 63, *63*
Bollihope Common, 57
Boltsburn, 92
Bonomi, Ignatius, 59
Bowes family, 39, 74
Bowes Moor, 178
Bowes Museum, 24–6, *26*
Bowlees Visitor Centre, 35
Bradley Hall, 68
Brampton, 162
Briarwood Bank, 136–7
Brigantes, 16, 24
Briggle Beck, 175, 176
Bronze Age, 61–2
Brotherlee, 56
Brough, 180–1
Brown, Wilf Swindle, 51, 52
Bruthwaite Forest, 164
Bulbeck, 88
Bulmer, 172
Burnfoot, 100–1
Burnhope Burn, 52, 85
Byerhope, 98–100, 101, 114
Byerhope Reservoir, 100, 105, 115

Caleb Reed, *146*
Calvert, John, 79
Calvertfold, 144
Carlisle, 14, 182
Carr Shield, 129, 131–2, 134
Carriers Way, 113, 115
Carrshield Moor, 134
Carterway Heads, 87, 91
Cartimandua, 24
Carts Bog, 136
Caryn, 33
Castle Carrock, 162
Castleside, 72
Catton, 112
Cauldron Snout, 18, 41, 42, *42,* 43, 44, 186, 187
Celts, 103–4, 107, 108, 153, 176, 179, 182, 185

Chopwell Wood, 76
Clifford, Robert de, 182
Coalcleugh, 104, 132–4, *132, 133,* 138
Coanwood, 138
Cold Fell, 162, 165
Coldberry End, 48
Coldberry Heights, 35–6, *36*
Collingwood, Frank, 151
Consett, 72, 74, 77, 79–80
Cotherstone, 26, 28, 30
Cotman, John Sell, 24
Countryside Commission, 50
Covenanters, 86–7
Cow Green Reservoir, 36, 41–2, *41,* 43–4
Cowshill, 48, 96, 114
Crag Head, 122, *123*
Cranswell family, 166
Crawley Engine, 57
Crawleyside Bank, 57
Croglin Bat, 166–7
Croglin Chase, *168*
Croglin Water, 166, 167–9
Cromwell, Oliver, 38, 177
Cronkley Fell, 38, 45
Cronkley Scar, 41, 45
Crooked Oak, 80, 82, 84
Cross Fell, 8, 11–15, *13,* 17, *19,* 43, 114, 115, 138, 145, 153, 163, 170–2, *171,* 175, 176, *183,* 184
Crow, Maddy, 116, 123–4

Daddry Shield, 55, 56
Dairy Bridge, 24
Dead Stones, 52
Deadwater, 138
Dent, Ray, 151
Dere Street, 76
Derwent, River, 8, 72
Derwent Gorge, 80–2, 120
Derwent Reservoir, 80, 84, 87, 88, 91, 115
Derwentdale, 72–93, *73*
Devil's Water, 88
Dickens, Charles, 12, 24, 79
Dickinson, George, 94
Dilston Castle, 88–9
Dirt Pot, 113, 114–15
Dixon, Robert, 104
Dower, John, 20
Dowgang Hush, 143
Dryden family, 148
Dufton, 44, 175, 186, 187–8
Dunham, Sir Kingsley, 54
Durham, 48
Durham, Prince Bishops of, 46, 55–6, 69

Durham Cathedral, 8, 56, 62
Durham County Council, 50
Durham Wildlife Trust, 35, 65
Dylan, Bob, 181

Eada Hall, 125
Easegill Head, 179
East Cumbria Countryside Project, 180
East Fellside, 160, 175–6, 180
East Fellside and Alston Moor Countryside
    Project, 147
Eastgate, 55, 57
Ebchester, 76–7, 78
Edale, 18
Eddy's Bridge, 87
Eden, River, 8, 14, 160–2, 184
Eden, Vale of, 151, 160–88
Eden Lacey, 174
Edmundbyers, *86,* 87, 91
Eggleston, 26, 27, 28, 30–2, 63, 65
Egglestone Abbey, 24, 26, *27*
Elia House, 101–3
Elpha Green, 104–5
Emerson, George, 53
English Heritage, 50
Eric Bloodaxe, King, 14–15, 180
Ethelreda, 131
Eudon Burn, 85
de Eure family, 68
European Development Fund, 50

Fairless, Eddie, 155
Fairy Holes, 61
Falcon Clints, *17,* 41, 44–5
Fawnlees Hall, 65
Featherstone Castle, 155–7, *156*
Featherstonehaugh family, 58, 156–7
Feg the Storyteller, 134
Fieldgarth, 166
Fisher, Isaac Daniel, 119
Flush, Dave, 114
Force Garth Farm, 36–8
Forest, Miles, 30
Forest Quarter, 55
Forest-in-Teesdale, 38, 39
Forestry Commission, 65, 74, 80
Forster, Katie, 134
Frankland, Raven, 181
Frizzle, Jane, 82
Frosterley, 62, 63

Gaels, 16
Gannister quarry, 54
Garrigill, 138, 143, *143,* 144–5
Gateshead, 72
Gelt, River, 162–3, 164
Geltsdale, 17, 159, 164–5, 169
General Strike (1926), 76
George VI, King, 121
Gibside, 72, 74–5
Gibson, Thomas, 35–6
Gibson's Cave, 36

Gilderdale Burn, 146, 153, 158
Glendue Fell, 17, 164
Goodfellow, Sarah, 97, 100
Great Dun Fell, 11, *11,* 43, 138
Great Musgrave, 178–9
Great North Salmon Run, 34–5
Greg's Hut, 145
Greta, River, 24
Greta Bridge, 24
Groverake, 54

Hadrian's Wall, 14, 16, 108, 134, 153, 162,
    163
The Hagg, 109
Hamsterley, 76
Hamsterley Forest, 65–7, *66, 67*
Hanging Walls of Mark Anthony, 18, 176
Hangman Hill, 108
Hannah's Well, 187
Haresceugh Fell, 169
Harrison, Thomas, 175
Harthope Moor, 46
Hartley, 180
Hartleyburn Common, 164
Hartside, 160, 169
Hay Rake, 108
Heathery Burn caves, 61–2
Helbeck Quarry, 181
Hell Beck, 162
Hell Gill, 184
Helm Wind, 172
Henry VIII, King, 132
Hexham, 108
High Cup Nick, *8,* 18, 44, 175, 184, 186–7
High Force, 16, 18, 22, 35, 36, *37,* 44, 45
High Mill, 70
High Seat, 184
High Shipley Lodge, 28–30
Highcrook, 137
Hildyard, E.J.W., 57
Hisehope Burn, 85
Hodgson, 141
Holwick Fell, 34, 36, 38
Hopper, Ken, 80–2, 84
Horsley Hall, 56–7
Horsleyhope Ravine, *81,* 82
Hudeshope, 32, 36
Hunstanworth Moor, 88, 90

Ice Ages, 28, 38, 43
Intake Farm, 39, 40, 41
Ireshopeburn, 48, 52–3, 56
Iron Age, 36

Kailash Bawan, 102–3, *103*
Killhope, 101, 115, 140
Killhope Burn, 52
Killhope Law, 103–4, 113, 114, 115, 134,
    138
Killhope Wheel, 48–51, *50,* 96
King's Forest of Geltsdale, 164
Kingswood Burn, 125

Kirk Yetholm, 18
Kirkby, Stephen, 178, 179–80, *180*
Kirkby, Thore, 176
Kirkcarrion, 33, *33*
Kirkhaugh, 153, 159
Kirkland, 145, 175–6
Kirkoswald, 166, 167, 169
Knock, 11, 175, 176
Knock Fell, 11, 143, 172, 176
Knock Pike, 187–8
Knoutberry Hill, 52, *52,* 140

Lacy, Colonel, 174
Lacy's Caves, 174, *174*
Langdon Beck, 39, 41, 43, 45, 46
Langdon Common, 18
Langley, 136
Langley, Cardinal, 68
Le Fleming, Michael, 175
Lintley, 159
Lintzford, 75–6, *76*
Little Dun Fell, 11, *11,* 43
Little Salkeld, 170, 174, 175
London Lead Company, 51, 141, 142
'The Long Drag', 107–8
Long Marton, 176
Long Meg and her Daughters, 170, 173–5,
    173
Lovelady Shield, 143
Low Geltbridge, 162–3
Low Potts, 187
Low Row, 159
Ludwell, 61
Lunedale, 32

McGrigor Phillips, Mrs, 177
Mackenzie, 126–7
Maddison, Liz and Bob, 98, 100
Maiden Way, 14, 16, 153, 159
Maize Beck, 44, 187
Mallerstang, *161,* 162, 181, 182, 184
Martin, John, 144–5
Mary, Queen of Scots, 125, 162
Melmerby Fell, 175
Methodism, 59, 60, 69
Mickle Fell, 38
Mickleton, 32
Middle Tongue Crag, 186–7
Middlehope Burn, 52
Middlehope Level, 71
Middlehope valley, 69
Middleton, 32, 33, 34, 48
Milburn, 175, 176
Milburn Beck, 176
Miles, John, 164–5, 170
Milburn, 175, 176
Minsteracres Monastery, 85
Moking Hurth, 41
Monk Wood, 119–21
Moor House, 17, 143–4
Moore, John, 175
Moore, Thomas, 57
Moorhouse National Nature Reserve, 144

Morralee Tarn, 136, 137
Morralee Wood, 137
Muggleswick, *10*, 84–7
Musgrave, Sir Richard, 185
Musgrave Fell, 178

Nag's Head, 52
National Trust, 74, 77, 136, 137, 177
Nature Conservancy Council, 32, 40, 82, 84, 143–4, 172
Nent, River, 132, 140, 142
Nent Force Level, 141–2
Nentdale, 135, 141
Nenthall, 143
Nenthead, 140, *140*, 141, *141*, 142–3
Newbiggin, 36, 176
Newcastle, 14
Nichol Chair, 187
Ninebanks, 129–32, *130, 131*
Noon Hill, 38
Noonestones Hill, 144
North Tynedale, 138
Nunnery Walks, 167–9, *168*

'Old Corpse Way', 145
Old Park Farm, 56
Oley family, 77, 78
Ord family, 126
Oswald, King, 169

Paine, James, 74
Park End Wood, 34
Parker, Willy, 102–3, 105–7, *105*, 151
Paulinus, St, 12, 170
Pease family, 65
Peel, Sir Robert, 64
Peeping Hill, 186–7
Pendragon Castle, 18, 181–2, *181*
Pennine Way, 11, 18
Penrith, 182
Percymere, *31*
Phillipson, George, 105
Philpotts, Dr, 59
Pike, Stan, 121–2, *121*
Pikeston Fell, 65
Pinkyn Wood, 157
Plankey Mill, 116, 136–7
Plenmellor Common, 155
Pontop and Jarrow Railway, 57
Premonstratensians, 26, 89, 91
Proctor, Hugh, 39

Raby Castle, 24, 26
Raby estate, 32, 155
Radcliffe family, 88–9
Randalholme, 148, *149*
Raven Beck, 169
Ravenglass, 182
Raven's Crag, 137
Ravenstonedale, 181, 185
Ray, John, 38
Redburn Skulls, 54

Rey Cross, 14, *14*, 15
Richardson, Neil, 178
Richardson, Rev. William, 12
Ridley College, 137
Rievaulx Abbey, 39
Risegreen Reservoir, 96
Ritson, Rev. Joseph, 131
Robinson, Rebecca and Margaret, 38
Rogerley Hall, 63
Rogerley quarry, 62
Rokeby Park, 24
Romaldkirk, 26–7, *27*, 28, 30
Romans, 16, 24, 76–7, 153, 159, 163, 182
Rookhope, 53–5, *53*, 56, 71, 88, 90, 96, 114
Rookhope Borehole, 54
Rookhope Burn, 52, 53, 55, 57
Rookhope Chimney, 54
Rookhope and Middlehope Railway, 70–1
Ross, Dr Ann, 108
Rowland's Gill, 72
Rowley Burn, 108
Royal Society for the Protection of Birds, 164, 169
Rutherford, John, 125

St John's Chapel, 46, 48, *49*
Saxons, 16, 39
Scarrowmanwick Fell, 167, *167*
Scots, 26, 56, 89
Scott, Alan, 40–1
Scott, Sir Walter, 8, 12, 22, 24, 30, 35, 54–5
Scutterhill incline, 56
Selset Reservoir, 32
Settle-Carlisle railway, 18, 169, 179–80
'Seven Sisters', 147
Shap Fell, 28
Shaw Side, 140
Shildon Burn, 92
Shipley Wood, 119–20
Shittlehope Burn, 61
Short, Denis, 151
Shotley Bridge, 75, 77–9
Silkin, Jon, 50
Simpson, Gordon, 65
Sinderhope, 107, *107*, 108–9
Sipton, *106*, 107
Sipton Cleugh, 107
Skirwith, 175–6
Slaggyford, 148, 151, 153, 158
Slaghill, *111*
Slaley Forest, 85, 87, 108
Slit Pasture, 71
Slit Wood, 70
Smiddy Shaw Reservoir, *85*, 85
Smith, Herbert, 65
Smith, Hubert, 46
Smith, Jane, 119
Snaisgill, 32
Sneep, 82–4, *83*
Snods Edge, 18
Snowball, Robert, 92
Solingen, 77

Sopwith, Sir Thomas, 98, 100, 142, 153
South Tynedale, 88, 138–59, *139*
South Tynedale Railway Preservation Society, 146, 158
Spartylea, 101–3, *101*, 104, 105–7, 108
Staindrop, 26
Stainmore, 155, 160
Stainmore, Pass of, 14, *14*, 15
Stanhope, 48, 57–61, *58, 59*
Stanhope Burn, 61
Stanhope Hall, 58
Stanhope and Tyne Railroad, 57
Stanners Garth, 64
Stanwick-St John, 24
Startforth, 26
Staward, 122–3, 136
Steukrith Bridge, 180
Stockton and Darlington Railway, 57, 62, 65
Stone Age, 15–16, 103–4, 173, 174
Stoney, Captain, 74–5
Strathmore, Earls of, 24, 74
Strathmore, Mary, Countess of, 74–5
Surtees, Robert, 156
Surtees family, 65
Swaledale Association, 151
Swinhope Burn, 104

Talkin Fell, 162
Talkin Tarn, 162
Tees, River, 8, 11, *11*, 24, *31*, 34, 144
Teesdale, 11, 17, 22–45, *23*
Temple Sowerby, 176, 177
Tennyson, Alfred, Lord, 84, 160, 163, 182
Thackeray, William Makepeace, 74
Thompson's Well Bridge, 158, 159
Tindale Tarn, 164, 165
Trundle Gill, 187
Tunstall Reservoir, 65
Turner, J.M.W., 12, 22, 24, 35, 36
Tyne, River, 8, 88, 143, 144, 145
Tyne Gap, 14, 108, 165
Tynedale, 138–59, *139*
Tynehead, 144

Uther Pendragon, 181

Van Mildert, Bishop, 56
Venutius, 24
Vielle Montagne, 142
Vikings, 14–15, 16, 30, 132, 182
Vindomora, 76–7

Walker, Brian, 65
Wallace, William, 145–6
Wallace family, 156
Wallish Walls, 18, 80
Walter the Molecatcher, 18, 116, 119, 122–5, *124*
Warcop, 18, 178, *179*
Waskerley Beck, 64–5
Waskerley, 85
Wear, River, 8

Weardale, 18, 46–71, *47*, 115, 151
Weardale Iron Company, 56, 64, 70–1
Weardale Mineral Holdings, 50
Weardale Museum, 52–3
Weardale and Shildon Water Company, 65
Wearhead, 52, 56
Weatherhill, 57
Weeds, 69
Wellhope Burn, 52
Wesley, John, 59
West Allen, 116–37, *117*
Westernhope Burn, 52
Westernhopeburn, 56, *56*
Westgate, 55, 56, 69

Wharnley Burn, 80
Wheel of the Tees, 42, 44
Wheeldale Sike, 43
Whetstonemea Burn, 134
Whin Sill, 33, 94, 175, 186–7
White Kirkley, 62, *62,* 63
White's Level, 70
Whitfield, 121–2, 127–8
Whitfield Brow, 63
Whitfield Hall, 116, 119–21, 125–7, *126,* 155
Whitley Castle, 153, 159
Whitleyshield Carrs, 134
Widdy Bank Pencil Mill, 45
Widdybank Fell, 38, 41, 44

Wild Boar Fell, 184–5, *184*
William Rufus, King, 56
Williamston Nature Reserve, 151, 158
Willisel, T., 38
Winton, 180
Wolsingham, 64, 68, 71, 72
Wolsingham Park, 65
Woodland Fell, 65
Wooley Burn, 109
Wordsworth, William, 160–2, 169
Written Rock of Gelt, 163
Wynch Bridge, 35

Young, Dr Robert, 57

ROGUES' GALLERY

The authors would like to thank the following persons and institutions, without whose help and collaboration, and in some cases hard work and friendship, this book could not have been written:

Vivien James, Anne Williams, Penny Mills, Walter Rutherford, Willy Parker, Herbert and Lucy Robson, Willy and Lena Wright, Muriel Paul, John and Elsie Heslop, Jennifer Hockey, Nicole Quayle, Kate Whiteworth, Laura Wilson, Colin Bainbridge, John Coulson, Margaret Peart, Ken Hopper, Stan Pike, Don Wilcock, Bob & Liz Maddison, Stuart Walker, George Phillipson, Economic and Social Research Council (ESRC), Maureen Oliphant, Rita Brownsword, Eggleston Village Adult Education Class 1983–84, Margaret Bradshaw, Nora Hancock and Raven Frankland.